FUZZY ENGINEERING EXPERT SYSTEMS WITH NEURAL NETWORK APPLICATIONS

FUZZY ENGINEERING EXPERT SYSTEMS WITH NEURAL NETWORK APPLICATIONS

ADEDEJI B. BADIRU
Department of Industrial Engineering
University of Tennessee
Knoxville, TN
JOHN Y. CHEUNG
School of Electrical and Computer Engineering
University of Oklahoma
Norman, OK

JOHN WILEY & SONS, INC.

Copyright © 2002 by John Wiley & Sons, New York. All rights reserved.

Published simultaneously in Canada.

This publication is designed to provide accurate and authoritative information in regard to the subject matter covered. It is sold with the understanding that the publisher is not engaged in rendering professional services. If professional advice or other expert assistance is required, the services of a competent professional person should be sought.

Wiley also publishes its books in a variety of electronic formats. Some content that appears in print may not be available in electronic books. For more information about Wiley products, visit our web site at www.wiley.com.

Library of Congress Cataloging-in-Publication Data:

Badiru, Adedeji Bodunde, 1952–
   Fuzzy engineering expert systems with neural network applications /
Adedeji B. Badiru, John Y. Cheung.
       p. cm.
     ISBN 0-471-29331-8
   1. Expert systems (Computer science)   2. Fuzzy systems.   3. Neural networks (Computer science)   I. Cheung, John Y. II. Title.
   QA76.76.E95 B24 2002
   006.3'3—dc21

                                                                    2002003706

Printed in the United States of America.

10 9 8 7 6 5 4 3 2 1

To Our Spouses, Iswat Amori Badiru, and Rose Kwan-Fun Cheung

CONTENTS

PREFACE

The definition of human intelligence has always been elusive. Despite years of research, scientists are still unable to describe accurately the reasoning process of the human brain. Scientific models have been used to describe the human reasoning process. Even though such models are never foolproof, they turn out to be suitable for most practical analyses of human intelligence. As new discoveries are made about the human brain, the descriptive models change to accommodate the new findings. Artificial intelligence (AI) is the combined attempt of mathematicians, engineers, and computer scientists to develop computers that perform acts normally associated with human intelligence. Since the term was coined by John McCarthy in the mid-1950s, artificial intelligence has undergone a remarkable transition from an object of research curiosity to a practical tool.

Specialized branches of AI have developed in recent years to accommodate specific application problems. The research and application domains of AI now cover diverse areas including speech recognition, pattern matching, natural language, artificial vision, game theory, robotics, learning, and theorem proving.

Expert systems (ES) constitute a class of modular computer programs developed to serve as electronic consultants in complex decision problems that would ordinarily require human expertise. Expert systems have been implemented for several practical purposes, the most successful being in medical diagnosis, equipment troubleshooting, mineral prospecting, and computer system configuration. New successful applications in other areas of human endeavors are reported frequently.

This book is designed to add to the existing body of printed materials on expert systems. The book presents a comprehensive discussion of all the basic concepts and procedures. The audience for the book includes students and teachers of expert systems, executives, managers, consultants, computer hobbyists, computer professionals, and nonprofessionals. It combines three popular and successful areas of artificial intelligence, the concepts of expert systems, fuzzy logic, and artificial neural networks. These concepts have been applied individually successfully in various academic, business, and industrial applications. But as the AI field matures and expands, it is increasingly necessary to combine these three areas. This is what the book delivers.

Artificial intelligence and expert systems have emerged from the laboratory into the realm of practical applications. Over the past several years, the interest in expert systems has increased dramatically. New basic developments and application avenues in science, business, and industry are being reported almost daily. Since this is a relatively new technology, there is still a shortage of printed material to educate researchers and practitioners on this very important computer-based tool. The publication of new books on expert systems has increased significantly in the past five years. Yet there are not enough books to satisfy both the academic and business needs. The authors frequently receive requests from the business and industry communities to recommend reading materials on expert systems.

It has become very important to train students and working professionals in the emerging technology of expert systems. Colleges and universities have been responding to this challenge by developing new courses in expert systems at both the undergraduate and graduate levels. Both authors now teach courses in expert systems or closely related fields.

In addition to presenting a practical and hybrid integration of expert systems, fuzzy logic, and artificial neural networks, this book includes simulation, which is a general computer tool.

ACKNOWLEDGMENTS

We graciously thank all of those who have supported us through the preparation of this book. It was a long and arduous process that we could not have completed without the contributions of several people. Particular thanks and appreciation go to Jeanette Myers, who diligently converted many old bits of the manuscript from an obsolete and archaic medium into a compatible and modern word-processing environment. Her cheerful response to each pressure situation kept the productivity juices flowing. We thank Dr. Monte P. Tull, Dr. Jim J. Sluss, Jr., and Dr. Joe P. Havlicek of the University of Oklahoma for contributing the application Chapters 10 and 11. These chapters enhance the overall quality of the book.

We also thank Jessica Gallus, editorial assistant to Senior Editor, Bob Argentieri. She kept the pressure on when crucial decisions had to be made. If not for her persistent checking on the status of the manuscript, things might not have moved along as fast as they did. Thanks, Jessica! As with our previous experiences with John Wiley & Sons, all of the editorial and production staff did a superb job of getting out a product of which we are all proud. We look forward to future associations with everyone.

FUZZY ENGINEERING EXPERT SYSTEMS WITH NEURAL NETWORK APPLICATIONS

1
ARTIFICIAL INTELLIGENCE

The background of artificial intelligence (AI) has been characterized by controversial opinions and diverse approaches. Despite the controversies, which have ranged from the basic definition of intelligence to questions about the moral and ethical aspects of pursuing AI, the technology continues to generate practical results. With increasing efforts in AI research, many of the prevailing arguments are being resolved with proven technical approaches. Expert systems, the main subject of this book, is the most promising branch of AI.

"Artificial intelligence" is a controversial name for a technology that promises much potential for improving human productivity. The phrase seems to challenge human pride in being the sole creation capable of possessing real intelligence. All kinds of anecdotal jokes about AI have been offered by casual observers. A speaker once recounted his wife's response when he told her that he was venturing into the new technology of artificial intelligence. "Thank God, you're finally realizing how dumb I've been saying you were all these years," was alleged to have been the wife's words of encouragement. One whimsical definition of AI is "Artificial Insemination of knowledge into a machine." Despite the derisive remarks, serious embracers of AI may yet have the last laugh. It is being shown again and again that AI may hold the key to improving operational effectiveness in many areas of applications. Some observers have suggested changing the term *artificial intelligence* to a less controversial one such as *intelligent applications* (IA). This refers more to the way that computer and software are used innovatively to solve complex decision problems.

Natural intelligence involves the capability of humans to acquire knowledge, reason with the knowledge, and use it to solve problems effectively. By contrast, *artificial intelligence* is defined as the ability of a machine to use simulated knowledge in solving problems.

1.1 ORIGIN OF ARTIFICIAL INTELLIGENCE

The definition of intelligence had been sought by many great philosophers and mathematicians over the ages, including Aristotle, Plato, Copernicus, and

1

Galileo. They attempted to explain the process of thought and understanding. The real key that started the quest for the simulation of intelligence did not occur, however, until the English philosopher Thomas Hobbes put forth an interesting concept in the 1650s. Hobbes believed that thinking consists of symbolic operations and that everything in life can be represented mathematically. These beliefs led directly to the notion that a machine capable of carrying out mathematical operations on symbols could imitate human thinking. This is the basic driving force behind the AI effort. For that reason Hobbes is sometimes referred to as the grandfather of artificial intelligence.

While the term "artificial intelligence" was coined by John McCarthy relatively recently (1956), the idea had been considered centuries before. As early as 1637 René Descartes was conceptually exploring the ability of a machine to have intelligence when he said:

> For we can well imagine a machine so made that it utters words and even, in a few cases, words pertaining specifically to some actions that affect it physically. However, no such machine could ever arrange its words in various different ways so as to respond to the sense of whatever is said in its presence—as even the dullest people can do.

Descartes believed that the mind and the physical world are on parallel planes that cannot be equated. They are of different substances following entirely different rules and can thus not be successfully compared. The physical world (i.e., machines) cannot imitate the mind because there is no common reference point.

The 1800s saw advancement in the conceptualization of the computer. Charles Babbage, a British mathematician, laid the foundation for the construction of the computer, a machine defined as being capable of performing mathematical computations. In 1833 Babbage introduced an analytical engine. This computational machine incorporated two unprecedented ideas that were to become crucial elements in the modern computer. First, it had operations that were fully programmable, and second, it could contain conditional branches. Without these two abilities the power of today's computers would be inconceivable. Due to a lack of financial support, Babbage was never able to realize his dream of building the analytic engine. However, his dream was revived through the efforts of later researchers. Babbage's basic concepts can be observed in the way that most computers operate today.

Another British mathematician, George Boole, worked on issues that were to become equally important. Boole formulated the laws of thought that set up rules of logic for representing thought. The rules contained only two-valued variables. By this, any variable in a logical operation could be in one of only two states: yes or no, true or false, all or nothing, 0 or 1, on or off, and so on. This was the birth of digital logic, a key component of the artificial intelligence effort.

In the early 1900s Alfred North Whitehead and Bertrand Russell extended Boole's logic to include mathematical operations. This not only led to the formulation of digital computers but also made possible one of the first ties between computers and thought process.

However, there was still no acceptable way to construct such a computer. In 1938 Claude Shannon demonstrated that Boolean logic consisting of only two-variable states (e.g., on–off switching of circuits) can be used to perform logic operations [93]. Based on this premise, ENIAC (Electronic Numerical Integrator and Computer) was built in 1946 at the University of Pennsylvania. ENIAC was a large-scale, fully operational electronic computer that signaled the beginning of the first generation of computers. It could perform calculations 1,000 times faster than its electromechanical predecessors. It weighed 30 tons, stood two stories high, and occupied 1500 square feet of floor space. Unlike today's computers, which operate in binary codes (0s and 1s), ENIAC operated in decimal (0, 1, 2, . . . , 9) and required 10 vacuum tubes to represent one decimal digit. With over 18,000 vacuum tubes, ENIAC needed a great amount of electrical power, so much that it was said that it dimmed the lights in Philadelphia whenever it operated.

1.2 HUMAN INTELLIGENCE VERSUS MACHINE INTELLIGENCE

Two of the leading mathematicians and computer enthusiasts between 1900 and 1950 were Alan Turing and John von Neumann. In 1945, von Neumann insisted that computers should not be built as glorified adding machines, with all their operations specified in advance. Rather, he suggested, computers should be built as general-purpose logic machines capable of executing a wide variety of programs. Such machines, von Neumann proclaimed, would be highly flexible and capable of being readily shifted from one task to another. They could react intelligently to the results of their calculations, could choose among alternatives, and could even play checkers or chess. This represented something unheard of at that time: a machine with built-in intelligence, able to operate on internal instructions.

Prior to von Neumann's concept, even the most complex mechanical devices had always been controlled from the outside, for example, by setting dials and knobs. Von Neumann did not invent the computer, but what he introduced was equally significant: computing by use of computer programs, the way it is done today. His work paved the way for what would later be called artificial intelligence in computers.

Alan Turing also made major contributions to the conceptualization of a machine that can be universally used for all problems based only on variable instructions fed into it. Turing's universal machine concept, along with von Neumann's concept of a storage area containing multiple instructions that can be accessed in any sequence, solidified the ideas needed to develop the programmable computer. Thus, a machine was developed that could perform logical operations and could do them in varying orders by changing the set of instructions that were executed.

Due to the fact that operational machines were now being realized, questions about the "intelligence" of the machines began to surface. Turing's other contribution to the world of AI came in the area of defining what constitutes intelligence. In 1950 he designed the Turing test for determining the intelligence of a system. The test utilized the conversational interaction between three players to try to verify computer intelligence.

The test is conducted by having a person (the interrogator) in a room that contains only a computer terminal. In an adjoining room, hidden from view, a man (person A) and a woman (person B) are located with another computer terminal. The interrogator communicates with the couple in the other room by typing questions on the keyboard. The questions appear on the couple's computer screen and they respond by typing on their own keyboard. The interrogator can direct questions to either person A or person B, but without knowing which is the man and which is the woman.

The purpose of the test is to distinguish between the man and the woman merely by analyzing their responses. In the test, only one of the people is obligated to give truthful responses. The other person deliberately attempts to fool and confuse the interrogator by giving responses that may lead to an incorrect guess. The second stage of the test is to substitute a computer for one of the two persons in the other room. Now the human is obligated to give truthful responses to the interrogator while the computer tries to fool the interrogator into thinking that it is human. Turing's contention is that if the interrogator's success rate in the human/computer version of the game is not better than his success rate in the man/woman version, then the computer can be said to be "thinking." That is, the computer possesses "intelligence." Turing's test has served as a classical example for artificial intelligence proponents for many years.

By 1952 computer hardware had advanced far enough that actual experiments in writing programs to imitate thought processes could be conducted. The team of Herbert Simon, Allen Newell, and Cliff Shaw was organized to conduct such an experiment. They set out to establish what kinds of problems a computer could solve with the right programming. Proving theorems in symbolic logic such as those set forth by Whitehead and Russell in the early 1900s fit the concept of what they felt an intelligent computer should be able to handle.

It quickly became apparent that there was a need for a new higher-level computer language than was currently available. First, they needed a language that was more user-friendly and could take program instructions that are easily understood by a human programmer and automatically convert them into machine language that could be understood by the computer. Second, they needed a programming language that changed the way in which computer memory was allocated. All previous languages would preassign memory at the start of a program. The team found that the type of programs they were writing would require large amounts of memory and would function unpredictably.

To solve the problem, they developed a list processing language. This type of language would label each area of memory and then maintain a list of all available memory. As memory became available it would update the list and when more memory was needed it would allocate the amount necessary. This type of programming also allowed the programmer to be able to structure his or her data so that any information that was to be used for a particular problem could be easily accessed.

The end result of their effort was a program called Logic Theorist. This program had rules consisting of axioms already proved. When it was given a new logical expression, it would search through all of the possible operations in an effort to discover a proof of the new expression. Instead of using a brute force search method, they pioneered the use of heuristics in the search method.

The Logic Theorist that they developed in 1955 was capable of solving 38 of 52 theorems that Whitehead and Russell had devised. It did them very quickly. What took Logic Theorist a matter of minutes would have taken years if it had been done by simple brute force on a computer. By comparison the steps that it went through to arrive at a proof to those that human subjects went through showed that it had achieved a remarkable imitation of the human thought process. This system is considered the first AI program.

1.3 THE FIRST AI CONFERENCE

The summer of 1956 saw the first attempt to establish the field of machine intelligence into an organized effort. The Dartmouth Summer Conference, organized by John McCarthy, Marvin Minsky, Nathaniel Rochester, and Claude Shannon, brought together people whose work and interest formally founded the field of AI. The conference, held at Dartmouth College in New Hampshire, was funded by a grant from the Rockefeller Foundation. It was at that conference that John McCarthy coined the term "artificial intelligence." This was the same John McCarthy who developed the LISP programming language, which has become a standard tool for AI development. In attendance at the meeting, in addition to the organizers, were Herbert Simon, Allen Newell, Arthur Samuel, Trenchard More, Oliver Selfridge, and Ray Solomonoff.

The Logic Theorist developed by Newell, Shaw, and Simon was discussed at the conference [73]. Newell, Shaw, and Simon were far ahead of others in actually implementing AI ideas. The Dartmouth meeting served mostly as an avenue for the exchange of information and, more importantly, as a turning point in the main emphasis of work in the AI endeavor. Instead of concentrating on the hardware to imitate intelligence, the meeting set the course for examining the structure of the data being processed by computers, the use of computers to process symbols, the need for new languages, and the role of computers for testing theories.

1.4 EVOLUTION OF SMART PROGRAMS

The next major step in software technology came from Newell, Shaw, and Simon in 1959. The program they introduced was called General Problem Solver (GPS). GPS was intended to be a program that could solve many types of problems. It was capable of solving theorems, playing chess, or doing various complex puzzles. GPS was a significant step forward in AI. It incorporates several new ideas to facilitate problem solving. The nucleus of the system was the use of means-end analysis, which involves comparing a present state with a goal state. The difference between the two states is determined and a search is done to find a method to reduce this difference. This process is continued until there is no difference between the current state and the goal state.

In order to improve the search further, GPS contained two other features. The first is that, if while trying to reduce the deviation from the goal state, GPS finds that it has actually complicated the search process, it was capable of backtracking to an earlier state and exploring alternate solution paths. The second is that it was capable of defining sub-goal states that, if satisfied, would permit the solution process to continue. In formulating GPS, Newell and Simon had done extensive work studying human subjects and the way they solved problems. They felt that GPS did a good job of imitating the human subjects. They commented on the effort by saying [72]:

> The fragmentary evidence we have obtained to date encourages us to think that the General Problem Solver provides a rather good first approximation to an information processing theory of certain kinds of thinking and problem-solving behavior. The processes of "thinking" can no longer be regarded as completely mysterious.

One criticism of GPs was that the only way the program obtained any information was through human input. The way and order in which the problems were presented was controlled by humans, thus the program was only doing what it was told to do. Newell and Simon argued that the fact that the program was not just repeating steps and sequences, but was actually applying rules to solve problems it had not previously encountered, is indicative of intelligent behavior.

There were other criticisms as well. Humans are able to devise new shortcuts and improvise. GPS would always go down the same path to solve the same problem, making the same mistakes as before. It could not learn. Another problem was that while GPS was good when given a certain area or a specific search space to solve, in solving problems it was difficult to determine what search space to use. Sometimes solving the problem is trivial compared to finding the search space. The problems posed to GPS were all of a specific nature. They were all puzzles or logical challenges; problems that could easily be expressed in symbolic form and operated on in a pseudomathematical approach. There are many problems that humans face that are not so easily expressed in symbolic form.

Also in 1959, John McCarthy came out with a tool that was to greatly improve the ability of researchers to develop AI programs. He developed a new computer programming language called LISP (list processing). It was to become one of the most widely used languages in the field.

LISP is distinctive in two areas: memory organization and control structure. The memory organization is done in a tree fashion with interconnections between memory groups. Thus, it permits a programmer to keep track of complex structural relationships. The other distinction is the way the control of the program is done. Instead of working from the prerequisites to a goal, it starts with the goal and works backwards to determine what prerequisites are required to achieve the goal.

In 1960 Frank Rosenblatt did work in the area of pattern recognition. He introduced a device called PERCEPTRON that was supposed to be capable of recognizing letters and other patterns. It consisted of a grid of 400 photo cells connected with wires to a response unit that would produce a signal only if the light coming off the subject to be recognized crossed a certain threshold.

During the latter part of the 1960s there were two efforts in another area of simulating human reasoning. Kenneth Colby at Stanford University and Joseph Weizenbaum at MIT wrote separate programs that were capable of interacting in a two-way conversation. Weizenbaum's program was called ELIZA. The programs were able to sustain very realistic conversations by using very clever techniques. For example, ELIZA used a pattern-matching method that would scan for keywords like "I," "you," "like," and so on. If one of these words was found, it would execute rules associated with it. If no match was found, the program would respond with a request for more information or with a noncommittal response.

It was also during the 1960s that Marvin Minsky and his students at MIT made significant contributions towards the progress of AI. One student, T. G. Evans, wrote a program that would perform visual analogies. The program was shown two figures that had some relationship to each other and was then asked to find another set of figures from a set that matched the same relationship. The input to the computer was not done by a visual sensor (like the one worked on by Rosenblatt), but instead the figures were described to the system.

In 1968 another student of Minsky's, Daniel Bobrow, came out with a linguistic problem solver called STUDENT. It was designed to solve problems that were presented to it in a word problem format. The key to the program was the assumption that every sentence was an equation. It would take certain words and turn them into mathematical operations. For example, it would convert "is" into "=" and "per" into "÷."

Even though STUDENT responded very much the same way that a real student would, there was a major difference in depth of understanding. While the program was capable of calculating the time two trains would collide given the starting points and speeds of both, it had no real understanding or even cared what a "train" or "time" was. Expressions like "perchance" and "this is it" could mean totally different things than what the program would assume. A human student would be able to discern the intended meaning from the context in which the terms were used.

In an attempt to answer the criticisms about understanding, another student at MIT, Terry Winograd, developed a significant program named SHRDLU. In setting up his program, he utilized what was referred to as a micro-world or blocks-world. This limited the scope of the world that the program had to try to understand. The program communicated in what appeared to be natural language.

The world of SHRDLU consisted of a set of blocks of varying shapes (cubes, pyramids, etc.), sizes, and colors. These blocks were all set on an imaginary table. Upon request, SHRDLU would rearrange the blocks to any requested configuration. The program was capable of knowing when a request was unclear or impossible. For instance, if it was requested to put a block on top of a pyramid it would request that the user specify more clearly what block and what pyramid. It would also recognize that the block would not sit on top of the pyramid.

Two other approaches that the program took that were new to programs were the ability to make assumptions and the ability to learn. If asked to pick up a larger block, it would assume that you meant a larger block than the one it was currently working on. If asked to build a figure that it did not know, it would ask for an explanation of what it was and, thereafter, it would recognize the object. One major sophistication that SHRDLU added to the science of AI programming was its use of a series of expert modules or specialists. There was one segment of the program that specialized in segmenting sentences into meaningful word groups, a sentence specialist to determine the relationship between nouns and verbs, and a scenario specialist that understood how individual scenes related to one another. This sophistication greatly enhanced the method in which instructions were analyzed.

As sophisticated as SHRDLU was at that time, other scholars were quick to point out its deficiencies. SHRDLU only responded to requests; it could not initiate conversations. It also had no sense of conversational flow. It would jump from performing one type of task to a totally different one if so requested. While SHRDLU had an understanding of the tasks it was to perform and the physical world in which it operated, it still could not understand very abstract concepts.

1.5 BRANCHES OF ARTIFICIAL INTELLIGENCE

The various attempts at formally defining the use of machines to simulate human intelligence led to the development of several branches of AI. Current subspecialities of artificial intelligence include:

1. *Natural language processing* deals with various areas of research such as database inquiry systems, story understanders, automatic text indexing, grammar and style analysis of text, automatic text generation, machine translation, speech analysis, and speech synthesis.
2. *Computer vision* deals with research efforts involving scene analysis, image understanding, and motion derivation.
3. *Robotics* involves the control of effectors on robots to manipulate or grasp objects, locomotion of independent machines, and use of sensory input to guide actions.
4. *Problem-solving and planning* involves applications such as refinement of high-level goals into lower-level ones, determination of actions needed to achieve goals, revision of plans based on intermediate results, and focused search of important goals.
5. *Learning* deals with research into various forms of learning including rote learning, learning through advice, learning by example, learning by task performance, and learning by following concepts.
6. *Expert systems* deals with the processing of knowledge as opposed to the processing of data. It involves the development of computer software to solve complex decision problems.

1.6 NEURAL NETWORKS

Neural networks, sometimes called connectionist systems, are networks of simple processing elements or nodes capable of processing information in response to external inputs. Neural networks were originally presented as models of the human nervous system. Just after World War II, scientists found out that the physiology of the brain was similar to the electronic processing mode used by computers. In both cases, large amounts of data are manipulated. In the case of computers, the elementary unit of processing is the *bit,* which is in either an "on" or "off" state. In the case of the brain, *neurons* perform the basic data processing. Neurons are tiny cells that follow a binary principle of being either in a state of firing (on) or not firing (off). When a neuron is on, it fires a signal to other neurons across a network of synapses.

In the late 1940s Donald Hebb, a researcher, hypothesized that biological memory results when two neurons are active simultaneously. The synaptic connection of synchronous neurons is reinforced and given preference over connections made by neurons that are not active simultaneously. The level of preference is measured as a weighted value. Pattern recognition, a major strength of human intelligence, is based on the weighted strengths of the reinforced connections between various pairs of simultaneously active neurons.

The idea presented by Hebb was to develop a computer model based on the way in which neurons form connections in the human brain. But the idea was considered to be preposterous at that time since the human brain contains

100 billion neurons and each neuron is connected to 10,000 others by a synapse. Even with today's computing capability, it is still difficult to duplicate the activities of neurons. In 1969, Marvin Minsky and Seymour Pappert criticized existing neural network research as being worthless [68]. It has been claimed that the pessimistic views they presented discouraged further funding for neural network research for several years. Funding was diverted instead to further research of expert systems, which Minsky and Pappert favored. Only recently have neural networks begun to make a strong comeback.

Because neural networks are modeled after the operations of the brain, they hold considerable promise as building blocks for achieving the ultimate aim of artificial intelligence. The present generation of neural networks uses artificial neurons. Each neuron is connected to at least one other neuron in a synapse-like fashion. The networks are based on some form of learning model. Neural networks learn by evaluating changes in input. Learning can be either supervised or unsupervised. In supervised learning, each response is guided by given parameters. The computer is instructed to compare any inputs to ideal responses, and any discrepancy between the new inputs and ideal responses is recorded. The system then uses this data bank to guess how much the newly gathered data are similar to or different from the ideal responses, that is, how closely the pattern matches. Supervised learning networks are now commercially used for control systems and handwriting and speech recognition.

In unsupervised learning, input is evaluated independently and stored as patterns. The system evaluates a range of patterns and identifies similarities and dissimilarities among them. However, the system cannot derive any meaning from the information without human assignment of values to the patterns. Comparisons are relative to other results, rather than to an ideal result. Unsupervised learning networks are used to discover patterns where a particular outcome is not known in advance, such as in physics research and the analysis of financial data. Several commercial neural network products are now available, such as NeuroShell from Ward Systems Group. The software is expensive but is relatively easy to use. It interfaces well with other software such as Lotus 1-2-3 and dBASE, as well as with C, Pascal, FORTRAN, and BASIC programming languages.

Despite the proven potential of neural networks, they drastically oversimplify the operations of the brain. The existing systems can only undertake elementary pattern-recognition tasks and are weak at deductive reasoning, math calculations, and other computations that are easily handled by conventional computer processing. The difficulty in achieving the promise of neural networks lies in our limited understanding of how the human brain functions. Undoubtedly, to model the brain accurately, we must know more about it. But a complete knowledge of the brain is still many years away.

1.7 EMERGENCE OF EXPERT SYSTEMS

In the late 1960s to early 1970s a special branch of AI began to emerge. The branch, known as expert systems, has grown dramatically in the past few years and represents the most successful demonstration of the capabilities of AI. Expert systems are the first truly commercial application of work done in the AI field and as such have received considerable publicity. Due to the potential benefits, there is currently a major concentration in the research and development of expert systems compared to other efforts in AI.

Unlike the desire to develop general problem-solving techniques that had characterized AI before, expert systems address problems that are focused. When Edward Feigenbaum developed the first successful expert system, DENDRAL, he had a specific type of problem that he wanted to be able to solve. The problem involved determining which organic compound was being analyzed in a mass spectrograph. The program was intended to simulate the work that an expert chemist would do in analyzing the data. This led to the term "expert system."

Between 1970 and 1980 numerous expert systems were introduced to handle several functions, from diagnosing diseases to analyzing geological exploration information. Of course, expert systems have not escaped the critics. Due to the nature of the system, critics argue that it does not fit the true structure of artificial intelligence. Because of the use of only specific knowledge and the ability to solve only specific problems, some critics are apprehensive about referring to an expert system as intelligent. Proponents argue that if the system produces the desired results, it is of little concern whether it is intelligent or not.

In 1972, Hubert Dreyfus initiated another debate of interest [24]. Joseph Weizenbaum presented similar views in 1976 [102]. The issues that both authors raised touched on some of the basic questions that dated back to the time of Descartes. One of Weizenbaum's reservations concerned what should ethically and morally be handed over to machines. He maintained that the path that AI was pursuing was headed in a dangerous direction. Some aspects of human experience, such as love and morality, cannot be adequately imitated by machines.

While the debates were going on over how much AI could do, the work on getting AI to do more continued. In 1972 Roger Shrank introduced the notion of script, the set of familiar events that can be expected from an often-encountered setting. This enables a program to assimilate facts quickly. In 1975 Marvin Minsky presented the idea of frames. Even though neither concept drastically advanced the theory of AI, they did help expedite research in the field.

In 1979 Minsky suggested a method that could lead to a better simulation of intelligence: the "society of minds" view, in which the execution of knowledge is performed by several programs working in conjunction simultaneously. This concept helped to encourage interesting developments such as present-day parallel processing.

During the 1980s AI gained significant exposure and interest. Artificial intelligence, once restricted to the domain of esoteric research, has now become a practical tool for solving real problems. While AI is enjoying its most prosperous period, it is still plagued with disagreements and criticisms. The emergence of commercial expert systems on the market has created both enthusiasm and skepticism. There is no doubt that more research and successful applications developments will help prove the potential of expert systems. It should be recalled that new technologies sometimes fail to convince all initial observers. IBM, which later became a giant in the personal computer business, hesitated for several years before getting into the market because the company never thought that those little boxes called personal computers would ever have any significant impact on the society. How wrong they were!

The effort in AI is worthwhile as long as it increases the understanding that we have of intelligence and enables us to do things that we previously could not do. Due to the discoveries made in AI research, computers are now capable of things that were once beyond imagination.

1.7.1   Embedded Expert Systems

More expert systems are beginning to show up, not as stand-alone systems, but as software applications in large software systems. This trend is bound to continue as systems integration takes hold in many software applications. Many conventional commercial packages, such as statistical analysis systems, data management systems, information management systems, project management systems, and data analysis systems, now contain embedded heuristics that constitute expert systems components of the packages. Even some computer operating systems now contain embedded expert systems designed to provide real-time systems monitoring and troubleshooting. With the success of embedded expert systems, the long-awaited payoffs from the technology are now beginning to be realized.

Because the technology behind expert systems has changed little over the past decade, the issue is not whether the technology is useful, but how to implement it. This is why the integrated approach of this book is very useful. The book focuses not only on the technology of expert systems, but also on how to implement and manage the technology. Combining neural networks technology with expert systems, for example, will become more prevalent. In combination, the neural networks might be implemented as a tool for scanning and selecting data while the expert system would evaluate the data and present recommendations.

2

FUNDAMENTALS OF EXPERT SYSTEMS

This chapter introduces the basic concepts of expert systems. The hierarchical process of developing expert systems is presented, as well as the essential characteristics of expert systems are presented. More specific details of the concepts introduced in this chapter are covered in subsequent chapters.

2.1   EXPERT SYSTEMS PROCESS

This book is organized in the structure of a strategic process for developing successful expert systems. Figure 2.1 presents the hierarchy of topics as they are presented here and in the subsequent chapters. The strategic process is recommended for anyone venturing into the technology of expert systems from the standpoint of training, research, or applications. This chapter covers the basic concepts of expert systems technology. A basic understanding of these concepts is essential to getting the most out of expert systems. More specific details of the concepts presented in this chapter are discussed in appropriate sections of the subsequent chapters. Chapter 3 covers problem analysis. To be effective, the right problems must be selected for expert systems implementation. The principle of "garbage in, garbage out" is also applicable here. Wrong problems lead to incorrect implementation of expert systems.

Chapter 4 covers knowledge engineering. Knowledge acquisition is a critical aspect of the expert systems effort. If the knowledge collected is garbage, the best that can be expected from a system is garbage. Chapter 5 presents probabilistic and fuzzy reasoning. Chapter 6 presents fuzzy systems techniques for handling uncertainty in expert systems. Chapter 7 presents neural networks.

Chapter 8 covers neural-fuzzy networks. Chapter 9 presents the technique of evolutionary computing. Chapter 10 presents an application to manufacturing. Chapter 11 presents an application to forecasting.

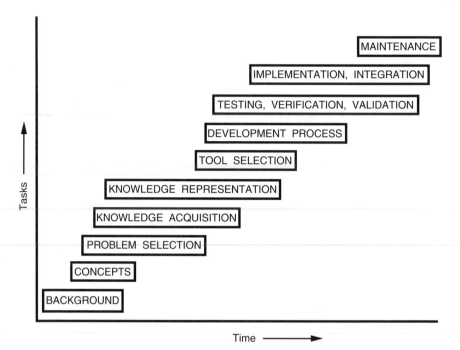

Figure 2.1. Hierarchy of expert systems development process.

2.2   EXPERT SYSTEMS CHARACTERISTICS

By definition, an expert system is a computer program that simulates the thought process of a human expert to solve complex decision problems in a specific domain. This chapter addresses the characteristics of expert systems that make them different from conventional programming and traditional decision support tools. The growth of expert systems is expected to continue for several years. With the continuing growth, many new and exciting applications will emerge. An expert system operates as an interactive system that responds to questions, asks for clarification, makes recommendations, and generally aids the decision-making process. Expert systems provide expert advice and guidance in a wide variety of activities, from computer diagnosis to delicate medical surgery.

Various definitions of expert systems have been offered by several authors. A general definition that is representative of the intended functions of expert systems is:

An *expert system* is an interactive computer-based decision tool that uses both facts and heuristics to solve difficult decision problems based on knowledge acquired from an expert.

An expert system may be viewed as a computer simulation of a human expert. Expert systems are an emerging technology with many areas for potential applications. Past applications range from MYCIN, used in the medical field to diagnose infectious blood diseases, to XCON, used to configure computer systems. These expert systems have proven to be quite successful. Most applications of expert systems will fall into one of the following categories:

- Interpreting and identifying
- Predicting
- Diagnosing
- Designing
- Planning
- Monitoring
- Debugging and testing
- Instructing and training
- Controlling

Applications that are computational or deterministic in nature are not good candidates for expert systems. Traditional decision support systems such as spreadsheets are very mechanistic in the way they solve problems. They operate under mathematical and Boolean operators in their execution and arrive at one and only one static solution for a given set of data. Calculation-intensive applications with very exacting requirements are better handled by traditional decision support tools or conventional programming. The best application candidates for expert systems are those dealing with expert heuristics for solving problems. Conventional computer programs are based on factual knowledge, an indisputable strength of computers. Humans, by contrast, solve problems on the basis of a mixture of factual and heuristic knowledge. Heuristic knowledge, composed of intuition, judgment, and logical inferences, is an indisputable strength of humans. Successful expert systems will be those that combine facts and heuristics and thus merge human knowledge with computer power in solving problems. To be effective, an expert system must focus on a particular problem domain, as discussed below.

2.2.1 Domain Specificity

Expert systems are typically very domain specific. For example, a diagnostic expert system for troubleshooting computers must actually perform all the necessary data manipulation as a human expert would. The developer of such a system must limit his or her scope of the system to just what is needed to solve the target problem. Special tools or programming languages are often needed to accomplish the specific objectives of the system.

2.2.2   Special Programming Languages

Expert systems are typically written in special programming languages. The use of languages like LISP and PROLOG in the development of an expert system simplifies the coding process. The major advantage of these languages, as compared to conventional programming languages, is the simplicity of the addition, elimination, or substitution of new rules and memory management capabilities. Some of the distinguishing characteristics of programming languages needed for expert systems work are:

- Efficient mix of integer and real variables
- Good memory-management procedures
- Extensive data-manipulation routines
- Incremental compilation
- Tagged memory architecture
- Optimization of the systems environment
- Efficient search procedures

2.3   EXPERT SYSTEMS STRUCTURE

Complex decisions involve intricate combination of factual and heuristic knowledge. In order for the computer to be able to retrieve and effectively use heuristic knowledge, the knowledge must be organized in an easily accessible format that distinguishes among data, knowledge, and control structures. For this reason, expert systems are organized in three distinct levels:

1. *Knowledge base* consists of problem-solving rules, procedures, and intrinsic data relevant to the problem domain.
2. *Working memory* refers to task-specific data for the problem under consideration.
3. *Inference engine* is a generic control mechanism that applies the axiomatic knowledge in the knowledge base to the task-specific data to arrive at some solution or conclusion.

These three pieces may very well come from different sources. The inference engine, such as VP-Expert, may come from a commercial vendor. The knowledge base may be a specific diagnostic knowledge base compiled by a consulting firm, and the problem data may be supplied by the end user. A knowledge base is the nucleus of the expert system structure. A knowledge base is not a data base. The traditional data base environment deals with data that have a static relationship between the elements in the problem domain. A knowledge base is created by knowledge engineers, who translate the knowledge of real human experts into rules and strategies. These rules and

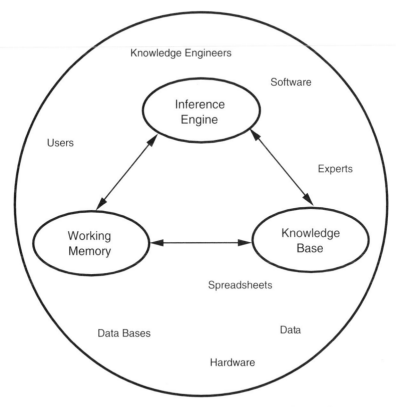

Figure 2.2. Expert systems organization and operating environment.

strategies can change depending on the prevailing problem scenario. The knowledge base provides the expert system with the capability to recommend directions for user inquiry. The system also instigates further investigation into areas that may be important to a certain line of reasoning but not apparent to the user.

The modularity of an expert system is an important distinguishing characteristic compared to a conventional computer program. Modularity is effected in an expert system by the use of three distinct components, as shown in Figure 2.2.

The knowledge base constitutes the problem-solving rules, facts, or intuition that a human expert might use in solving problems in a given problem domain. The knowledge base is usually stored in terms of if–then rules. The working memory represents relevant data for the current problem being solved. The inference engine is the control mechanism that organizes the problem data and searches through the knowledge base for applicable rules. With the increasing popularity of expert systems, many commercial inference engines are coming onto the market. A survey of selected commercial infer-

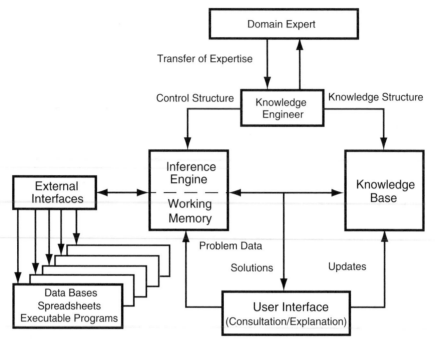

Figure 2.3. Integration of expert systems components.

ence engines is presented in the Appendix at the end of this book. The development of a functional expert system usually centers around the organization of the knowledge base. A functional integration of expert systems components is shown in Figure 2.3.

A good expert system is expected to grow as it learns from user feedback. Feedback is incorporated into the knowledge base as appropriate to make the expert system smarter. The dynamism of the application environment for expert systems is based on the individual dynamism of the components. This can be classified as follows:

- *Most dynamic: Working memory.* The contents of the working memory, sometimes called the data structure, changes with each problem situation. Consequently, it is the most dynamic component of an expert system, assuming, of course, that it is kept current.
- *Moderately dynamic: Knowledge base.* The knowledge base need not change unless a new piece of information arises that indicates a change in the problem solution procedure. Changes in the knowledge base should be carefully evaluated before being implemented. In effect, changes should not be based on just one consultation experience. For example, a rule that is found to be irrelevant under one problem situation may turn out to be crucial in solving other problems.

• *Least dynamic: Inference engine.* Because of the strict control and coding structure of an inference engine, changes are made only if absolutely necessary to correct a bug or enhance the inferential process. Commercial inference engines, in particular, change only at the discretion of the developer. Since frequent updates can be disruptive and costly to clients, most commercial software developers try to minimize the frequency of updates.

2.3.1 The Need for Expert Systems

Expert systems are necessitated by the limitations associated with conventional human decision-making processes, including:

1. Human expertise is very scarce.
2. Humans get tired from physical or mental workload.
3. Humans forget crucial details of a problem.
4. Humans are inconsistent in their day-to-day decisions.
5. Humans have limited working memory.
6. Humans are unable to comprehend large amounts of data quickly.
7. Humans are unable to retain large amounts of data in memory.
8. Humans are slow in recalling information stored in memory.
9. Humans are subject to deliberate or inadvertent bias in their actions.
10. Humans can deliberately avoid decision responsibilities.
11. Humans *lie, hide,* and *die.*

Coupled with these human limitations are the weaknesses inherent in conventional programming and traditional decision-support tools. Despite the mechanistic power of computers, they have certain limitations that impair their effectiveness in implementing human-like decision processes. Conventional programs:

1. Are algorithmic in nature and depend only on raw machine power
2. Depend on facts that may be difficult to obtain
3. Do not make use of the effective heuristic approaches used by human experts
4. Are not easily adaptable to changing problem environments
5. Seek explicit and factual solutions that may not be possible

2.3.2 Benefits of Expert Systems

Expert systems offer an environment where the good capabilities of humans and the power of computers can be incorporated to overcome many of the limitations discussed in the previous section. Expert systems:

1. Increase the probability, frequency, and consistency of making good decisions
2. Help distribute human expertise
3. Facilitate real-time, low-cost expert-level decisions by the nonexpert
4. Enhance the utilization of most of the available data
5. Permit objectivity by weighing evidence without bias and without regard for the user's personal and emotional reactions
6. Permit dynamism through modularity of structure
7. Free up the mind and time of the human expert to enable him or her to concentrate on more creative activities
8. Encourage investigations into the subtle areas of a problem

Expert Systems Are For Everyone. No matter which area of business one is engaged in, expert systems can fulfill the need for higher productivity and reliability of decisions. Everyone can find an application potential in the field of expert systems. Contrary to the belief that expert systems may pose a threat to job security, expert systems can actually help to create opportunities for new job areas. Presented below are some areas that hold promise for new job opportunities:

- Basic research
- Applied research
- Knowledge engineering
- Inference engine development
- Consulting (development and implementation)
- Training
- Sales and marketing
- Passive or active end user

An active user is one who directly uses expert systems consultations to obtain recommendations. A passive user is one who trusts the results obtained from expert systems and supports the implementation of those results.

2.3.3   Transition from Data Processing to Knowledge Processing

What data has been to the previous generations of computing, knowledge is to the present generation of computing. Expert systems represent a revolutionary transition from the traditional data processing to knowledge processing. Figure 2.4 illustrates the relationships between the procedures for data processing and knowledge processing to make decisions. In traditional data processing the decision maker obtains the information generated and performs an explicit analysis of the information before making his or her decision. In

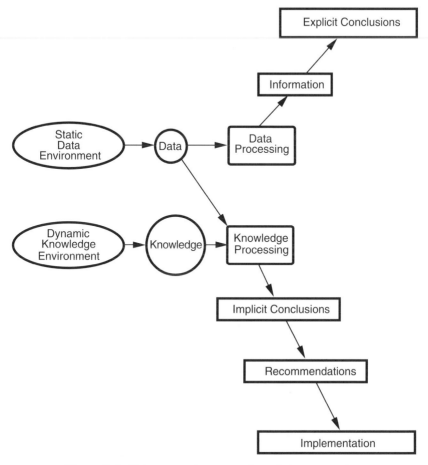

Figure 2.4. Data processing versus knowledge processing.

an expert system knowledge is processed by using available data as the proc-essing fuel. Conclusions are reached and recommendations are derived im-plicitly. The expert system offers the recommendation to the decision maker, who makes the final decision and implements it as appropriate. Conventional data can now be manipulated to work with durable knowledge, which can be processed to generate timely information, which is then used to enhance hu-man decisions.

2.4   HEURISTIC REASONING

Human experts use a type of problem-solving technique called heuristic rea-soning. Commonly called rules of thumb or expert heuristics, it allows the expert to arrive at a good solution quickly and efficiently. Expert systems base their reasoning process on symbolic manipulation and heuristic inference procedures that closely match the human thinking process. Conventional programs can only recognize numeric or alphabetic strings and manipulate them only in a preprogrammed manner.

2.4.1   Search Control Methods

All expert systems are search intensive. Many techniques have been employed to make these intensive searches more efficient. Branch and bound, pruning, depth-first search, and breadth-first search are some of the search techniques that have been explored. Because of the intensity of the search process, it is important that good search control strategies be used in the expert systems inference process.

2.4.2   Forward Chaining

This method involves checking the condition part of a rule to determine whether it is true or false. If the condition is true, then the action part of the rule is also true. This procedure continues until a solution is found or a dead end is reached. Forward chaining is commonly referred to as data-driven reasoning. Further discussions of forward chaining are presented in subsequent chapters.

2.4.3   Backward Chaining

Backward chaining is the reverse of forward chaining. It is used to backtrack from a goal to the paths that lead to the goal. Backward chaining is very good when all outcomes are known and the number of possible outcomes is not large. In this case, a goal is specified and the expert system tries to determine what conditions are needed to arrive at the specified goal. Backward chaining is thus also called goal-driven. More details are provided on the backward chaining process in Chapter 5.

2.5   USER INTERFACE

The initial development of an expert system is performed by the expert and the knowledge engineer. Unlike most conventional programs, in which only programmers can make program design decisions, the design of large expert systems is implemented through a team effort. A consideration of the needs of the end user is very important in designing the contents and user interface of expert systems.

2.5.1 Natural Language

The programming languages used for expert systems tend to operate in a manner similar to ordinary conversation. We usually state the premise of a problem in the form of a question, with actions being stated much as when we verbally answer the question, that is, in a "natural language" format. If, during or after a consultation, an expert system determines that a piece of its data or knowledge base is incorrect or is no longer applicable because the problem environment has changed, it should be able to update the knowledge base accordingly. This capability would allow the expert system to converse in a natural language format with either the developers or users.

Expert systems not only arrive at solutions or recommendations, but can give the user a level of confidence about the solution. In this manner, an expert system can handle both quantitative and qualitative factors when analyzing problems. This aspect is very important when we consider how inexact most input data are for day-to-day decision making. For example, the problems addressed by an expert system can have more than one solution or, in some cases, no definite solution at all. Yet the expert system can provide useful recommendations to the user just as a human consultant might do.

2.5.2 Explanations Facility in Expert Systems

One of the key characteristics of an expert system is the explanation facility. With this capability, an expert system can explain how it arrives at its conclusions. The user can ask questions dealing with the what, how, and why aspects of a problem. The expert system will then provide the user with a trace of the consultation process, pointing out the key reasoning paths followed during the consultation. Sometimes an expert system is required to solve other problems, possibly not directly related to the specific problem at hand, but whose solution will have an impact on the total problem-solving process. The explanation facility helps the expert system to clarify and justify why such a digression might be needed.

2.5.3 Data Uncertainties

Expert systems are capable of working with inexact data. An expert system allows the user to assign probabilities, certainty factors, or confidence levels to any or all input data. This feature closely represents how most problems are handled in the real world. An expert system can take all relevant factors into account and make a recommendation based on the best possible solution rather than the only exact solution.

2.5.4 Application Roadmap

The symbolic processing capabilities of AI technology lead to many potential applications in engineering and manufacturing. With the increasing sophisti-

Figure 2.5. Application roadmap for expert systems.

cation of AI techniques, analysts are now able to use innovative methods to provide viable solutions to complex problems in everyday applications. Figure 2.5 presents a structural representation of the application paths for artificial intelligence and expert systems.

2.5.5   Symbolic Processing

Contrary to the practice in conventional programming, expert systems can manipulate objects symbolically to arrive at reasonable conclusions to a prob-

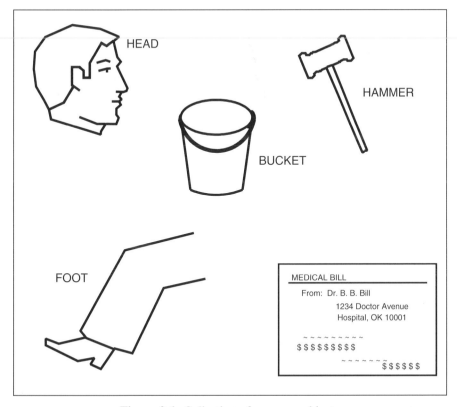

Figure 2.6. Collection of common objects.

lem scenario. The object drawings in this section are used to illustrate the versatility of symbolic processing by using the manipulation of objects to convey information. Let us assume that we are given the collection of five common objects as shown in Figure 2.6. The objects are Head, Hammer, Bucket, Foot, and Bill (as in doctor's bill). We can logically arrange a subset of the set of given objects to convey specific inferences. In Figure 2.7, four of the five objects are arranged in the order Hammer, Head, Foot, and Bucket. This unique arrangement may be represented by the equation presented below:

$$\text{Hammer} \sim \text{Head} = \text{Foot} \sim \text{Bucket}$$

It is desired to infer a reasonable statement of the information being conveyed by the symbolic arrangement of objects in Figure 2.7. Figure 2.8 presents an alternative arrangement of another subset (hammer, foot, foot, and bill) of the given objects. This alternative arrangement may be represented by the equation shown below:

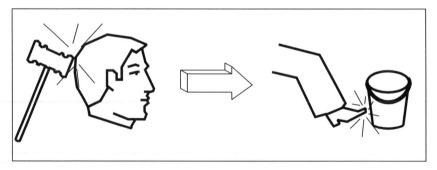

Figure 2.7. Arrangement of common objects.

Hammer ~ Foot = Foot ~ Bill

It is desired to infer a reasonable statement from Figure 2.8. It should be noted that ordinary mathematical reasoning concerning the equation hammer ~ foot = foot ~ bill might lead to Hammer = Bill. However, in artificial intelligence symbolic reasoning, the context of the arrangement of the objects will determine the proper implication.

Figure 2.7: If Hammer smashes Head, then victim kicks the bucket (i.e., dies). In this case, the action part of the statement relates to an action (a fatal one) by the victim of the assault.

Figure 2-8: If Hammer smashes Foot, then assailant foots the bill. In this case, the action part of the statement relates to a compensatory action (restitution) by the assailant.

Using a finite set of symbolic objects, we can generate different pieces of information with different permutations of the objects. A particularly interesting aspect of symbolic processing is noted in Figure 2.8. The object Foot

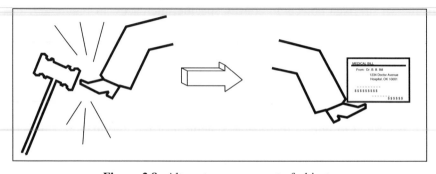

Figure 2.8. Alternate arrangement of objects.

conveys one meaning when concatenated with one given object (Hammer) and another totally different meaning when concatenated with another object (bill). In fact, the identification of the object Bill is itself symbolically conveyed by the contents of the medical bill in Figure 2.6. With the illustrated capability of symbolic processing, very powerful AI-based tools can be developed for practical applications. However, more research and development efforts will be needed before many of those practical applications can be realized.

3
PROBLEM ANALYSIS

This chapter addresses the problem of selecting an appropriate problem for expert systems application. This is the first step in the expert systems development process and must be carefully investigated.

3.1   PROBLEM IDENTIFICATION

The selection of an appropriate problem is extremely important and is a major factor in determining the success of expert systems. A good problem for expert systems is one that has the following characteristics:

1. The problem affects many people.
2. There is enough concern about the problem.
3. The problem is in a domain where experts are in short supply.
4. Solving the problem has the potential for significant time and cost savings.
5. There is a reliable and accessible source of knowledge to be acquired.

Problem identification refers to the recognition of a situation that constitutes a problem to the organization. Problem identification requires the recognition of a window of opportunity to utilize expert systems. Both the problem domain and the specific problem must be identified. A problem domain refers to the general functional area in which the problem is located. For example, the general problem of engineering design constitutes a problem domain that design engineers will be interested in. Within engineering design, the specific problem may be that of designing a flexible manufacturing system. The identification of a problem may originate from any of several factors. Some of the factors are:

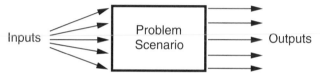

Figure 3.1. Input/output interface in problem scenario.

1. Internal needs and pressures
2. External motivation, such as market competition
3. Management requirement
4. Need for productivity improvement
5. Desire to stay abreast of the technology
6. Technological curiosity
7. Compliance with prevailing rules and regulations
8. Deficiencies in the present process

Once the general problem area has been identified, the next function is to decide what to do about the problem. Several options may be available in addressing the problem. These include:

1. Ignoring the problem
2. Denying that the problem exists
3. Devising an alternative that circumvents the problem
4. Deferring a solution to the problem
5. Confronting the problem and finding a solution to it

If the problem is to be confronted and solved, then a thorough analysis of the problem must be performed. The results of the analysis will indicate the specific approach that may be suitable in tackling the problem.

3.2 PROBLEM ANALYSIS

Problem analysis involves the evaluation of the characteristics associated with a given problem. The input–output process of the problem should be examined. Figure 3.1 presents a representation of the interface between inputs and outputs in a problem scenario. An analysis of the problem may reveal that computer solution is either not necessary or very essential. One should not embark upon a computer approach without first understanding the fundamental issues involved in the problem. Expert systems should be seen as a tool to solving a problem rather than the focus of the problem. The specific issues to be analyzed are presented below. For example, in engineering applications there may be a tendency to place too much emphasis on computer applications rather than engineering fundamentals. Expert systems should be used to implement engineering fundamentals after the fundamentals are fully understood in the light of the prevailing problem.

3.2.1   Scope of the Problem

The problem to be considered for expert system application should be well bounded and focused to prevent combinatorial explosion in the solution structure.

3.2.2   Symbolic Nature of the Problem

Problems that are numerically involved and algorithmic in nature may not be suitable for expert systems. The potential for symbolic representation and processing in the given problem should be evaluated. Symbolic processing refers to the use of symbols or strings of characters and data structures to convey problem characteristics. Conventional high-level programming languages such as FORTRAN and BASIC are good for numeric processing but poor for symbolic processing. Symbolic processing requires special-purpose languages such as LISP (List Processing) and PROLOG (Programming in Logic). If a problem does not have the characteristics suitable for symbolic representation, it may not be a suitable candidate for expert systems application.

3.2.3   Solution Time

The length of time needed to generate a solution to the problem is a major factor in determining the suitability for expert systems application. If a problem requires several weeks to solve, then it may not be suitable for an expert system. In such a large problem, an expert system may help provide intermediate solutions that are needed to arrive at the overall solution. Thus, an expert system can serve as an aid in a multistage solution process. On the other hand, if a problem requires very little time to solve, for example a few seconds, it may be too trivial to justify the expense of developing an expert system.

3.2.4   Frequency of Problem Occurrence

The frequency with which a problem occurs can also determine the approach to addressing the problem. A problem that occurs frequently enough to be a nuisance to regular operations is a good candidate for expert systems. A problem that occurs only once in a long while may not be a good candidate

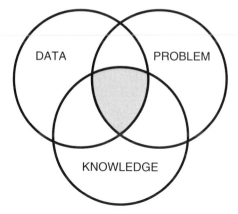

Figure 3.2. Intersection of data, knowledge, and problem.

unless it is very difficult to solve when it does occur and possesses the potential for great catastrophe if it is not solved.

3.2.5 Optimization versus Satisficing

A decision on whether to accept a satisfactory solution in place of the best solution can affect whether or not a problem needs the services of an expert system. Optimization requires the best solution available for a specific problem. Optimal solutions are normally produced by algorithmic models. These models can be implemented conveniently in conventional programming environments and do not need expert systems application. Satisficing models provide trade-off strategies for achieving a satisfactory solution to a problem within given constraints. These models are helpful for cases when time limitation, resource shortage, and performance requirements constrain the solution of a problem or in cases where an optimal solution is not possible. If the trade-off between best and satisfactory solutions is acceptable, then an expert system may be required.

3.2.6 Data and Knowledge Availability

A complete analysis of a problem will help determine if the data needed to solve the problem can be obtained. A match must be made between data availability, knowledge availability, and problem characteristics, as shown in Figure 3.2. The objective is to increase the intersection of the data availability, knowledge availability, and problem requirements as much as possible. Not only must an expert with the right knowledge be available, but the expert must also be willing to make his or her expertise available for solving the problem under consideration.

Most engineering problems have essential elements in common. If these elements are clearly outlined, an engineer can properly perceive, formulate, structure, and analyze the problem environment. The essential elements of engineering problems include problem statement, information, performance measure, solution model, and solution implementation. The steps involved in the solution approach are outlined below:

Step 1: Problem statement. A problem involves choosing between competing, and probably conflicting, alternatives. The components of problem-solving in engineering include:

- Describing the problem.
- Defining a model to represent the problem.
- Solving the model.
- Testing the solution.
- Implementing and maintaining the solution.

Problem definition is not a trivial task. In many cases, we recognize *symptoms* of a problem more readily than we recognize its *cause* and *location*. Even after the problem is accurately identified and defined, a benefit/cost analysis may be needed to determine if the cost of solving the problem is justified.

Step 2: Data and information requirements. Information is the driving force or fuel for any solution. Information clarifies the relative states of past, present, and future events in the problem scenario. The collection, storage, retrieval, organization, and processing of raw data are important components for generating information. Without data, there can be no information. Without good information, there cannot be any valid solution. The essential requirements for generating information for solving a problem include:

- Ensuring that an effective data-collection procedure is followed.
- Determining the type and the appropriate amount of data to collect.
- Evaluating the cost of collecting the required data.
- Evaluating the data collected with respect to information potential.

For example: Suppose a manager is presented with a recorded fact that says, "Sales for the last quarter are 10,000 units." This constitutes ordinary data. There are many ways of using these data to make a decision, depending on the manager's value system. An engineering analyst, with the aid of an expert system, can ensure the proper use of the data by transforming it into information, such as "Sales of 10,000 units for last quarter are low." With this type of information, the manager could develop a more definite course of action.

Step 3: Performance measure. The decision maker assigns a perceived worth or value to the available alternatives. Setting a measure of performance is crucial to the process of defining and generating recommendations in an expert system environment.

Step 4: Solution model. A solution model provides the basis for the analysis and synthesis of information and is the platform over which competing alternatives are compared. To be effective, a solution model must be based on a systematic and logical framework for guiding solution steps. A solution model can be a verbal, graphical, or mathematical representation of the ideas in the solution process. A solution model has the following characteristics:

- It is a simplified representation of an actual situation.
- It explains, simulates, and predicts the actual situation.
- It need not be complete or exact in all respects.
- It emphasizes the most important relationships in the decision process.
- It permits experiments that advance the understanding of the problem.
- It can be used repeatedly for similar problem scenarios.

The formulation of a solution model has three essential components:

1. *Abstraction:* Determining the relevant factors in the problem
2. *Construction:* Combining the factors into a logical model
3. *Validation:* Ensuring that the model adequately represents the problem

There are five basic types of solution models applicable to engineering and manufacturing problems:

1. *Descriptive models* directed at describing a decision scenario and identifying the associated problem. For example, a project analyst might use a critical path method (CPM) network model to identify bottleneck tasks in a project.
2. *Prescriptive models* furnish procedural guidelines for implementing actions. A managerial model for achieving communication, cooperation, and coordination in a problem environment is an example of a prescriptive model.
3. *Predictive models* are used to predict future events in a problem environment. They are typically based on historical data about the problem

situation. For example, a regression model based on past data may be used to predict future productivity gains associated with expected levels of resource allocation in a manufacturing operation.

4. *Satisficing models* provide satisfactory solutions rather than optimized solutions to a problem. The models are needed for cases where optimal solution may not be achievable.

5. *Optimizing models* are designed to find the best available solution to a problem subject to a certain set of constraints. For example, a linear programming model can be used to determine the optimal product mix in a production environment.

In many situations, two or more of the above models may be involved in the solution of a problem. For example, a descriptive model might provide insights into the nature of the problem, an optimization model might provide the optimal set of actions to take in solving the problem, a satisficing model might modify the optimal solution based on practicality, a prescriptive model might suggest the procedures for implementing the selected solution, and a predictive model might predict the expected outcome of implementing the solution. A good analysis of the problem to be solved will indicate where an expert system may be suitable in the overall problem scenario.

Step 5: Obtaining the solution. Using the available data, information, and the solution model, an expert system can determine the real-world actions that are needed to solve the problem at hand. These actions are then presented to the user in terms of recommendations. A sensitivity analysis may be incorporated into the design of the expert system to determine what changes in parameter values might cause a change in the solution.

Step 6: Implementing the solution. A solution represents the selection of an alternative that satisfies the objective stated in the problem statement. A good solution is useless until it is implemented. Therefore, an important aspect of a solution generated by an expert system is the strategy needed to implement the solution. Some of the factors that may affect the implementation of a solution include:

- Technical aspects of the solution.
- Managerial aspects of the solution.
- Resources required to implement the solution.
- Cost of implementing the solution.
- Time frame needed for implementing the solution.

3.3   DATA REQUIREMENT ANALYSIS

A good problem for an expert system is one in which there is a general agreement on the facts of the problem domain and in which clear boundaries of the problem area and data sets can be determined. Just like human experts, expert systems do not always arrive at the best possible solutions at all times. An expert system will sometimes generate better solutions than a real expert and will sometimes generate inferior solutions based on the prevailing set of data. A problem selected for an expert system implementation should be such that the user is willing to accept imperfect solutions based on whatever imperfection may be associated with the available data. Consequently, a careful analysis of the data requirements for expert systems problems should be performed.

An expert system knowledge engineer often deals with different types of measurement scales depending on the particular problem being considered. The problem analysis and solution approach will be influenced by the types of data and measurement scales to be used. The symbolic processing approach of expert systems requires an understanding of the different types of data available in a problem. The different types of data-measurement scales are presented below:

Nominal scale is the lowest level of measurement scales. It classifies items into categories. The categories are mutually exclusive and collectively exhaustive. That is, the categories do not overlap and they cover all possible categories of the
characteristics being observed. Examples of data using the nominal scale are sex, job classification, color, and name.

Ordinal scale is distinguished from a nominal scale by the property of order among the categories. An example is the process of assigning course grades based on the order of student scores. A grade of A is known to be better than a grade of B, but there is no indication of how much better it is. Similarly, first is ahead of second, which is ahead of third, but there is no indication of the relative spacings between the categories. Other examples of data on an ordinal scale are high/medium/low, thick/thin, good/bad, and so on.

Interval scale is distinguished from an ordinal scale by having equal intervals between the units of measure. The assignment of scores ranging from 0 to 100 to student projects is an example of a measurement on an interval scale. A score of zero on a project does not imply that the student getting the zero knows absolutely nothing about the subject of the project. Temperature is a good example of an item that is measured on an interval scale. Even though there is a zero point on the temperature scale, it is an arbitrary relative measure. It cannot be determined that an item is $0°$ cold simply by touching it because different people will have different levels of sensitivity to cold. Other examples of interval scale are IQ measurements and aptitude ratings.

Ratio scale has the same properties of an interval scale, but with a true zero point. For example, an estimate of zero processing time for a computer task is a ratio scale measurement. Other examples of items measured on a ratio scale are volume, length, height, weight, and inventory level. In an expert system, a mixture of the different types of data scales will be needed in implementing heuristics to arrive at acceptable solutions.

In addition to the measurement scale, data can be classified based on their inherent nature. Examples of the relevant classifications are transient data, recurring data, static data, and dynamic data.

Transient data is defined as a volatile set of data that is encountered once during an expert system consultation and is not needed again. Transient data need not be stored in a permanent database record unless it may be needed for future analysis or uses.

Recurring data refers to data that are encountered frequently enough to necessitate storage on a permanent basis. Recurring data may be further categorized into *static data* and *dynamic data*. Recurring data that are static will retain their original parameters and values each time they are encountered during an expert system consultation. Recurring data that are dynamic have the potential for taking on different parameters and values each time they are encountered.

3.4 EXPERT SYSTEM JUSTIFICATION

Expert systems are suitable for knowledge-intensive problems that are typically solved by human experts. Because expert systems depend on human knowledge, if human experts are unable to solve a given problem, no successful expert system can be developed to solve the problem either. When the demand for human expertise surpasses the availability of experts, an expert system may be the tool for handling the situation. The justification of using an expert system for a selected problem depends on the primary goal of the organization and the types of alternatives available.

This section presents the use of analytic hierarchy process (AHP) in the justification of expert systems. Expert system justification should be performed after an appropriate problem has been selected and before too much time and effort have been committed to the development effort. Many of the expert systems now under development for various applications are being developed without any formal attempt to justify the need for them. The lack of proper justification is partly responsible for the cases where some expert systems have not delivered the much-advertised benefits. Expert systems may be developed for several reasons, including strategic necessity, tactical needs, and economic consideration. A proper justification of expert systems will ensure that the systems are developed and deployed in the most appropriate functions with the greatest potential for success. The potential of expert systems can be best matched with practical applications through formal justification processes.

The justification of an expert system is essentially the same as the justification of any new technological tool, where the quantification of the specific cost improvements based on experience may be difficult or impossible. The justification of an expert system will be determined by the system's effectiveness in major and subtle areas of improvement such as reduction in inventories, better raw material management, better control of work in progress, more accurate decisions, better resource utilization, reduction in rework and rehandling, improved employee morale, productivity improvement, better planning, increased consistency, and better service delivery. Robust justification techniques can help in handling both the qualitative and quantitative as well as the subjective aspects of the contribution of an expert system in solving a problem of value to the organization.

The consistency, promptness, and accuracy of decisions offered by expert systems can facilitate better throughput in a production environment or improve personnel productivity in a service environment. Machine times that previously had been idle could then be put to productive use. The increased capacity and output (subject to market constraints) can generate real economic benefits for the organization. Many production facilities have inherent flexibilities that can only be identified through automated reasoning tools such as expert systems. With its capability to process large amounts of data and resident knowledge, an expert system can point out areas where flexibilities such as equipment substitution or material replacement are possible without jeopardizing the desired product quality. The consistency of decisions and actions provided by expert systems can help in producing products with consistent quality characteristics.

The increased utilization of equipment and resources due to the effect of using expert systems may be quantitatively evaluated as shown below. Every system has an output that has a value per unit. If an expert system reduces the idle time of equipment by reducing down time or forced idle time, then the cost gain may be computed as:

$$V = v\Delta T$$

where

V = value produced per unit time of operation
v = revenue per unit of standard time
ΔT = increased production time (reduction in idle time)

Transition costs can be defined if the value (V) of an employee at a full experience level can be defined. There are some jobs in which job experience and not training is the major determinant of effectiveness. Examples are shipping clerks, who must know railroad freight rate systems, insurance clerks, merchandise clerks, inspectors, and so on. A reasonable argument is that an employee's value is worth his or her direct cost plus overhead plus profit on total cost. If such an employee is only 50% efficient, then one-half of this value is lost per day. On the other hand, if the employee is 50% more efficient due to the use of expert systems, then one-half of his or her cost will be saved. Suppose an employee has a job whose task is difficult, "difficult" being defined as the fact that a task can be performed with probability p and not performed with probability $1 - p$ by a normally effective employee. If an employee increases his probability of performance by δ, then his new real value is $(1 + \delta)V$. This can then be translated to measurable units for inclusion in the justification process. The preceding discussions present some of the factors that may be relevant to the justification process. These factors and other qualitative and quantitative measures can be incorporated into comprehensive multiattribute evaluation methodologies.

To evaluate properly whether the installation of an expert system is justified, we must first determine exactly what the system is expected to accomplish. This is why a thorough problem analysis is essential. The specification for an expert system can begin as general statements of the expectations, but it must be reduced to a list of measurable criteria before a justification approach can be implemented. We must determine how the performance or the contribution of the expert system can be measured or estimated. This is the most difficult portion of the justification process and certainly one of the most important. Many of the sources for the data needed for justification will have some subjective nature. For this reason, methodologies that permit the incorporation of subjective data are of utmost importance in the justification of expert systems. Such a methodology is the analytic hierarchy process.

Economic analysis is the process of evaluating alternatives on the basis of cost and revenue implications. The conventional methods of justification are based on quantitative measures of worth of an alternative. In expert systems technology, many tangible and intangible, quantitative and qualitative factors intermingle to compound the justification process. Multiattribute methodologies integrate both objective and subjective factors. Expert systems may be justified on the basis of an integrated evaluation of economic, analytic, and strategic attributes.

Examples of strategic benefits of expert systems include better employee morale, better competitive edge, better insulation against labor uncertainties, better use of information resources, and ability to keep pace with technology. Examples of tactical benefits of expert systems include reduced processing time, higher throughput, better process control, improved quality, improved productivity, better consistency, faster response time, more accurate decisions, and improved data utilization. Examples of economic benefits of expert systems include higher return on investment, better equipment utilization, reduced labor costs, shorter processing times, and lower operating overheads. Analytic hierarchy process is an excellent method for evaluating the potential hierarchical interactions of the several aspects of implementing expert systems.

The analytic hierarchy process (AHP) is a practical approach to solving complex decision problems involving the comparisons of attributes or alternatives. The technique has been used extensively in practice to solve many decision problems. Golden et al. present a comprehensive survey of the technique and its various applications [32]. Based on the previous successful applications of the technique, it can be applied to the comparison of characteristics and attributes involved in the justification of expert systems.

In general, AHP enables decision makers to represent the hierarchical interaction of many factors, attributes, characteristics, or alternatives. For example, in expert systems technology transfer, AHP can be used to identify which attribute should be the determining factor in selecting technology transfer strategies. The general approach to using AHP includes the following steps:

1. Develop the hierarchical structure for the decision problem.
2. Determine the relative weights of each alternative with respect to the characteristics and subcharacteristics in the hierarchy.
3. Determine the overall priority score of each alternative.
4. Determine the indicators of consistency in making pairwise comparisons of the characteristics and alternatives.
5. Make a final decision based on the results.

The hierarchy should be constructed so that elements at the same level are of the same class and must be capable of being related to some elements in the next higher level. In a typical hierarchy, the top level reflects the overall objective or focus of the decision problem. Criteria, factors, or attributes on which the final objective is dependent are listed at intermediate levels in the hierarchy. The lowest level in the hierarchy contains the competing alternatives through which the final objective might be achieved. After the hierarchy has been constructed, the decision maker must undertake a subjective prioritization procedure to determine the weight of each element at each level of the hierarchy. Pairwise comparisons are performed at each level to determine the relative importance of each element at that level with respect to each element at the next-higher level in the hierarchy. Figure 3.3 presents a flowchart of the implementation of AHP.

Figure 3.4 presents an example of a decision hierarchy for decision aid alternatives for productivity improvement. The objective is to select and justify the best overall decision aid to satisfy a specified productivity improvement need in an organization. Three possible systems or alternatives are available. The justification problem is summarized as shown below:

Objective: Select best overall decision aid

Alternative 1:   Manual process

Alternative 2:   Expert systems

Alternative 3:   Conventional program

The alternatives are to be compared on the basis of factors that the organization considers to be very important. Such factors may be determined based on a combination of objectives relating to productivity improvement, quality improvement, better customer satisfaction, better employee morale,

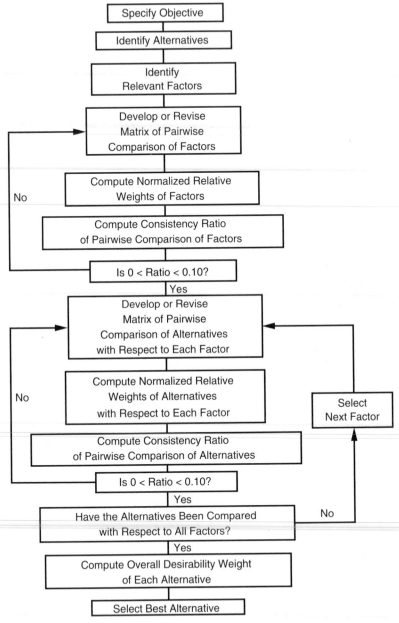

Figure 3.3. Flowchart of AHP methodology.

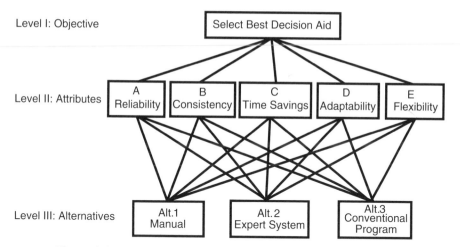

Figure 3.4. Analytic hierarchy process for decision aid alternatives.

economic feasibility, strategic importance, and so on. For the purpose of this illustration, the following five attributes are used in comparing the alternatives:

Attribute A:	Reliability
Attribute B:	Consistency
Attribute C:	Time savings
Attribute D:	Adaptability
Attribute E:	Flexibility

The first step in the AHP procedure involves developing relative weights for the five attributes with respect to the objective at the next higher level in the hierarchy. To come up with the relative weights, the attributes are compared pair-wise with respect to their respective contributions to the objective. The pairwise comparison is done through subjective evaluation by the decision maker(s). Table 3.1 shows the tabulation of the pairwise comparison of the five attributes. Each of the attributes listed along the rows of the table is compared against each of the attributes listed in the columns. Each number in the body of the table indicates the degree of importance of one attribute over the other on a scale of 1 to 9. A typical question that may be used to arrive at the relative rating is:

"Do you consider consistency to be more important than time savings in the selection of a decision aid for productivity improvement?"

"If so, how much more important is it on a scale of 1 to 9?"

TABLE 3.1. Pairwise Rating of Decision Attributes

Attributes	Reliability	Consistency	Time savings	Adaptability	Flexibility
Reliability	1	1/3	5	6	5
Consistency	3	1	6	7	6
Time savings	1/5	1/6	1	3	1
Adaptability	1/6	1/7	1/3	1	1/4
Flexibility	1/5	1/6	1	4	1

Similar questions are asked iteratively until each attribute has been compared with each of the other attributes. For example, in Table 3.1, attribute B
(Consistency) is considered to be more important than attribute C (Time savings), with a degree of 6 with respect to the selection of a decision aid. In
general, the numbers indicating the relative importance of the attributes are
obtained by using the following rules:

Equally important: Degree = 1
    If attribute A is equally as important as attribute B,
    Then the importance rating of A over B is 1.
Weakly more important: Degree = 3
    If attribute A is weakly more important than attribute B,
    Then the importance rating of A over B is 3.
Strongly more important: Degree = 5
    If attribute A is strongly more important than attribute B,
    Then the importance rating of A over B is 5.
Very strongly more important: Degree = 7
    If attribute A is very strongly more important than attribute B,
    Then the importance rating of A over B is 7.
Absolutely more important: Degree = 9
    If attribute A is absolutely more important than attribute B,
    Then the importance rating of A over B is 9.

Intermediate numbers are used as appropriate to indicate intermediate levels of importance. If the comparison order is reversed (e.g., B versus A rather
than A versus B), then the reciprocal of the importance rating is entered in
the pairwise comparison table. For example, the following statements are
equivalent:

Consistency is more important than Time savings, with a degree of 6.
Time savings is more important than Consistency, with a degree of 1/6.

Because of its fractional rating, the second statement actually implies that
Time savings is less important than Consistency. The relative evaluation rat-

TABLE 3.2. Matrix of Pairwise Comparisons of the Five Attributes

Attributes	A	B	C	D	E
A	1.000	0.333	5.000	6.000	5.000
B	3.000	1.000	6.000	7.000	6.000
C	0.200	0.167	1.000	3.000	1.000
D	0.167	0.143	0.333	1.000	0.250
E	0.200	0.167	1.000	4.000	1.000
Column Sum	4.567	1.810	13.333	21.000	13.250

ings in Table 3.1 are converted to a matrix of pairwise comparisons, as shown in Table 3.2. The entries in this Table are then normalized to obtain Table 3.3. The normalization is done by dividing each entry in a column by the sum of all the entries in the column. For example, the first cell in Table 3.3 (i.e., 0.219) is obtained by dividing 1.000 by 4.567. Note that the sum of the normalized values in each attribute column is 1.

The last column in Table 3.3 shows the normalized average rating associated with each attribute. For example, the first entry in that column (i.e., 0.288) is obtained by dividing 1.441 by 5 since there are five attributes. These averages represent the relative weights (between 0.0 and 1.0) of the attributes that are being evaluated. The relative weights show that attribute B (Consistency) has the highest importance rating, 0.489. Thus, consistency is considered to be the most important factor in the selection of a decision aid for productivity improvement. Table 3.4 presents a summary of the relative weights of the attributes. Figure 3.5 presents a graphical representation of the relative weights.

The relative weights of the attributes are denoted as w_i. Thus, if the attributes are numbered from 1 to 5, we would have the following:

$$w_1 = 0.288; \ w_2 = 0.489; \ w_3 = 0.086; \ w_4 = 0.041; \ \text{and} \ w_5 = 0.096$$

These attribute weights are valid only for the particular goal specified in

TABLE 3.3. Normalized AHP Matrix of Paired Comparisons

Attributes	A	B	C	D	E	Row Sum	Row Average
A	0.219	0.184	0.375	0.286	0.377	1.441	0.288
B	0.656	0.551	0.450	0.333	0.454	2.444	0.489
C	0.044	0.094	0.075	0.143	0.075	0.431	0.086
D	0.037	0.077	0.025	0.048	0.019	0.206	0.041
E	0.044	0.094	0.075	0.190	0.075	0.478	0.096
Column Sum	1.000	1.000	1.000	1.000	1.000		1.000

TABLE 3.4. Summary of Attribute Weights

Attributes	Weights
Reliability	0.288
Consistency	0.489
Time savings	0.086
Adaptability	0.041
Flexibility	0.096

the AHP model for the problem. If another goal is specified, the attributes would need to be reevaluated with respect to that new goal.

Since the initial pairwise comparisons of the attributes are done based on subjective opinions of the people involved in the decision making, it is quite possible that some elements of bias and inconsistency will be present in the evaluations. To minimize bias and ensure some level of consistency, Saaty

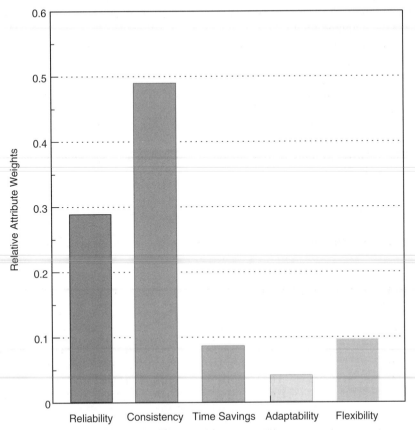

Figure 3.5. Relative weights of five attributes.

TABLE 3.5. Pairwise Rating of Alternatives on the Basis of Reliability

Alternatives	Alt 1	Alt 2	Alt 3
Alt 1	1	1/3	1
Alt 2	3	1	2
Alt 3	1	1/2	1

proposed a procedure for calculating the consistency ratio associated with the AHP methodology [87]. The consistency ratio gives a measure of the consistency of the decision maker in comparing attributes and alternatives. All the consistency ratios for the above example fall within the acceptable limit of 0.0 to 0.10.

After the relative weights of the attributes are obtained, the next step is to evaluate the alternatives on the basis of the attributes. In this step, relative evaluation rating is obtained for each alternative with respect to each attribute. The procedure for the pairwise comparison of the alternatives is similar to the procedure for comparing the attributes. Table 3.5 presents the tabulation of the pairwise comparisons of the three alternatives with respect to attribute A (Reliability). The table shows that alternative 1 and alternative 3 have the same level of importance based on reliability. Examples of questions that may be useful in obtaining the pair-wise rating of the alternatives are:

"Is alternative 1 better than alternative 2 with respect to reliability?"
"If so, how much better is it on a scale of 1 to 9?"

It should be noted that the comparisons shown in Table 3.5 are valid only when the reliability of the alternatives is being considered. Separate pairwise comparisons of the alternatives must be done whenever another attribute is being considered. Consequently, for our example, we would have five separate matrices of pairwise comparisons of the alternatives, with one matrix associated with each attribute. Table 3.5 is the first one of the five matrices. The other four are not shown due to space limitations. Each matrix is analyzed and normalized by using the same procedure shown previously for Table 3.1. The normalization of the entries in Table 3.5 yields the following relative weights of the alternatives with respect to reliability:

Alternative 1: 0.21
Alternative 2: 0.55
Alternative 3: 0.24

Table 3.6 shows a summary of the normalized relative ratings of the three alternatives with respect to each of the five attributes. The attribute weights shown earlier in Table 3.4 are now combined with the system weights con-

TABLE 3.6. Relative Weights of the Three Alternatives with Respect to Each Attribute

	Attributes				
Alternatives	Reliability	Consistency	Time Savings	Adaptability	Flexibility
Alternative 1	0.21	0.12	0.50	0.63	0.62
Alternative 2	0.55	0.55	0.25	0.30	0.24
Alternative 3	0.24	0.33	0.25	0.07	0.14

tained in Table 3.6 to obtain the overall relative weights of the alternatives as shown below:

$$\alpha_j = \sum_i (w_i k_{ij})$$

where

α_j = *overall* weighted evaluation for alternative j.
w_i = relative weight for attribute i.
k_{ij} = evaluation rating for alternative j with respect to attribute i. This is often referred to as the *local* weight of the alternative.
$w_i k_{ij}$ = a measure representing the *global* weight of alternative j with respect to attribute i. The sum of the global weights associated with an alternative represents the overall weight, α_j, of that alternative.

Table 3.7 shows the summary of the final AHP analysis for the example. The three alternatives have been evaluated on the basis of all five attributes. The question addressed by the AHP approach in this example is to determine which alternative should be selected to satisfy the stated production goal based on weighted evaluation of the relevant attributes. The summary in Table 3.7 shows that alternative 2 (Expert systems) should be selected since it has the highest weighted rating, 0.484.

TABLE 3.7. Summary of AHP for Decision Aid Alternatives

	Attributes					
	A $i = 1$	B $i = 2$	C $i = 3$	D $i = 4$	E $i = 5$	
$w_i \Rightarrow$	0.288	0.489	0.086	0.041	0.096	
System j			k_{ij}			α_j
System 1	0.21	0.12	0.50	0.63	0.62	0.248
System 2	0.55	0.55	0.25	0.30	0.24	0.484
System 3	0.24	0.33	0.25	0.07	0.14	0.268
Column Sum	1.000	1.000	1.000	1.000	1.000	1.000

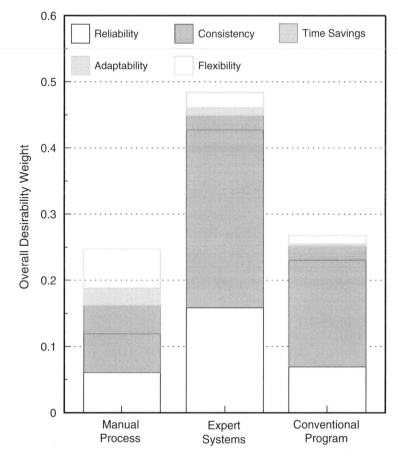

Figure 3.6. Histogram of overall weights of three alternatives.

Figure 3.6 presents a bar chart of the relative weights of the three alternatives. The segments in each bar represent the respective rating of each alternative with respect to each of the five attributes. The overall weighted rating of an alternative is sometimes referred to as the alternative's *desirability index* or *weight*. Our illustrative example shows that expert systems are the most desirable of the three alternatives considered.

3.4.1 Problem-Selection Guidelines

Summarized below are guidelines for selecting expert systems problems. The guidelines are useful as a checklist to be used in conjunction with the other discussions presented earlier in this chapter.

1. The expert system development effort should not address a problem so difficult that it cannot be solved with the available resources and within

the limits of anticipated development time. An experienced knowledge engineer should develop a small prototype system and then evaluate the results of this effort to decide whether or not to proceed with the full development.

2. An expert system should alleviate the difficulty that motivated the development. Otherwise, the system will end up solving only a subset of the problem that needs to be solved. When defining the problems to solve, the development team should consider the needs of both the overall organization and the end users and try to resolve any basic conflicts between them before seriously undertaking the project.

3. The expert system should be concise and to the point. The system with the largest number of rules is not necessarily the best system. If a problem appears to be too large, the scope of the project should be reduced.

4. Choosing a problem that no one has ever solved will create an insurmountable bottleneck in the knowledge-acquisition process.

5. The domain expert should have a collection of real cases readily available. These can be used for the perception of the difficulty of the task and the system's performance.

6. Avoid problems that require strict structures and those that are numeric in nature. These do not require much of the capabilities of expert systems because they do not require heuristics in their solutions. They can be best handled by algorithmic computer programs.

7. Make sure the pertinent knowledge in the problem can be represented. For instance, interpretations made from certain sound and visual characteristics are extremely difficult to represent in problems dealing with pattern recognition.

After the expert system has been justified to be suitable for solving the selected problem, the real task of acquiring the required knowledge, coding the knowledge, and developing the expert system can start.

4

KNOWLEDGE ENGINEERING

Knowledge acquisition is one of the key elements in the development of an expert system. It is the process by which knowledge engineers acquire and encode the knowledge that domain experts use to solve a given problem. The success of an expert system depends on its ability to represent accurately the problem-solving techniques of at least one domain expert. Because of its criticality in the development process, knowledge acquisition is often associated with what is known as the knowledge acquisition bottleneck.

Much research on knowledge acquisition has been carried out in the last few years. Many differing theories exist on the subject. This chapter discusses the several aspects that must be considered in the knowledge-acquisition process and some procedures for enhancing the process. Because of the relative importance of the domain expert, discussions are presented on the desired characteristics of the expert and methods for choosing (and working with) a good one. Several accepted knowledge acquisition techniques are explored. The pros and cons of each technique are presented.

4.1 KNOWLEDGE-ACQUISITION PHASES

Knowledge acquisition is implemented in multiple phases. The phases involve finding a good knowledge engineer, establishing the characteristics of the knowledge to be acquired, choosing the domain expert, and transferring/acquiring of knowledge.

4.1.1 The Knowledge Engineer

A knowledge engineer assumes the responsibility of modeling human reasoning and expertise in the form of a computer program. The variety of techniques includes written documentation, past examples of human performance, domain experts, and the knowledge engineer's own expertise.

49

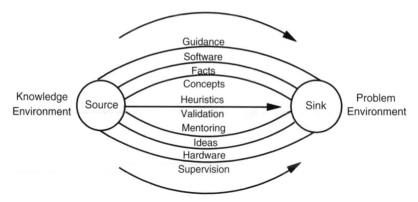

Figure 4.1. Knowledge transfer formats.

Characteristics of a Good Knowledge Engineer. A good knowledge engineer should have many of the following desirable characteristics:

- Patience
- Perseverance
- Attentiveness
- Inquisitiveness
- Result orientation
- Willingness to learn
- Congenial personality
- Technical credibility
- Good motivational skills
- Good organization skills
- Good technical background
- Receptiveness to suggestions
- Excellent communication skills

4.1.2   Knowledge Characteristics

The characteristics of knowledge to be acquired depend both on the nature of the problem to be solved and on the type and level of expertise of the domain expert. Figure 4.1 presents a model of knowledge transfer.

Sources of Knowledge. The characteristics of knowledge are often dictated by the source of the knowledge to be acquired. Typical sources of knowledge are:

- Direct consultation with human experts
- Printed materials such as books
- Direct task observation
- Direct task performance
- Third-party accounts of expert procedures

Of all the available sources of knowledge, direct consultation with human experts poses the greatest difficulty but offers the highest level of reliability. By contrast, third-party accounts are the least reliable method of acquiring knowledge. Books and other printed materials are particularly suitable as stable sources of knowledge. Handbooks, magazines, journals, and printed guides can form the basis for an initial knowledge base. The initial knowledge base may then be expanded with the aid of one or more experts. To acquire knowledge from an expert, one must first choose the expert and secure the expert's cooperation.

4.1.3 Choosing the Expert

Experts can serve as knowledge engineers and knowledge engineers can serve as experts. In some cases, expert systems are best designed, developed, and implemented by experts themselves. That is, the domain expert can also be the knowledge engineer. This is true for problems where the transfer of knowledge is extremely complex. The domain expert can also serve as the knowledge engineer in cases where the expert wishes to learn and experiment with expert systems to capture his own expertise. If an expert becomes proficient in the creation of knowledge bases, he or she may find that it offers the most productive way of documenting new problem-solving techniques. The experience may also increase the expert's awareness of his own techniques. The process of knowledge extraction from oneself may reveal prevailing inefficiencies in the expert's problem-solving approaches and help identify potential avenues for improvement.

In other cases, the consolidation of the roles of domain expert and knowledge engineer is not recommended because bias may be introduced into the expert system development process. For example, the choice of a development tool, knowledge-representation scheme, and specific contents of the knowledge base may be biased by the characteristics and background of the person making the choice. A domain expert acting also as a knowledge engineer may have preferences that a trained knowledge engineer might not even consider.

Several criteria may be used in identifying the best expert for a given problem scenario. Some of the most common criteria are:

1. The expert must be able and willing to communicate personal knowledge and experience.

2. The expert must be outwardly cooperative.
3. The expert must be able to coordinate multiple functional responsibilities.
4. The expert must have developed his or her domain expertise by actual practice over a reasonable length of time.
5. The expert must be able to explicitly explain the methods used to apply his or her expertise to the problem under consideration.
6. The expert must be easy to work with.
7. The expert must be willing to commit a substantial amount of time to the development process.

One of the most significant criteria that can be used is the expert's wide acceptance as a true expert by his peers. If he is recognized by others in his field as an expert, then his judgment is respected and reliable. Domain experts should not be directly paid for their contribution to the knowledge-acquisition process. Direct financial remuneration can be counterproductive because it can lead to knowledge prostitution, in which case the expert furnishes his knowledge to the highest bidder.

The Paradox of the Excellent Expert. One of the difficulties that may arise in the selection of an expert is the inability of some experts to describe their own reasoning techniques. They may be so proficient in solving the problems in their domain that most of the processes are ingrained. Thus, experienced experts solve problems without the use of conscious reasoning. This, of course, makes it difficult for them to explain their solution approaches. A better expert may be the one who is good at solving problems but is still at the stage where he or she has to evaluate his or her actions and reasoning approaches consciously. Such a fledgling expert may be better able to transfer knowledge for expert systems purposes.

Due to their familiarity with the domain, good experts may also ignore their own "simple" knowledge in an effort to extract deep knowledge. In many cases, it is the simple knowledge that solves most of the problems. Unfortunately, a very good expert may trivialize simple knowledge and thereby deprive the expert system of an important resource. In general, good domain experts should possess certain characteristics that must be considered when selecting an expert for knowledge acquisition purposes:

1. A well-developed sense of perception
2. Ability to distinguish between relevant and irrelevant information
3. Ability to simplify and organize complicated problem scenarios
4. Strong oral and written communication skills
5. A strong sense of responsibility and accountability for decisions
6. Ability to adapt to changing problem conditions

7. Ability to perform under stress
8. Innovativeness
9. Respect for professional service

According to Harmon and King, a world-class expert has 50,000 to 100,000 bits of heuristic information about his particular specialty [35]. Further, it is believed that it takes at least 10 years to accumulate 50,000 bits. Therefore, as a minimum, the candidates being considered as experts should have 10 years of study and practice in their fields. The view of this author is that the length of experience is not as crucial as some authors suggest. In some tasks, particularly in high-technology operations, the learning curve may be such that a person can learn much within a short period of time. In other tasks, the learning curve may be relatively flat, thereby precluding fast learning.

4.1.4 Knowledge Extraction versus Knowledge Acquisition

Sometimes it is essential to make distinctions between knowledge extraction and knowledge acquisition [100]. Knowledge extraction may be viewed as the actual solicitation of knowledge by asking or watching an expert. On the other hand, knowledge acquisition can be viewed as the process that provides for the creation of new concept structures or the rules that govern the structures. In other words, knowledge acquisition gives the person acquiring the knowledge the opportunity to generate independently new approaches to solving problems in the domain under consideration. By comparison, knowledge extraction merely uses the person doing the extracting as a medium for getting knowledge from one point (the expert) to another point (the knowledge base).

Knowledge Discovery. One of the preliminary requirements of a knowledge engineer is to become familiar with the domain in which he or she will be working. This is the knowledge-discovery phase. Knowledge discovery is necessary in the process of defining the size and characteristics of the domain. It also allows the knowledge engineer to get a feel for the typical reasoning scenarios, basic rules, and concepts of the domain. The knowledge engineer must also learn the terminology of the domain at this time. Without an understanding of the language, consultation with experts will be difficult.

During the knowledge-discovery phase, it is important for the knowledge engineer to keep an open mind. Preliminary consultations with several experts and end users will uncover subtle problems inherent to the domain. For example, the knowledge engineer may want to interview end users to find out whether they prefer a long explanation of the decision by the expert system or just a simple recommendation. An initial prototype of the high-level system may be designed by the knowledge engineer before the formal knowledge extraction using this discovered knowledge. This prototype can incorporate

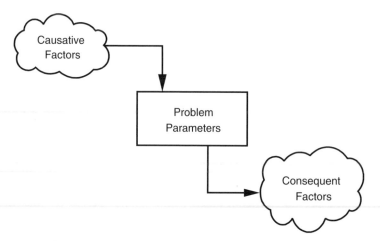

Figure 4.2. Causative and consequential relationships.

the basic structure of the task, such as the form of input and output to be used by the expert system and the typical solutions or classes of solutions. In acquiring knowledge, the knowledge engineer must evaluate the causative and consequential relationships among the parameters in a problem. Figure 4.2 presents a model of the input/output relationships of problem parameters.

4.2   METHODS OF EXTRACTING KNOWLEDGE FROM EXPERTS

Knowledge acquisition is not a science with predictable results. Expert systems developers must use knowledge-acquisition methodologies that fit the problem situation and the needs of those involved in the acquisition process. The domain expert is a key player in the knowledge acquisition process. The knowledge engineer serves as the facilitator for knowledge elicitation, acquisition, and representation. One or more experts may be consulted during the preliminary stages of an expert system effort. This may be needed, for example, to determine the scope of the problem domain. The first in-depth attempt to elicit knowledge usually takes place after the initial knowledge discovery. Hoffman discusses the problems of extracting knowledge from experts [42]. Presented below are some of the techniques for knowledge elicitation from an expert.

4.2.1   Interviews

The most popular and widely used form of expert knowledge extraction is the interview. In the unstructured method of interview, the knowledge engineer sits with the expert and goes through the process of solving a problem. The expert may describe the process verbally only or verbally while a task is being performed. The knowledge engineer records the information and asks spontaneous questions in order to obtain more information concerning the expert's problem-solving approaches. Some specific methods that are often used during interviews for knowledge extraction include:

1. *Problem discussion* explores the kind of data, knowledge, and procedures needed to solve specific problems.
2. *Problem description* requires that the expert describe a prototype problem for each category of answer in the domain.
3. *Problem analysis* presents the expert with a series of realistic problems to solve explicitly while probing the rationale behind the reasoning steps.
4. *Refinement* requires that the expert present a series of problems to solve using the knowledge acquired during previous interviews.
5. *Examination* requires that the expert examine and critique the prototype rules and control structure.
6. *Validation* requires the presentation of the sample problems solved by the expert and the prototype system to other outside experts.

An unstructured interview may be used first in the preliminary stage of the knowledge acquisition to obtain a large amount of general information. Later a structured interview can be used to gain specific information about one particular aspect of the expert's technique. It is also useful to record the interview on audio or videotape. Recording helps to document the interview and also provides a way for the knowledge engineer to analyze the expert's verbal and facial gestures. However, recording alone is not enough; the knowledge engineer must take good notes during interviews. Privacy is very important, and interruptions during interview sessions should be kept to a minimum.

4.2.2   Open-Ended Interviews

This type of interview requires either a pilot knowledge base (possibly from unstructured interviews) or a knowledge engineer with a significant amount of domain knowledge. When a preliminary knowledge base exists, the expert goes over the contents, making comments on each one. This way additions or deletions may be made very quickly and easily. Tape recording this interview may not be necessary, since the expert can write notes directly on a copy of the pilot knowledge base. When the knowledge engineer possesses a large amount of domain knowledge, the same process can take place. The interview consists of specific questions directed at certain aspects of the domain. The expert answers the questions and elaborates where necessary.

4.2.3 Advantages and Disadvantages of Interviews

In general, unstructured interviews have the advantage of generating a large amount of data. This is especially true in the early stages of expert systems development. It is the job of the knowledge engineer to keep the expert from digressing to other unrelated topics and control the amount and detail of the expert's comments. The main disadvantage of interviews is that they are very time-consuming. Unstructured interviews may take weeks to conduct and may be very inefficient due to their informal nature.

Structured interviews may also be very time consuming because preliminary knowledge bases, by nature, may be very long and covering the material may take a long time. This method, however, tends to be more efficient than unstructured interviews.

In terms of the validity of the data, the effectiveness of interviews depends mainly upon the skill of the interviewer in asking the right questions and the skill of the expert in conveying his or her knowledge and techniques. Not all experts have this skill. Some of the shortcomings associated with interviews are:

1. There is often a tendency to focus on the leading items in a sequence of events when reasoning about the entire problem sequence.
2. Easily available data sets are often utilized without regard to their relevance.
3. There is often a tendency to be conservative in complex decision problems.
4. The manner in which data are presented may affect the ability to retrieve the inherent information.
5. Too much unnecessary data may complicate the problem scenario and overwhelm the knowledge engineer.
6. People believe a fact because it is thought to be important. Conversely, what is thought to be important is believed to be a fact.
7. There is often a tendency to use past successful strategies whether or not they fit new situations.
8. There is often a tendency to remember the first and last items in a sequence better than the middle ones.
9. There is often a tendency not to explore the subtle aspects of the problem domain.
10. Dynamic memory is required when handling multiple pieces of information with multiple levels of interactions.

4.2.4 Task Performance and Protocols

Observing an expert performing a familiar problem-solving task can be a very productive way to gather detailed knowledge. In the case of early data gathering, the task may be simple or routine. This gives the knowledge engineer the framework of the expert's thought process. The expert must be encouraged to think aloud while performing the task. Care must be taken, however, not to interrupt this thought process except for reminders to keep to the subject matter. The process may be videotaped or audio taped in order to obtain an accurate record of the expert's words and actions. The tapes can be analyzed later by the knowledge engineer. The knowledge engineer may also ask the expert to repeat the task, adding detailed comments as the process continues. In this method of knowledge acquisition, the study of the expert's actions is sometimes called protocol analysis.

4.2.5   Analyzing the Expert's Thought Process

After observing a knowledge acquisition task, the knowledge engineer should conduct a structured interview in order to analyze the sequence of events associated with the task. Questions that should be asked include:

"What led you from this conclusion to the next?"
"What data did you consider?"
"What past experiences came to mind at this point?"

These questions are necessary to elicit further thoughts from the expert. Verbal explanations must be evaluated in an effort to extract any of the expert's factual and heuristic knowledge. Internal dialogue used by the expert may be indicated by phrases such as:

"Something tells me . . ."
"I bet that is it . . ."
"This reminds me of . . ."
"The last time I saw this . . ."

These phrases help to indicate the expert's attempt to relate current problem situation to previous experiences. The knowledge engineer must take care to understand the expert's reasoning process and adequately document it rather than introducing his own methods of reasoning into the knowledge-acquisition process. The performance of a simple task and the subsequent analysis of the data gathered can be a very good source of detailed knowledge. The knowledge engineer must be very observant, inquisitive, and skillful in his approach to knowledge acquisition.

4.2.6   Constrained Task

The constrained task approach involves asking the expert to perform a task under a certain constraint. The constraint can be a limit on the time allotted to examine a piece of evidence or reach a conclusion based on the facts presented. This method provides information on the strategies and high-level structures of the expert's thought process. The objective of the constrained task approach is to challenge the expert and bring out his or her intuitive problem-solving approach.

4.2.7   Tough Case Method

The tough case method of knowledge acquisition involves providing the expert with a tough test problem to solve. The test problems are selected from a rare set of problems that occur only occasionally in the expert's normal function. The expert may be requested to use a tape recorder to record the account of how a tough case is solved whenever it is encountered. The expert is requested to think aloud during the solution process.

4.2.8   Questionnaires and Surveys

Questionnaires and surveys are other methods of knowledge acquisition. Open-ended questionnaires ask the expert to describe the methods and reasoning used to solve a problem. This may be useful in the knowledge-discovery stage to provide broad information. The disadvantage of this approach is that the knowledge engineer is not present to moderate the expert and make sure the responses are really relevant to the questions.

An alternative is to use a short-answer questionnaire format to elicit the opinion of multiple experts quickly and easily. The information that can be gathered with this method is usually limited to simple descriptions or techniques. The knowledge engineer should be sufficiently educated in the domain in order to create meaningful questions to be useful for short-answer questionnaires.

Forced-answer questionnaires can be used as a knowledge base-validation tool. These questionnaires call for "yes" or "no" or multiple-choice answers. For example, forced-answer questionnaires may be used to validate a production rule by asking whether the "if" clause really yields the "then" clause.

4.2.9   Documentation and Analysis of Acquired Knowledge

Proper documentation should be accumulated throughout the knowledge-acquisition effort. Written documentation, audio, and video records of the knowledge acquisition sessions are essential for clarifying the expert's reasoning process during the actual development of the knowledge base. Data related to the acquired knowledge should be kept in an organized and easily accessible format. The transcription of the interviews and verbal information generates a great deal of additional written information. The documentation and analysis should address the following:

1. *Transcription:* Verbal exchanges during knowledge acquisition should be documented in writing.
2. *Phrase indexing:* Key phrases in the problem domain should be indexed with proper notes and references attached.
3. *Knowledge coding:* Knowledge elements acquired should be grouped into descriptive and procedural categories.

The analysis of the acquired knowledge may be performed concurrently with the knowledge-acquisition process. It is not necessary to wait until the acquisition stage is complete before beginning the analysis. Concurrent analysis and validation can help identify areas that should be explored further during the knowledge acquisition process.

4.2.10 Expert's Block

Like writers that experience the legendary writer's block, domain experts can experience expert's block. This happens when the expert cannot generate any additional output for the knowledge-acquisition process. A skilled knowledge engineer can help the expert by providing appropriate hints and posing probing questions that can resuscitate the expert's reasoning process. If a complete problem analysis has been performed as presented in Chapter 3, it should not be very difficult to identify subtle elements of the problem domain that will be useful in generating additional links to new problem-solving rules. If the block persists, the knowledge-acquisition session should be temporarily terminated and recommenced at a later time. The mutual interaction of the knowledge engineer and the domain expert is presented in Figure 4.3. The knowledge engineer provides the leads necessary for the expert to come up with additional inferences.

4.3 KNOWLEDGE-ACQUISITION MEETINGS

Meetings are an important component of the knowledge-acquisition process. Being able to manage knowledge-acquisition meetings effectively is an important skill for the knowledge engineer. If a knowledge-acquisition meeting is poorly organized, improperly managed, or called at the wrong time, valuable cooperation may be lost very quickly. Meetings are essential for communication and decision making related to the problem to be solved by the proposed expert system. Some important points should be kept in mind for knowledge acquisition meetings, including:

1. Carefully review the items to be discussed at the meeting and determine which can be more effectively disseminated through brief memoranda.

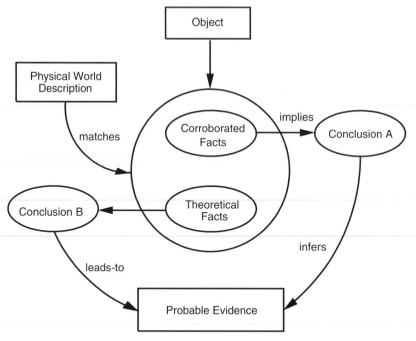

Figure 4.3. Interaction between domain expert and knowledge engineer.

The powers of desktop computers and electronic mail should be fully exploited to complement knowledge-acquisition meetings.

2. Ensure that only those who need to be at the knowledge-acquisition meeting are invited to be there. The point of diminishing returns for any meeting is equal to the number of people actually needed for the meeting. The larger the number of people at a meeting, the lower the productivity of the meeting. The extra attendees only serve to generate unconstructive and conflicting ideas that impede the success of the meeting.

3. Those not invited to the knowledge-acquisition meeting should, however, be informed of how they may contribute to the process and how the proceedings of the meeting may affect them.

4. The prospective end users of the proposed expert system should be offered avenues through which may contribute to the knowledge-acquisition process.

5. A knowledge acquisition meeting should not be allowed to degenerate into a social gathering.

Some guidelines for conducting knowledge-acquisition meetings more effectively are:

1. Do pre-meeting homework:
   - Clarify the problem area.
   - Identify the topics to be discussed.
   - Establish the desired outcome for each topic.
   - Determine how the outcome will be verified.
   - Determine who really needs to be there.
   - Evaluate the suitability of meeting time and venue.
   - Allow enough time to address each topic.
   - Identify complementary communication media (telephone, mail, etc.).
2. Circulate a written agenda of the knowledge-acquisition process prior to the meeting.
3. Emphasize the importance of the problem domain and the criticality of the knowledge-acquisition process in solving the problem.
4. Start the meeting on time.
5. Review the knowledge-acquisition agenda at the beginning.
6. Get everyone present at the meeting involved in the knowledge-elicitation process by posing direct questions to each participant.
7. Keep to the agenda; do not add new items unless absolutely essential.
8. Quickly resolve conflicts that may develop from diverging views of domain experts.
9. Keep digression from the knowledge-acquisition mission to a minimum.
10. Recap the accomplishments of each topic before going to the next.
11. Let those who have made commitments know what is expected of them.
12. Evaluate meeting success relative to specified goals.
13. Adjourn the meeting on time.
14. Prepare and distribute the minutes or proceedings of the meeting.
15. Highlight the knowledge acquired through the knowledge-acquisition meeting.

4.4   GROUP KNOWLEDGE ACQUISITION

Many problem situations are complex and poorly understood. No one person has all the information to make all decisions accurately. As a result, crucial decisions are better made by a group of people. Some organizations use outside consultants with appropriate expertise to make recommendations for important problem decisions. Other organizations, choosing not to go outside the organization, set up their own internal consulting groups that attend to decision problems. Many companies now have internal expert systems consulting groups geared towards providing technical assistance for expert systems development throughout the company. Decisions can be made through linear responsibility, in which case one person makes the final decision based on input from other people. Alternatively, decisions can be made through shared responsibility, in which case a group of people shares the responsibility for making joint decisions. The major advantages of group decision making are:

1. *Ability to share experience, knowledge, and resources:* Many heads are better than one. A group will possess greater collective ability to solve a given decision problem.
2. *Increased credibility:* Decisions made by a group of people often carry more weight in an organization.
3. *Improved morale:* Personnel morale can be positively influenced because many people have the opportunity to participate in the decision-making and knowledge-acquisition processes.
4. *Better rationalization:* The opportunity to observe other people's views can lead to an improvement in an individual's reasoning process.

Knowledge acquisition through group decision making can be achieved using several approaches. Some of these approaches are discussed below.

4.4.1   Brainstorming

Brainstorming is a way of generating many new ideas. In brainstorming, the decision group comes together to discuss alternative ways of solving a decision problem. The members of the brainstorming group may be from different departments, may have different backgrounds and training, and may not even know one another. The diversity of the constituents to create a stimulating environment for generating many different ideas. The technique encourages free outward expression of new ideas no matter how remote the ideas may appear. No criticism of any new idea is permitted during the brainstorming session. A major concern in brainstorming is that extroverts may take control of the discussions. For this reason, an experienced and respected leader is needed to manage the brainstorming discussions. The group leader establishes the procedure for proposing ideas, keeps the discussions in line with the group's mission, discourages disruptive statements, and encourages the participation of all members.

After the group runs out of ideas, open discussions are held to weed out the unsuitable ones. It is expected that even the rejected ideas may stimulate the generation of other ideas, which may eventually lead to other favored ideas. Some guidelines for improving the brainstorming session for knowledge acquisition are:

- Focus on a specific problem to be solved.
- Keep ideas relevant to the intended knowledge-acquisition mission.
- Be receptive to all new ideas.
- Evaluate the ideas on a relative basis after exhausting new ideas.
- Maintain an atmosphere conducive to cooperative discussions.
- Maintain documentation of the ideas generated and how they impact the knowledge-acquisition process.

4.4.2   Delphi Method

The traditional approach to group decision making is to obtain the opinion of experienced experts through open discussions. An attempt is then made to reach a consensus among the experts. However, open group discussions are often biased because of the influence of or even subtle intimidation by dominant individuals. Even when the threat of a dominant individual is not present, opinions may still be swayed by group pressure. This is often called the bandwagon effect.

The Delphi method attempts to overcome these difficulties by requiring individuals to present their opinions anonymously through an intermediary. The method differs from the other interactive group methods because it eliminates face-to-face confrontations. It was originally developed for forecasting applications, but it has been modified in various ways for application to different types of decision making. The method can be quite useful for knowledge-acquisition purposes. It is particularly effective when decisions must be based on a broad set of factors. The Delphi method is normally implemented as follows:

1. *Problem definition:* A decision problem that is considered significant to the organization is identified and clearly described.
2. *Group selection:* An appropriate group of experts or experienced individuals is formed to address the particular decision problem. Both internal and external experts may be involved in the Delphi process. A leading individual is appointed to serve as the administrator of the decision process. The group may operate through the mail or gather together in a room. In either case, all opinions are expressed anonymously on paper. If the group meets in the same room, care should be taken to provide enough room so that each member does not have the feeling that someone may accidentally or deliberately spy on his or her responses.

3. *Initial opinion poll:* The technique is initiated by describing the problem to be addressed in unambiguous terms. The group members are requested to submit a list of major areas of concern in their specialty areas as they relate to the decision problem.

4. *Questionnaire design and distribution:* Questionnaires are prepared to address the areas of concern related to the decision problem. The written responses to the questionnaires are collected and organized by the administrator. The administrator aggregates the responses in a statistical format. For example, the average, mode, and median of the responses may be computed. This analysis is distributed to the decision group. Each member can then see how his or her responses compare with the anonymous views of the other members.

5. *Iterative balloting:* Additional questionnaires based on the previous responses are passed to the members. The members submit their responses again. They may choose to alter or not to alter their previous responses.

6. *Silent discussions and consensus:* The iterative balloting may involve anonymous written discussions of why some responses are correct or incorrect. The process is continued until a consensus is reached. A consensus may be declared after five or six iterations of the balloting or when a specified percentage (e.g., 80%) of the group agrees on the questionnaires. If a consensus cannot be declared on a particular point, it may be displayed to the whole group with a note that it does not represent a consensus.

In addition to its use in technological forecasting, the Delphi method has been widely used in other general decision making. Its major characteristics of anonymity of responses, statistical summary of responses, and controlled procedure make it a reliable mechanism for obtaining numeric data from subjective opinion. The major limitations of the Delphi method are:

1. Its effectiveness may be limited in cultures where strict hierarchy, seniority, age, or devout reverence for expertise influence decision-making processes.

2. Some experts may not readily accept the contribution of nonexperts to the group decision-making process.

3. Since opinions are expressed anonymously, some members may take the advantage of the situation to make ludicrous statements. However, if the group composition is carefully reviewed, this problem can be avoided.

4.4.3 Nominal Group Technique

Nominal group technique is a silent version of brainstorming. Rather than asking people to state their ideas aloud, the team leader asks each member to jot down a minimum number of ideas, for example, five or six. A single list of ideas is then composed on a chalkboard for the whole group to see. The group then discusses the ideas and weeds out some iteratively until a final decision is reached. The nominal group technique is easier to control. Unlike brainstorming, where members may get into shouting matches, it permits members to present their views silently. In addition, it allows introverted members to contribute to the decision without the pressure of having to speak out too often.

In all of the group decision-making techniques, an important procedure that can enhance and expedite the decision-making process is to require that members review all pertinent data before coming to the group meeting. This will ensure that the knowledge-acquisition process is not impeded by trivial preliminary discussions. Some disadvantages of group decision making are:

1. Peer pressure in a group situation may influence a participant's opinion and contributions.
2. In a large group, some members may not get to participate effectively in the discussions.
3. A member's relative reputation in the group may influence how well his or her opinion is received.
4. A member with a dominant personality may overwhelm the other members in the discussions.
5. The limited time available to the group may create time pressure that forces some members to present their opinions without fully evaluating the ramifications of the available data.
6. It is often difficult to get all members of a decision group together at the same time.

Despite the noted disadvantages, group decision making has many advantages that can alleviate the shortcomings. The advantages as presented earlier will have varying levels of effect from one problem situation to another. Team knowledge acquisition can be enhanced by following the guidelines below:

1. Get a willing group of experts together.
2. Set an achievable goal for the group.
3. Determine the limitations of the group.
4. Develop a set of guiding rules for the group.
5. Create an atmosphere conducive to group synergism.
6. For major expert systems projects and extended knowledge-acquisition activities, arrange for team training that allows the group to learn the decision rules and responsibilities involved in the problem.

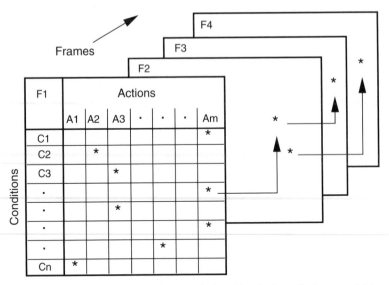

Figure 4.4. Multidimensional factor relationships in knowledge acquisition.

4.5 KNOWLEDGE-ACQUISITION SOFTWARE

To aid in the difficult process of knowledge acquisition, knowledge engineers and programmers have been developing software tools designed to gather knowledge by interacting directly with the expert. Knowledge-acquistion software offers distinct advantages over the traditional pencil-and-paper approach. One of the advantages of knowledge-acquisition software is that the expert may contribute to the knowledge base at his or her pace and convenience. The tools can be classified into two categories: knowledge-elicitation tools and induction-by-example tools.

4.5.1 Knowledge Elicitation Tools

These consist of computer programs that interact directly with the expert. The expert enters information about the domain directly into a computer. The program guides the expert through the classification and clarification processes of knowledge-acquisition. Knowledge-acquisition software can interactively manipulate the data collected from the expert by using various statistical, clustering, and multidimensional data-organization techniques. Figure 4.4 shows a model of the interaction of knowledge elements in a multidimensional format. Knowledge base rules are generated from the organized data. Knowledge-acquisition software tools have been shown to be successful alternatives to the traditional interactions between the knowledge engineer and the expert [23, 96].

Newquist describes a knowledge-acquisition tool known as the Knowledge Acquisition Module (KAM) [74]. This PC-based program can scan text and create rules, relationships, if–then statements, and heuristics based on constraints set by the expert. The program can scan the text of an interview with an expert and generate relevant rules. Prerau discusses the techniques used for acquiring knowledge for a multiparadigm expert system named COMPASS (Central Office Maintenance Printout Analysis and Suggestion System) [83]. COMPASS was developed by GTE laboratories for telephone switching system maintenance. OPAL (Oncology Protocol Acquisition Laboratory) is a computer-based knowledge-acquisition tool developed at Stanford University for the Oncocin project. Domain experts (physicians) interact directly with the software to encode their knowledge. This removes the potential for knowledge-acquisition bottleneck. OPAL has the advantage of giving the domain expert some experience as a knowledge engineer.

One of the first commercial interactive knowledge-acquisition products was AutoIntelligence, developed by IntelligenceWare, Inc. AutoIntelligence is an automatic knowledge-acquisition system that captures the knowledge of an expert through interactive interviews, condenses the knowledge, and then automatically generates an expert system. Through AutoIntelligence, the time and money spent in the interview process with the knowledge engineer is saved and it is not necessary to know how to type in rules, since rules are generated automatically. The system helps experts without a knowledge engineer to capture their own expertise.

4.5.2   Induction-by-Example Tools

In this method, a program will infer rules based on examples generated by the expert. The program models the decision-making process of the expert based on the conclusions reached in the examples. Because there is a limit to the number of unique examples the expert may generate, induction-by-example programs are most effective for small expert systems. However, new software techniques are being used to enhance the capability of induction-based knowledge-acquisition programs so that they can handle large problem domains.

Di Piazza and Helsabeck discuss a knowledge-acquisition program named Laps [23]. Laps is a software package designed for interviewing experts. It combines the functions of gathering, organizing, and testing knowledge related to specified problems. Laps begins with a case in the form of a sample solution path elicited from the domain expert. This sample solution path is refined by a process called dechunking, which facilitates finding a model of the expert's reasoning process. The model guides the determination of the structure of alternatives by using an effective level of abstraction. The information gathered is organized into tables that the expert uses to generate additional rows of knowledge elements. The process is continued until a complete knowledge base is developed. Knowledge-acquisition software should not be developed to replace the roles of the knowledge engineer. Rather, the software should be developed to aid both the expert and the knowledge engineer produce more effective knowledge bases quickly.

4.6   CHARACTERISTICS OF KNOWLEDGE

The purpose of knowledge representation is to organize the required knowledge into a form such that the expert system can readily access it for decision-making purposes. Knowledge does not always come compiled and ready for use. The term "knowledge" is used to describe a variety of bits of understanding that enable people and machines to perform their intended functions.

4.6.1   Types of Knowledge

Knowledge can be broadly classified into two types: *surface knowledge* and *deep knowledge*. The classification is based on the prevailing information circumstances and the intended (conscious or subconscious) uses of knowledge. Surface knowledge is based on heuristics and experience acquired from having successfully solved many similar problems. Deep knowledge involves reasoning from basic principles involving laws of nature and complex behavioral models. Some of the characteristics of the two types are:

Surface knowledge:
- Composed of situation and action pairs
- Capable of solving simple domain problems
- Often used in cursory situations
- Faster to implement

Deep knowledge:
- Composed of cause-and-effect relationships
- Based on hierarchical cognition of events
- Involves goals and plans to achieve the goals
- Capable of solving difficult problems

Knowledge, whether surface or deep, must be extracted and encoded into usable forms for solving problems. When deep knowledge is organized, indexed, and stored in such a way that it is easily retrieved for solving problems, we obtain what is known as *compiled knowledge*. Sometimes the source of knowledge may be so dormant that a great deal of effort must be made to extract it. Once extracted, an element of knowledge must undergo other transformations before it can achieve an operational form. Extraction involves eliciting the basic concepts of the problem domain from a reliable knowledge source. The two major sources of knowledge are *active human expertise* and *latent expertise*.

Active human expertise relates to the expertise available from an expert who is currently active in solving problems in the problem domain. Latent expertise refers to the type of knowledge available in the form of printed material. This type of expertise is dormant until someone derives some use from it by converting the printed material into a usable form. Knowledge extraction from the source of expertise is performed to obtain enough problem-solving knowledge to develop an expert system knowledge base. Heuristics constitute the key product of knowledge extraction from the source of expertise. Once enough knowledge is available, the knowledge engineer selects an appropriate scheme or technique for representing the knowledge. The encoding of the knowledge base begins after the knowledge engineer has selected the framework and knowledge-representation techniques. Before encoding, knowledge may be subdivided into *declarative knowledge,* which refers to facts and assertions, and *procedural knowledge,* which refers to sequence of actions and consequences. Declarative knowledge is associated with knowing *what* is involved in solving a problem. Procedural knowledge is associated with knowing *how* to apply appropriate problem-solving strategies to solve a given problem. Declarative knowledge representation uses logic-based and relational approaches. Logical representation involves the use of propositional and predicate logic. Relational models are implemented by using decision trees, graphs, or semantic networks. Procedural knowledge representation involves the use of rule-based approaches to store the knowledge of how to solve problems. The example below illustrates the difference between declarative and procedural knowledge.

The complete table of the standard normal random variable widely used in probability and statistics analysis represents declarative knowledge encompassing a large body of knowledge of the relationship between a value of the random variable and the probability of observing a value less than or equal to that particular value. By comparison, procedural knowledge refers to the compiled sequence of the procedures and actions showing how to compute probabilities using the normal table.

Declarative knowledge representation is usually more comprehensive and difficult to implement, while procedural knowledge representation is more compact and easy to implement. Many practical problems will require the use of both declarative and procedural representations. The choice of a representation model will be dictated by the nature of the problem to be solved and the type of knowledge available.

4.7 KNOWLEDGE-REPRESENTATION MODELS

A knowledge-based expert system performs the tasks that would normally be performed by experts. For the expert system to be effective, the knowledge acquired from the expert must be properly represented to prevent ambiguities in the problem-solving procedures. Different knowledge-representation techniques are available. Some techniques are suitable for a majority of problems typically encountered by expert systems. There are, however, some problems that require unique knowledge representation approaches. The major knowledge-representation models are:

1. Semantic networks
2. Frames
3. Production rules
4. Predicate logic
5. O-A-V (object-attribute-value) triplets
6. Hybrids
7. Scripts

4.7.1   Semantic Networks

Semantic networks are the most general and perhaps the oldest representational structure for expert system knowledge base. They serve as the basis for other knowledge representations. A semantic network structure is a scheme for representing abstract relations among objects in a problem domain, such as membership in a class. Since most reasoning processes associate objects based on classes and relationships of known objects, the semantic network structure provides a general framework from which other representation methods can be derived.

Semantic networks consist of a collection of nodes that are linked to form object relationships. Arcs linking nodes carry notations that indicate the type of relationships. The nodes in a semantic network typically represent objects or facts. Examples of object relationships are:

Gear is-a part-of a Rotor Assembly.
Gear can-be produced by Machining.
Machining is-done-in The-shop.
Rotor Assembly needs Inspection.

Such relationships may be represented graphically by a network of nodes and links where nodes represent objects and links represent the relationships among the objects. In this case the nodes would represent the objects Gear, Rotor Assembly, Machining, The-shop, and Inspection. The links would represent the relations IS-A, PART-OF, CAN-BE, IS-DONE-IN, and NEEDS. The network as a whole forms a taxonomy of the available knowledge. An example of a semantic network for manufacture and inspection of a gear is presented in Figure 4.5.

The IS-A relation establishes a property of inheritance in object hierarchy in the network. Items lower in the network can inherit properties from items higher up in the network. This permits concise representation since information about similar nodes does not have to be repeated at each node. Se-

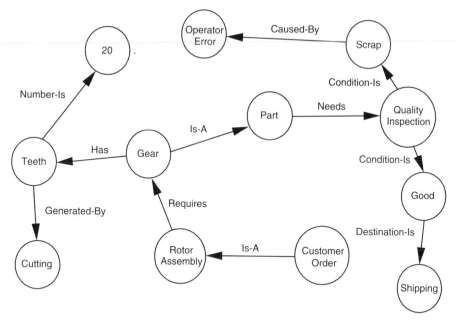

Figure 4.5. Example of semantic network.

mantic networks have been used successfully to represent knowledge in domains that use well-established taxonomies to simplify problem solving. Some of the advantages of semantic networks are:

1. Flexibility in adding, modifying, or deleting new nodes and arcs
2. Ability to inherit relationships from other nodes
3. Ease of drawing inferences about inheritance hierarchy

The major disadvantage of semantic networks is the lack of a formal definitive structure which makes it difficult to implement in an operational setting. However, simple representation forms such as frames and rules can be derived from the network.

4.7.2 Frames

A frame consists of a collection of slots that contain attributes to describe an object, a class of objects, a situation, an action, or an event. Frames differ from semantic networks in that frames contain a subset of the items that may be represented in a semantic network. In a semantic network, information about an object can be randomly placed throughout the knowledge base. By contrast, in a frame, the information is grouped together into a single unit called a frame. Frames are used for representing declarative knowledge. As

Gear	
Teeth Number	20
Assembly	Rotor
Production Method	Cutting
Delivery Date	9/2/91

Figure 4.6. Frame representation for gear production.

discussed earlier, declarative knowledge is knowledge that cannot be immediately executed but can be stored and retrieved as needed to provide information for solving a problem.

Frames provide a description of an object by using a tabulation of information associated with the object. This organization of useful relationships helps to mimic the way an expert typically organizes the information about an object into chunks of data. Psychologists believe that when experts recall the information about a particular object, all the typical attributes of the objects are recalled at the same time as a group. This grouping of object attributes is what is known as a frame. Frame-based reasoning is based on seeking items that fill the slots of information required to solve a problem. If a frame is not relevant to a given problem situation, control will move to another frame. Advantages of frames are:

1. Frames are arranged in a hierarchical manner such that they can inherit relationships from other frames.
2. Frames facilitate faster searches of the knowledge base through the concise and compact representation of information.
3. Frames permit the representation of inheritance relationships among objects.

Using the earlier gear example, a frame representation might be constructed as shown in Figure 4.6. The knowledge base analyzes the problem of buying or leasing an asset. Once a buy or lease conclusion has been reached, the knowledge base determines the best financing method for the acquisition of the asset. The consultation process involves three goal parameters ordered as follows:

How-to-Acquire → Payment → Finance-It

How-To-Acquire represents the buy or lease decision option, Payment represents the installment payment needed to acquire the asset, and Finance-It

TABLE 4.1. Root Frame and Subframe Organization

Root Frame	Subframe

Frame Name: ASSET
PARMS:
  LESSEE-CASH
  CASH-RESERVE-NEEDED
  PRESERVES-CASH
  CANNOT-BORROW
  ACQUIRE-BY
RULES:
1. IF LESSEE-CREDIT = POOR
   THEN CANNOT-BORROW
   AND ACQUIRE = LEASE
2. IF CANNOT-BORROW OR PRE-
   SERVES-CASH THEN HOW-TO-
   ACQUIRE = LEASE AND
   ACQUIRE-BY = LEASE
3. IF LESSEE-CREDIT = FAIR
   AND LESSEE-CASH = FAIR
   AND CASH-RESERVE-NEEDED
   THEN PRESERVES-CASH
4. IF HOW-TO-ACQUIRE IS NOT
   KNOWN THEN HOW-TO-AC-
   QUIRE = BUY-THE-ASSET AND
   ACQUIRE-BY = PURCHASE
 	
GOALS:
HOW-TO-ACQUIRE, PAYMENT
	Frame Name: FINANCE
	PARMS:
	  FINANCE-INTEREST
	  FINANCE-PERIOD
	  DOWN-PAYMENT
	  ASSET-COST
	
	RULES:
	1. IF ACQUIRE-BY = PURCHASE
	   THEN FINANCE-IT (calculation)
	
	2. IF ACQUIRE-BY = LEASE THEN
	   FINANCE-IT = (external calcula-
	   tion)
	
	3. IF FINANCE-IT IS KNOWN
	   THEN PAYMENT =
	   (external calculation)
	
	GOAL:
	FINANCE-IT

represents the finance method appropriate for the particular scenario of the client. It seems logical to organize the knowledge base rules into frames according to their relationships with the goal parameters. As shown in Table 4.1, rules relevant to How-to-Acquire and Payment are located in the root frame while rules relevant to Finance-It are in the subframe. When dealing with large knowledge bases, it is helpful to have an analytical tool for investigating the relationships and logical groupings of the knowledge elements. Frames facilitate such an efficient organization.

4.7.3   Scripts

Script is a knowledge-representation technique suggested by Schank [90]. Scripts are a special form of frames. A script describes a stereotyped sequence of events in a particular context. It presents the expected sequence of events and their associated information in a linked time-based series of frames. For example, the frame discussed previously for gear production may be linked to other frames which contain detailed information on the cutting operation in the time sequence of events in the production schedule. Details of script representation are presented by Schank and Abelson [89], Minsky [67], Kuipers [58], and Hayes [38]. The components of a script include the following:

1. *Entry conditions:* Conditions for entering the script.
2. *Results:* Outcomes that are expected after the events described in the script have occurred.
3. *Props:* Slots representing objects in the script. Recall that a script is a collection of frames where each frame is associated with a certain object.
4. *Roles:* Slots representing entities (e.g., people) that perform the actions specified in the script.
5. *Track:* Specific case of a general pattern that is represented by a specific script. For example, at a professional conference, several tracks of technical presentations are conducted simultaneously under the general theme of the conference.
6. *Scenes:* Actual sequences of events that occur. Typical scenes at a professional conference might be registration, selection of sessions to attend, attendance at the sessions, and adjournment.

4.7.4   Rules

Rules are the most popular and versatile of all the representation schemes. Rules provide a formal way of representing recommendations, directives, or strategies. If–then rules link antecedents to their associated consequents. Rules are appropriate for a variety of expert systems problem domains. The if–then structure of rules links pairs of objects or attributes as shown below:

If premise, **then** conclusion
If input, **then** output
If condition, **then** action
If antecedent, **then** consequent
If action, **then** outcome
If data, **then** goal

Premise refers to the fact that must be true before a certain conclusion can be drawn. *Input* refers to the data that must be available before a certain output can be obtained. *Condition* refers to circumstances that must prevail before a certain action can be taken. *Antecedent* refers to the situation that must occur before a certain consequence can be observed. *Action* refers to the activities that must be undertaken before a certain outcome can be expected. Note that the action that is an antecedent in this particular case was generated as a consequent from a condition/action pair. *Data* refers to the information that must be available before a certain goal can be realized. In subsequent discussions, the terms *premise, condition,* and *antecedent* are used interchangeably.

The antecedent typically contains several clauses linked by the logical connectives AND and OR. The consequent consists of one or more phrases that specify the action to be taken. Advantages of rules are:

1. They are flexible in that individual rules can be easily added, removed, or updated.
2. They provide a straightforward representation of knowledge that is easy to interpret.
3. They are structured in a way similar to the way people rationalize to solve problems.
4. They are useful for representing the interaction between declarative and procedural knowledge.

The major disadvantage of rules is the requirement for a very efficient search mechanism for finding appropriate rules during an expert system consultation. An example of a rule that might be used in the gear-production example is:

Antecedent: **If** thickness for any tooth is large and circular pitch is small and face width is medium
Consequent: **Then** production method is cutting

Rules can be classified into two categories: First-order rules and meta rules (higher-order). A First-order rule is a simple rule consisting of antecedents and consequents. A meta rule is a rule whose antecedents and consequents contain information about other rules. Examples are:

First-order rule:
    If node j is inactive and arc i has a reliability < 0.9
    Then set $(1, n)$ connectedness $= 0$
Meta rule:
    If arc k has a failure rate similar to arc m
    And arc k uses rule R1
    Then activate rule R1

A familiar example of a meta rule is the popular office sign that reads:

Rule Number One:
  The boss is always right.
Rule Number Two:
  If the boss is wrong
  Then refer to Rule Number One

Rules are versatile and widely applicable for representing knowledge in a variety of problem domains. However, there are certain unique problem domains where rules may not be readily applicable. Pattern recognition or machine vision are two problem domains where rules might be difficult to apply. Machine vision problems lend themselves to solutions using frames and scripts or other related techniques. Rules might be used during a postprocessing part after enough features have been extracted from a particular vision scenario.

4.7.5 Predicate Logic

Propositional calculus is an elementary system of formal logic that is used to determine whether a given proposition is true or false. Predicate calculus adds the capability of specifying relationships and making generalizations about propositions. Logical expressions use predicate calculus to generate inferences by asserting the truthfulness or otherwise of propositional statements. Adding functions and other analytical features to predicate calculus creates first-order predicate calculus. A function is a logical construct that yields a value. For example, when a function defined as "is-made-by" is applied to the object gear, the result might be "machining." That is,

(Is-Made-By (Gear Machining))

The statement "Gear is-a machined part" is either true or not-true in the context of the problem being addressed. Many forms of logic have been developed for use within AI, including propositional calculus, predicate calculus, first-order logic, modal logic, temporal logic, and fuzzy logic. First-order logic, an extension of predicate logic, is perhaps the most commonly used. A predicate symbol expresses a statement about individual elements, either singly or in relation to other elements. A function symbol expresses a mapping from one element or a group of elements to another element. For example, in the formula below, the predicate (noun) Product denotes a relationship between three arguments: a particular class of item, material, and shape.

Product (Shaft, Metal, Cylindrical)

The predicate will return a value of "true" if a given item matches the description of a cylindrical metal shaft. Similarly, the function symbol "Use" in the formula below maps metal shafts to a particular usage category.

Product (Shaft, Metal, Use (Crankshaft))

If "crankshaft" is used as the argument in the function "use," the function will most probably return the value "cylindrical" since most crankshafts are cylindrical in shape. The value "cylindrical" is then used by the predicate "Product" to identify a specific type of product. Subsets of product types can be formed, for example, by further classifying cylindrical metal shafts into diameter size categories. Thus, product inheritance relationships can be represented by considering the predicate "part-of" as shown in the formula below:

$$\{\text{Part-of } (x, y)\} \cap \{\text{Part-of } (y, z)\} = \text{part-of } (x, z)$$

Predicate logic relies on the truth and rules of inferences to represent symbols and their relationships to each other. It can be used to determine the truthfulness or falsity of a statement and can also be used to represent statements about specific objects or individuals. The advantages of predicate logic include:

1. Simplicity of notation allows descriptions to be readily understandable,
2. Modularity allows statements to be added, deleted, or modified without affecting other statements in the knowledge base
3. It is concise because each fact has to be represented only once.
4. Theorem-proving techniques can be used to derive new facts from old ones

Predicate logic is best used in domains of concise and unified theories such as physics, chemistry, and other mathematical or theoretical fields. The disadvantages of predicate logic are:

1. Difficulty in representing procedural and heuristic knowledge
2. Difficulty in managing large knowledge bases due to restricted organizational structure
3. Limited data-manipulation procedures

4.7.6 O-A-V Triplets

An O-A-V triplet is a common type of semantic network commonly used within the framework of other representation models. It is divided into three parts, *object, attribute,* and *value.* The representation presents a serial list of an object and an attribute of interest. Objects are viewed as physical or conceptual entities. Attributes are general properties defining the object, while the values indicate the specific descriptions of the attribute. Using a segment of the semantic network presented earlier in Figure 4.5, an example of O-A-V triplet for the gear production problem is:

Object	Attribute	Value
Gear	Number of teeth	20

O-A-V representation is used within the framework of other representation techniques. For example, in semantic network, each object may have an attribute of interest identified and the associated value of the attribute may be used in determining further links within the network structure.

4.7.7 Hybrids

Each knowledge-representation technique has its advantages and disadvantages. For example, rules are especially useful for representing procedural knowledge (methods for accomplishing goals). Semantic networks are good for representing relations among objects. Frame-based semantic networks can concisely store a large amount of knowledge about object properties and relations. Predicate logic provides a means for explicitly expressing different types of knowledge. Early expert systems tended to use one technique or another exclusively. More recently the tendency has been to combine different representation techniques, so as to take advantage of the capabilities of each technique within the context of the prevailing problem. A system might use rules to define procedures for discovering attributes of objects, semantic networks to define the relationships among the objects referenced in the rules, and frames to describe the objects' typical attributes. The frame example presented earlier in Table 4.1 is a good example of combining rule and frame representations.

4.7.8 Specialized Representation Techniques

Specialized representation techniques are sometimes needed to address the unique characteristics of certain problem domains. The specialized approaches may be needed to take advantage of specific search strategies. For example, Badiru presents a Cantor set representational technique. described below [4].

Cantor Set Model for Knowledge Representation. The Cantor set is often referred to as the set of the excluded middle thirds [88]. A unique property of the Cantor set is that it contains an infinite number of elements, but its representative points occupy no space, in the geometric sense, on the real number line. The concept of excluded middle thirds may have relevance in certain problem domains requiring specialized search strategies. These are domains where associative property inheritance relationships exist among the elements of the knowledge base such that the elements can be stored in an ordered fashion using a key property. Examples of such domains are:

1. *Computer-aided design* (CAD): Knowledge bases where design elements are stored by some design characteristic. For example, drive shaft designs that are stored in order of shaft diameters and bending stresses.
2. *Group technology:* Group technology and process planning applications where items are grouped into product families in a predetermined sequence.
3. *Chemical analysis:* Knowledge bases where materials are stored in order of some key property, say atomic weight or electrical conductivity. Experimental searches for materials properties are a suitable application for cantor set search approach.

Mathematically, the Cantor set is denoted as:

$$C = \left\{ x \in \Omega \mid x \in \bigcup_{k=0}^{\infty} \delta_k \right\}$$

where $\Omega = [0, 1]$. The interval, δ_k, is as explained below.

Consider the closed interval $\Omega = [0, 1]$ and the open intervals generated by successive removal of the middle thirds of intervals left after previous removals. The interval deletions are shown geometrically in Figure 4.7. Note that:

$$\bigcup_{k=0}^{\infty} \delta_k = [0, 1]$$

The interval δ_k is the union of the open intervals deleted from Ω after the kth search iteration. The deleted intervals are represented mathematically below:

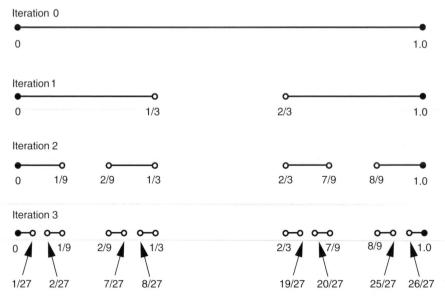

Figure 4.7. Cantor set representation.

$$\delta_0 = \phi \text{ (null set)}$$

$$\delta_1 = \left[\frac{1}{3}, \frac{2}{3}\right]$$

$$\delta_2 = \left[\frac{1}{9}, \frac{2}{9}\right] \cup \left[\frac{1}{3}, \frac{2}{3}\right] \cup \left[\frac{7}{8}, \frac{8}{9}\right]$$

.

.

.

If Ω is considered as the universal set, then we may also express the Cantor set as the complement of the original set C. That is, alternately,

$$C = \left(\bigcup_{k=0}^{\infty} \delta_k\right)^c$$

which, by DeMorgan's law, implies

$$C = \bigcap_{k=0}^{\infty} (\delta_k)^c$$

If we use the following simplifying notation for the complement,

$$(\delta_k)^c = \lambda_k$$

we would obtain the following alternate representation:

$$C = \bigcap_{k=0}^{\infty} \lambda_k$$

where

$$\lambda_0 = [0, 1]$$

$$\lambda_1 = \left[0, \frac{1}{3}\right] \cup \left[\frac{2}{3}, 1\right]$$

$$\lambda_2 = \left[0, \frac{1}{9}\right] \cup \left[\frac{2}{9}, \frac{1}{3}\right] \cup \left[\frac{2}{3}, \frac{7}{9}\right] \cup \left[\frac{8}{9}, 1\right]$$

.

.

.

It should be noted that λ_k is the remaining search space available for the kth search iteration. Also note that λ_k consists of 2^k closed and nonoverlapping intervals each of real length $(1/3^k)$.

Application of the Cantor Set Approach. Knowledge bases for expert systems consist of pieces of information on the basis of which inferences are drawn for a particular problem situation. For large domain problems, the knowledge base lookup or search can easily lead to a combinatorial explosion of possibilities. For example, if we have 50 pieces of evidence, each of which is either true or false, then there are 2^{50} possible combinations. From a practical point of view, we need search procedures that can considerably reduce the dimensionality of the search space.

In a manufacturing context, two physical objects are exactly alike only if they are fully interchangeable. In an actual manufacturing situation, items in a group will not necessarily have characteristics that are fully identical. Recalling the earlier example of shafts, a group of objects may consist of items that are related by their classification as "shafts." Differences within the group may pertain to the items' diameters or any other characteristic of interest. For example, we may be interested in diameters that range from 3 in. to 7 in. Arranging shaft designs in increasing or decreasing order of shaft diameter can be used to indicate the degree of relationship or the level of property inheritance of the items in the group. Thus, in a knowledge base, inferences can be drawn to relate to certain subsets of a given set of the knowledge

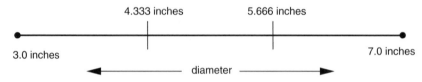

Figure 4.8. Range of shaft diameters as a search space.

elements. Graphically, the shaft example may be represented as shown in Figure 4.8.

Suppose we are interested in a shaft that meets a certain quality characteristic. We can conduct an exhaustive search to check if each shaft meets the desired quality characteristic. But exhaustive searches are very costly and time consuming, particularly where we have a large number of items to search. An efficient search strategy would be helpful in reducing the time and expense of finding the item that meets the specified characteristic. Suppose we know the distribution of the shaft diameters over the range of 3 in. to 7 in. If the distribution can be reasonably expected to follow a bell-shaped curve such as the normal distribution shown in Figure 4.9, then the Cantor set strategy may be employed. The search strategy would proceed as follows:

Step 1. Identify a known property of the items to be searched (e.g., diameter sizes).

Step 2. Determine the range of values of the known property. This establishes the search space.

Step 3. Specify the desired characteristic of the item to be searched (e.g., quality characteristic).

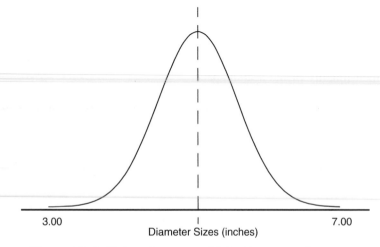

Figure 4.9. Bell-shaped curve model for Cantor search strategy.

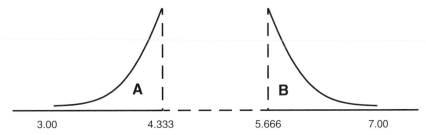

Figure 4.10. Search space for the second iteration of Cantor search.

Step 4. Determine the distribution of the items based on the known property (e.g., bell-shaped).

Step 5. Sort the items in increasing or decreasing order of the known
property.

Step 6. Apply the Cantor set search procedure iteratively until an item
matching the specified characteristic is found.

Instead of conducting an exhaustive search over the entire search interval,
we would check the middle third first. If the item that meets the requirement
is not found in that interval, we would delete the interval from further consideration. The middle thirds of the remaining intervals are then searched in
successive iterations.

Comments on the Search Procedure

1. If the distribution of the items is bell-shaped, then searching the first
   middle third before any other interval is logical since that is where the
   majority of the items are located.
2. The largest search effort will involve the first middle third. The search
   process becomes less efficient as more iterations are needed to find the
   desired item.
3. In the second and subsequent iterations, a decision must be made concerning which middle third interval to search next. For example, Figure
   4.10 shows the search space left after deleting the first middle third. We
   have the option of first searching the middle third of interval A and
   then the middle third of interval B and vice versa. Since the intervals
   are equally likely to contain the desired item, one can flip a coin to
   determine which interval to search first. The decision becomes more
   difficult in the third iteration since, as shown in Figure 4.11, the remaining four intervals are not equiprobable. Figure 4.12 shows the
   search intervals for the first three iterations of the Cantor search strategy.

In the Cantor search procedure, the desired item is found only when it is
located in the middle third of some interval. If the value of interest is in the

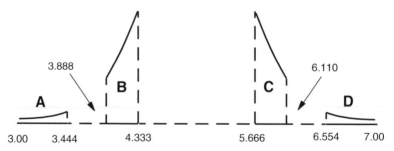

Figure 4.11. Search space for the third iteration of Cantor search.

interval (4.333, 5.666), then only one interval search will be needed to find it. If it is in the interval (3.444, 3.888) ∪ (6.110, 6.554), then at most three interval searches will be needed. If the value is in the interval (3.148, 3.296) ∪ (4.036, 4.184) ∪ (5.814, 5.962) ∪ (6.702, 6.85), then at most seven interval searches will be needed. In general, the maximum number of interval searches, N, needed to locate an item in a Cantor set search strategy is one of the following:

$$N_k = 1, 3, 5, 7, 15, 31, \ldots$$

where k is the iteration number. That is,

$$N_0 = 0$$

$$N_k = N_{k-1} + 2^{k-1}$$

$$= \sum_{j=0}^{k-1} 2^j$$

$$= (2^k) - 1$$

It should be noted that if the distribution of the items to be searched is skewed to the right or left (e.g., chi-squared or lognormal distributions), as shown in Figure 4.13, then the basic Cantor set search strategy will not be appropriate.

Modified Search Procedure. The deficiency mentioned in the third comment on the Cantor search procedure can be overcome by using the following modification of the procedure. The modification improves the efficiency of the search strategy.

Consider the search intervals to be used for the second iteration (shown earlier in Figure 4.10). Instead of considering the intervals [3.00, 4.333] and [5.666, 7.00] as separate search intervals, we can merge the intervals as shown

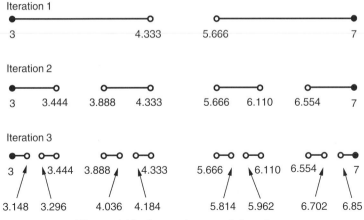

Figure 4.12. Successive search iterations.

in Figure 4.14. Then the next middle third to be searched during the second iteration will be [3.89, 6.11]. Recall that the items in the interval [4.333, 5.666] have already been deleted in the first iteration and are not contained within the modified middle third interval of [3.89, 6.11]. This process is repeated consecutively until the desired item is found. Figure 4.15 shows the search interval for the third iteration using the merged interval modification.

Alternate Search Preference. The conventional Cantor set search strategy gives first preference to the middle third of the ordered set of items to be searched. As mentioned previously, this is suitable if the distribution of the property of interest is bell-shaped. If, by contrast, the distribution is bimodal

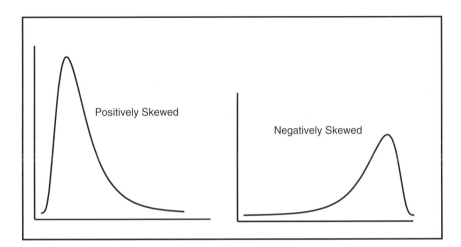

Figure 4.13. Skewed distributions not suitable for Cantor search.

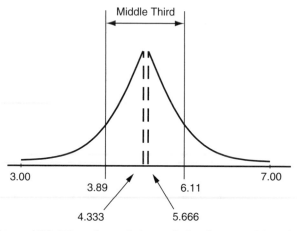

Figure 4.14. Merged search intervals for the second iteration.

end-heavy, then an alternate ordering of the items may be required. An example of a bimodal end-heavy distribution is shown in Figure 4.16, which is representative of typical hazard functions in product reliability analysis. The bathtub-shaped distribution is a special form of the beta distribution with shape parameters of $\alpha = 0.001$ and $\beta = 0.001$.

It is noted that most of the items to be searched are located in the regions close to the minimum and maximum points. An alternate arrangement of the items is achieved by bisecting the ordered set through the median and flipping over the half-sets generated. This is shown graphically in Figure 4.17. This alternate arrangement gives first preference to the end points of the original set of the items to be searched.

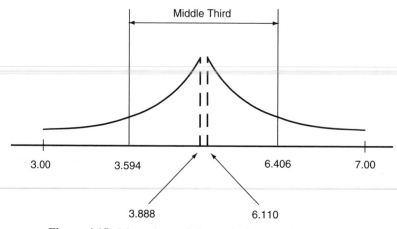

Figure 4.15. Merged search intervals for the third iteration.

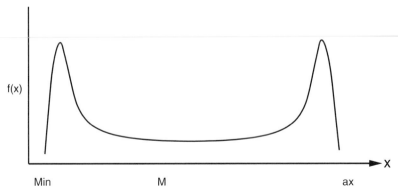

Figure 4.16. Bathtub-shaped distribution.

4.8   CONCEPT OF KNOWLEDGE SETS

Experts differ in personal cognitive reasoning skills and will follow different patterns of reasoning. The peculiar features of a problem domain are important in determining how the knowledge acquired in the domain should be represented. The organization of medical knowledge, for example, would have certain unique characteristics and requirements compared to the representation of financial management knowledge. Medical information concerning specific patient data may be more dynamic than the information in other problem domains. These differences must be taken into account in organizing knowledge into an efficient form for problem solving.

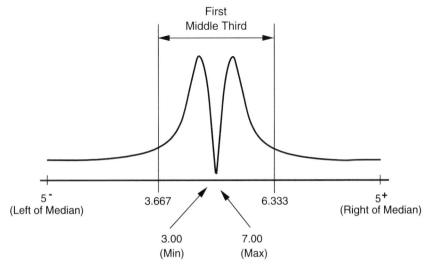

Figure 4.17. Bisected and flipped search interval.

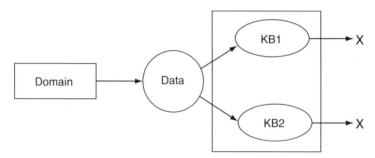

Figure 4.18. Equivalent knowledge bases.

4.8.1   Properties of Knowledge Sets

Badiru presents a collection of concepts based on set theory for organizing elements in expert systems knowledge bases [5]. A knowledge set may be defined as a collection of heuristics or facts that constitute a problem-solving technique. Specific distinguishable contents of the knowledge set are the knowledge elements. When the knowledge set is applied to a specific problem domain, then we have what is referred to as a knowledge base. Presented below are some set properties defined in the context of knowledge base organization.

Equivalent Knowledge Bases. Two knowledge bases A and B are equivalent if and only if they both yield the same consultation result for the same problem scenario. That is:

$$A \equiv B$$

As shown in Figure 4.18, the two knowledge bases, KB1 and KB2, are equivalent if they both yield the same conclusion, X, for the same given set of data. An evaluation of the equivalence of knowledge bases may be useful in a comparative analysis of competing products that are designed to solve the same problem with comparable performance.

Equality of Knowledge Bases. Knowledge bases A and B are equal if and only if they contain identical knowledge elements. That is:

$$A = B \ni \forall x \in A, \qquad x \in B$$

and

$$B = A \ni \forall x \in B, \qquad x \in A$$

Figure 4.19 shows the equality of two knowledge base sets. If A is equal

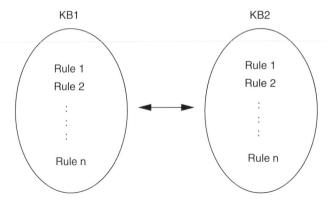

Figure 4.19. Equality of knowledge bases.

to B, then an element x belonging to A implies that B also contains x. Knowledge bases that are equal are not necessarily equivalent, since different organizations of the knowledge elements can lead to different reasoning paths and thus yield different results.

Subjugation of Knowledge Sets. Let A and B be knowledge bases. If every rule element of A is a rule element of B, then A is a subset of B and B is a superset of A as presented mathematically below and graphically in Figure 4.20.

$$A \subseteq B \ni \forall x \in A \rightarrow X \in B$$

A true subset of a knowledge base should solve a subproblem of the main problem that the knowledge base is designed to solve. In terms of expert systems consultation, a subset of a knowledge base is that portion of the

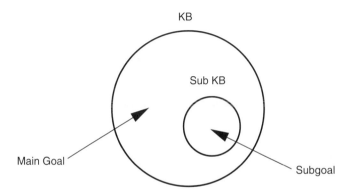

Figure 4.20. Formation of a subset of a knowledge base.

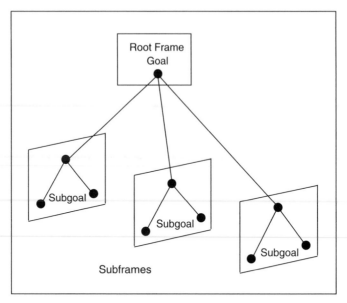

Figure 4.21. Partition of problem into subframes.

knowledge that would yield a subgoal of the main goal. This concept is useful for problem partition purposes. The partitions (or subsets) of a given knowledge base may be used to construct subframes associated with specific subgoals, as shown in Figure 4.21. The union of the root frame and subframes make up the entire knowledge base.

Ordered Pairs of Knowledge Elements. Given any two objects a and b, we may form a new object (a, b), called the "ordered pair (a, b)," with the property that:

$$(a, b) \neq (b, a)$$

Two ordered pairs (a, b) and (c, d) are equal if and only if $a = c$ and $b = d$. The concept of ordered pairs is useful in the symbolic representation technique of artificial intelligence. For example, the words "Down" and "Town" can form two distinct ordered pairs, "Down Town" and "Town Down." The first pair represents a central location of a geographic area, while the second may be viewed as describing the "Down" or depressed condition of the geographic region. Obviously,

$$\text{Down-Town} \neq \text{Town-Down}$$

To elaborate further the concept of ordered knowledge elements in symbolic representation, we may consider the words "bills" and "foot." They may be ordered symbolically to yield ordered pairs with two distinct interpretations:

1. (Bills-Foot) referring to a part of the body of a person named Bill
2. (Foot-Bills) referring to an action state (i.e., to incur consequential expenses)

Similarly, the TV commercial that says "no salt is sodium-free" may be used to illustrate an ordered pair. For example, "(No-Salt) is sodium-free" implies that the product named "no-salt" contains no sodium. By comparison, "No-(Salt) is sodium-free" implies that there is no salt that is sodium-free (i.e., all salts contain sodium). In an analogous manner, the phrase "No news is good news" indicates that there is no news that is good news, whereas the phrase "No-news is good news" declares the object "no-news" as being "good news."

Cartesian Products of Knowledge Sets.   Let A and B be two knowledge sets. The set of all ordered pairs (a, b), where a and b are specific parameters of objects, with a belonging to A and b belonging to B, is the Cartesian product of A and B, denoted by $A\mathbf{X}B$.

$$A\mathbf{X}B = \{(a, b) \mid a \in A, \qquad b \in B\}$$

For example:

$$\text{Let } A = \{\text{Hammer, Foot, Kick}\}$$

and

$$B = \{\text{Head, Bill, Bucket}\}$$

Then:

$A\mathbf{X}B = \{$(Hammer, Head), (Hammer, Bill), (Hammer, Bucket), (Foot, Head), (Foot, Bill), (Foot, Bucket), (Kick, Head), (Kick, Bill), (Kick, Bucket)$\}$

Some of the elements of $A\mathbf{X}B$ may be combined to obtain symbolic representations that convey different inferences. For example, as discussed in Chapter 2,

$$\text{(Hammer-Head)-(Kick-Bucket)}$$

could be the symbolic representation for the statement: "If the victim's head is hammered, then the victim may kick the bucket." Likewise,

(Kick-Head)-(Foot-Bill)

could symbolically represent the statement "If victim's head is kicked, the assailant will foot the bill incurred as a result of the injury." We note that the words "head" and "kick" are common to the two representations above. However, the way they are ordered in combination with two other words creates two different meanings.

Knowledge Set Relations. Given knowledge sets A and B, not necessarily distinct, a relation $\mathbf{R}$ from A to B is a subset of the Cartesian product $A \mathbf{X} B$. Thus, an element a of A is related to another element b of B by the relation $\mathbf{R}$. This relation is written as:

$$a\mathbf{R}b \text{ to indicate that } (a, b) \in \mathbf{R}$$

The symbol $a\mathbf{R}b$ is read as "a is $\mathbf{R}$-related to b." Several distinct relations can be defined within a given knowledge base. For example, relations may be of "equality," "opposite," "synonym," and so on. If the sets A and B are the same set, say K, then $\mathbf{R}$ is defined as a relation in K instead of a relation from K to K. In a community of people denoted by C, the symbol "(Paul)$\mathbf{H}$(Joan)" may define a relation $\mathbf{H}$ (of being the husband of . . .) and imply that Paul is the husband of Joan. Thus, we are considering an ordered pair (Paul, Joan) in the relation $\mathbf{H}$. The order can be reversed to define a different relation. For example, (Joan)$\mathbf{W}$(Paul) defines a relation $\mathbf{W}$ (of being the wife of . . .) in C. As another illustration of relations, we can define a relation, $\mathbf{S}$, for synonyms with the example of:

$$(\text{Large})\mathbf{S}(\text{Big})$$

The synonym relation can have useful applications in knowledge base searches since it would permit consultations to proceed successfully on the basis of the instantiation of synonym parameters rather than the specific parameters requested. A relation $\mathbf{R}$ is said to be *symmetric* if and only if $x\mathbf{R}y$ implies $y\mathbf{R}x$—for example, a brother-to-brother relation. The relations $\mathbf{H}$ and $\mathbf{W}$ discussed above are not symmetric. But the $\mathbf{S}$ relation is symmetric since large is a synonym for big and big is a synonym for large. Here, "big" and "large" represent specific values of an attribute of a given object. The relation $\mathbf{R}$ is said to be *transitive* if and only if $x\mathbf{R}y$ and $y\mathbf{R}z$ imply that $x\mathbf{R}z$—for example, brother-to-brother-to-brother relations.

Inverse Relations. Each knowledge base relation, $\mathbf{R}$, may have an inverse that is defined as:

$$\mathbf{R}^- = \{(b, a) \mid (a, b) \in \mathbf{R}\}$$

The inverse relation may be used to obtain parameter negation instead of explicitly reversing parameter values. In a knowledge base, particularly one of those dealing with natural language applications, it may be necessary to define a relation of synonym as well as an inverse relation of antonym. In quantitative analysis, a relation of "greater-than" and the relation of "less-than" may be of interest. Using the earlier synonym relation as an example, a parameter, P, can be instantiated by any synonym of the word "known" as shown below:

$$P = x \in \{a \mid a\mathbf{S}\text{known}\}$$

So, any word "x" that is a synonym for "known" can be a suitable value for the instantiation of P. Thus, we have

$$(\text{KNOWN})synonym(\text{x})$$

where x may be any element in the set of words given by:

$A = \{$available, accessible, handy, ready, within-reach, identified, recognized, specified, understood, asserted, justified, stated, inferred, given, observed, realized$\}$

Instead of defining another parameter value of "unknown" to achieve parameter negation for "known," a generic inverse relation can be used. This is shown mathematically as:

$$P = x \in \{a \mid a\mathbf{S}^{-1} \text{ known}\}$$

Thus, the inverse relation facilitates a compact representation of a large body of knowledge. The major advantage of the inverse relation is that a single relation can be applied generally across various parameters within a given knowledge base.

Domain of Knowledge Set Relations. If $\mathbf{R}$ is a relation from set A to set B, then the domain of $\mathbf{R}$ is the set of all parameter a belonging to A such that $a\mathbf{R}b$ for some parameter b belonging to B. That is,

$$\text{Dom}(\mathbf{R}) = \{a \in A \mid (a, b) \in \mathbf{R} \text{ for some } b \in B\}$$

As an example, consider the two frames in Figure 4.22. Let frame A contain the subgoals $a1$, $a2$, $a3$, $a4$, $a5$ while frame B contains the subgoals $b1$, $b2$, $b3$, $b4$, $b5$, $b6$, $b7$, $b8$. Define a relation $\mathbf{Z}$ from A to B such that an element a belonging to A is related to an element b belonging to B if and only if there is a rule in B that has a as a premise and b as a conclusion.

Now suppose only the following rules exist in frame B:

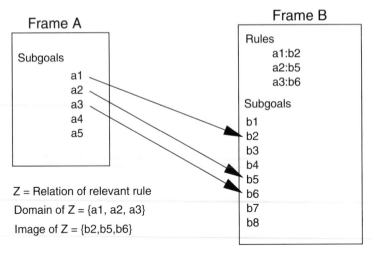

Figure 4.22. Relations defined on knowledge base sets.

If $a1$, **then** $b2$

If $a2$, **then** $b5$

If $a3$, **then** $b6$

The domain of **Z** is then given by the set:

$$\text{Dom}(\mathbf{Z}) = \{a1, a2, a3\}$$

since the elements $a1$, $a2$, and $a3$ are the only elements of A that can successfully trigger rules in B. The image of the relation, **R**, is defined as:

$$\text{Im}(\mathbf{R}) = \{\in B \mid (a, b) \in \mathbf{R} \text{ for some } a \in A\}$$

Thus, the image of the relation **Z** is:

$$\text{Im}(\mathbf{Z}) = \{b2, b5, b6\}$$

which corresponds to the set of rules that are triggered in frame B. A special kind of relation on knowledge sets is parameter mapping in which there is one-to-one correspondence between parameters in knowledge subsets. An example of parameter mapping is shown in Figure 4.23. An identification of the specific correspondence between parameters in the subsets of a knowledge can lead to a better control of the inference process. For example, in Figure 4.24, parameter j is known to be capable of producing only subgoal i.

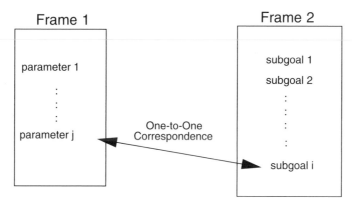

Figure 4.23. Parameter mapping in knowledge base frames.

Identity Relations on Parameters. An identity relation in a knowledge base is a relation that relates every knowledge element with itself such that:

$$\mathbf{R} = \{(a, a) \mid a \in A\}$$

This is referred to as the reflexive property of the relation $\mathbf{R}$. For example, a relation defined as **DIVISION-BY-ONE** will preserve the characteristics of any given element to which it is applied. For example,

$$\text{DIVISION-BY-ONE(argument)} = \text{argument}$$

By contrast, a relation defined as SQUARE is not a reflexive relation, since

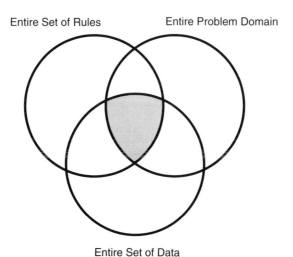

Figure 4.24. Intersection of domain, knowledge, and data sets.

it does not preserve the characteristics of all the arguments to which it is applied.

Binary Operations on Knowledge Sets. A binary operation on a knowledge set S is a function from the Cartesian square $S \mathbf{X} S$ to S, that is, an operation that uses an ordered pair from $S \mathbf{X} S$ to produce another element of S. For example, let S be the set of groups of words in a knowledge base dictionary. An operation may be defined for the process of forming natural language statements (or new groups of words) in the set. The new groups of words belong to the original set of words.

Mapping of Knowledge Sets. If the set C is a subset of the Cartesian product $A \mathbf{X} B$, of the knowledge sets A and B, then C is a mapping from A to B such that for each a belonging to A there is exactly one b belonging to B for which (a, b) belong to C. In order words, the mapping, C, is the collection of the elements of $A \mathbf{X} B$ that have one-to-one correspondence with the elements of A and B. The elements of the sets A, B, and C are specific parameters of objects contained in the knowledge base of interest.

In the example presented earlier, $C = A \mathbf{X} B$ since each element a of A, in combination with each element b of B, yields a unique (distinct) ordered pair of words. In the experiment of tossing two fair dice and observing the sum of the faces that show, only two of the 36 elements of the sample space can form a mapping. The element "sum $= 2$" can be obtained in only one way, $(1 + 1)$, while the element "sum $= 12$" can also be obtained in only one way $(6 + 6)$. The other number combinations produce sums that are not unique. For example, $1 + 2 = 3$ and $2 + 1 = 3$. An understanding of the mapping of parameters is quite useful in the organization of parameter data for knowledge base construction. The knowledge engineer can analyze and identify what combinations of parameters produce which instantiations. Thus, redundancy can be identified and eliminated.

Intersection of Knowledge Sets. Successful parameter instantiation can occur only in the intersection of the domain, knowledge, and data sets. This intersection is not the same as in the physical sense of conventional sets. It is a conceptual intersection that relates to which data fit which problem situation and the contents of the knowledge base. This is shown graphically in Figure 4.24. Set A is the set of all available parameters in the knowledge base rules, set B is the set of problem domain parameters, and set C is the set of all parameters in the available data.

It is obvious that not all available rules will match the problem domain and the available data simultaneously. To reduce the processing time for expert systems consultation, the minimum most applicable set of knowledge base should be used. This minimum set can be identified by finding the conceptual intersection of the three sets A, B, and C. There is a tendency to measure the robustness of an expert system by the number of rules it contains.

But a close and careful review may reveal that a large percentage of the rules included in a knowledge base are irrelevant for the type or amount of data available.

Integration of Set Concepts. As expert systems and artificial intelligence products find their ways into various areas of applications, the need to make those products more compact and efficient will become a major concern. Many researchers are now beginning to address the problems associated with the shortcomings of the present systems. An integration of the set concepts presented in the preceding sections should be applicable to the solution of the prevailing problems in knowledge base organization.

4.9   REASONING MODELS

Once problem-solving knowledge has been identified, the way it is encoded for drawing inferences depends on the reasoning approach desired for the chosen problem domain. The search strategy, inference process, and control structure are all important for knowledge-representation purposes. The structure of the problems in some domains will dictate which reasoning approach would be most applicable or effective. *Reasoning* is the process of drawing inferences from known or assumed facts. An *inference* is the logical conclusion or implication based on available information. Sometimes it is possible to draw an inference based on *intuition*. In such a case, one reaches a conclusion without a conscious use of reasoning. Presented below are some important concepts and models for drawing inferences during expert systems consultation.

Deductive reasoning is the process of reasoning from general information about a class of objects or events to specific information about a given member of the class.

In *inductive reasoning,* one draws a general conclusion based on specific facts. For example, the specific information about individual members of a class of objects or events may lead to a general conjecture about the whole class.

Monotonic reasoning involves a unidirectional parameter instantiation. Parameter instantiation is to the assignment of a specific value to a parameter. In monotonic reasoning, parameter instantiation is irrevocable regardless of whatever new information may become available. For example, the statement, "Once a thief, always a thief" conveys the notion of monotonic reasoning. The observer's view of a thief never changes, regardless of any new information that may indicate the rehabilitation of the thief.

In *nonmonotonic reasoning,* parameters can be reinstantiated if new information warrants the assignment of a new value to the parameter.

Forward chaining, commonly known as *forward reasonsing* or *data-driven search,* is the process of reasoning forward from a given set of data to some possibly remote goal state or conclusion. Forward chaining is generally of the heuristic form:

If (data condition)

Then (conclusion)

If we can assume that people normally like those that they trust, then a forward chaining rule to convey that assumption is:

If *person x* trusts *person y*

Then *person x* likes *person y*

The conclusion part of a rule may become the condition part of another rule. Thus, we can extend the above example to the one below:

If *person x* likes *person y*

Then *person x* enjoys-the-company-of *person y*

In *backward chaining,* also called *backward reasoning* or *goal-driven,* the reasoning process starts from a goal state and backtracks to the paths that might have led to the goal. Backward chaining is generally of the form:

Goal state

If (data condition)

A backward chaining rule based on the previous example is:

person x likes *person y*
If *person x* trusts *person y*

This example asserts that liking someone requires a precondition of trust. As discussed below, such an assertion may not be precise. If, for example, only 80% of the population fell in the category of the rule assertion, then we could assign some level of certainty or confidence to the rule. Then the rule might be stated as:

person x likes *person y*

If *person x* trusts *person y* (certainty factor = 0.80)

Backward chaining is often implemented in expert systems in the coding format of a forward chaining rule. In that case, the goal is specified in the antecedent of the rule and the condition leading to the goal is specified in the

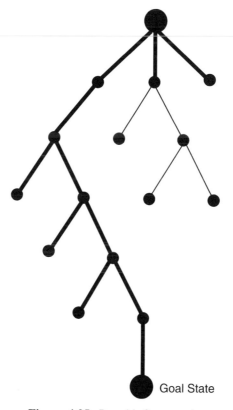

Figure 4.25. Breadth-first search.

conclusion part of the rule. For the example of interpersonal relationship, the backward chaining rule can be written as:

If *person x* is-to-like *person y*

Then *person x* must-trust *person y*

The process of drawing inferences using an expert system knowledge base involves searching for parameters and values that match certain conditions. In *breadth-first search,* all the available premises at a decision node are evaluated before the deeper details of each premise are gone into. Figure 4.25 shows an example of a breadth-first search. All the branches at each decision node are evaluated before the branch to follow for the next search is selected. The breadth-first search generates all nodes in the search tree at level *k* before investigating the nodes at level *k* + 1. The complexity of the search process is thus a function of the number of nodes investigated.

Since the procedure exhaustively investigates the branches at each level before proceeding to the next lower level, breadth-first search will always find

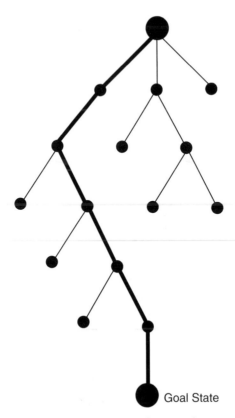

Goal State

Figure 4.26. Depth-first search.

the search path of shortest length. Thus, if search path length is the basis for evaluating the efficiency of the search, then breadth-first search is optimal. However, it is time consuming and sometimes impractical, particularly if the goal state is located deep in the search tree and there are many branches at each node. If the search tree has X branches at each node and there are Y levels in the tree, then there are X^Y alternate paths to be investigated. However, not all searches will go to the same depth and not all nodes will have the same number of branches. So it is necessary to develop some aggregate measure of branches and levels to determine the number of alternate paths to be investigated.

Depth-first search involves the evaluation of all the ramifications of each premise before going to the next one. This is shown in Figure 4.26. An important aspect of depth-first search is that it only requires keeping track of the current path, and consequently storage and memory requirements to perform a depth-first search are less than for a breadth-first search. For this reason, depth-first search is often preferred to breadth-first search. An advantage of breadth-first search is that if a solution path exists and there are a finite number of branches in the search tree, then there is a guarantee that the solution will be found.

An example of the comparison of depth-first search to breadth-first search may be drawn from the screening of job applicants. Under breadth-first search, all the applicants are broadly reviewed before whom to invite for interview is decided, whereas under depth-first search, the first applicant is reviewed, interviewed, and evaluated before other applicants are considered.

Modus ponens is one of the most common inference strategies in knowledge-based systems. This is a logical reasoning that states that when the premise of a rule is known to be true, then it is valid to believe that the conclusion is true. For example, *modus ponens* allows us to reach the conclusion about *B* as shown below:

Given rule: **If** *A* is true, **then** *B* is true

Known fact: *A* is true

Valid conclusion: *B* is true

Modus tollens is the converse of *modus ponens*. *Modus tollens* reasoning states that if the premise of a rule must be true for the rule's conclusion to be true, then the falsity of the conclusion implies the falsity of the premise. As an example, consider the rule below:

Given rule: **If** SAT-SCORE is-greater-than 1200, **then** ADMISSION = yes

Known fact: ADMISSION = no

Modus tollens conclusion: SAT-SCORE is-not-greater-than 1200

As can be seen in this example, *modus tollens* reasoning may not necessarily hold in many practical problem scenarios. The fact that ADMISSION = no does not necessarily imply that the applicant did not have an SAT score greater than 1200. Admission might have been denied for other reasons besides SAT score. When it can be shown to be applicable, however, *modus tollens* reasoning can be a powerful inference strategy.

Blackboard architecture is a special type of knowledge-based system, that uses a form of opportunistic reasoning whereby several knowledge sources contribute to the reasoning strategy [25, 34, 76]. The basic characteristics of blackboard architecture are:

1. There are multiple sources of knowledge willing to contribute to the problem solving process. Each knowledge source is considered to be an expert in some limited aspect of the problem to be solved. That is, each knowledge source can solve a subset of the overall problem.

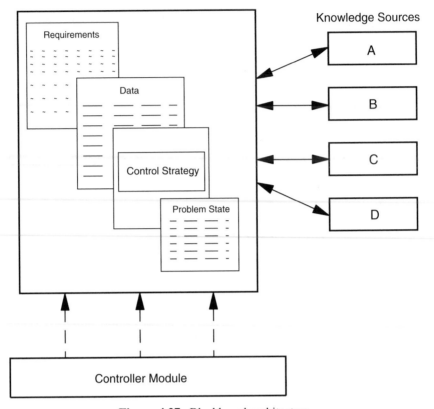

Figure 4.27. Blackboard architecture.

2. The knowledge sources may contain knowledge in the form of procedures, rules, or other knowledge-representation schema.
3. The knowledge sources work collectively to achieve synergism needed
   to solve the overall problem.
4. A globally accessible data base structure, the blackboard, is available.
   The blackboard contains information about the current state of the problem being solved. Each knowledge source checks the blackboard to find
   out what information is required for the next stage of the solution and
   determines how it may contribute to that next solution step. The knowledge sources make changes to the blackboard data incrementally until
   the desired solution is reached.
5. The knowledge sources cannot communicate with each other directly.
   Communication and interactions between the knowledge sources are
   accomplished solely through the blackboard.
6. Control information for the blackboard architecture may be contained
   within the knowledge sources, on the blackboard itself, or in a separate
   data base module. The controller monitors the changes to the blackboard
   and determines the next immediate requirement in the solution process.
   Figure 4.27 presents the components of the blackboard architecture.

5

PROBABILISTIC AND FUZZY REASONING

This chapter presents common techniques for handling uncertainty in expert systems. Expert systems consultations for practical problems often require that some simplifying assumptions be made. The assumptions may involve the elimination of certain parameters, the truncation of certain data sets, or the inclusion of facts that have little bearing on the problem domain. Unfortunately, these simplifying assumptions, coupled with other natural limitations in the inference process, create uncertainties that complicate our reasoning processes.

5.1 HUMAN REASONING AND PROBABILITY

How human reasoning differs from machine reasoning has been a subject of intense research for many years. Humans possess definite advantages over computers when it comes to structural reasoning. Humans have intuitive insight, which has thus far been difficult to implement in computer-based systems. Uncertainty is a reality in human reasoning and decision making. In many practical situations, it is difficult to have problem conditions that involve certain, complete, and consistent facts. Uncertainty can arise from several sources. For example, the information available may be incomplete, the information may be very volatile, the facts of the decision problem may be unstable, important data may be missing, the problem scenario may be too dynamic, key facts may be imprecise, the problem statement may be too vague, and so on. All of these situations compound the decision-making environment.

Several techniques have been developed to handle uncertainty in decision making. Many of these techniques are now being incorporated into expert systems. Probability analysis appears to be the most natural way to handle uncertainty in expert systems. However, it has certain limitations that make it difficult to implement. Simplified techniques that do not resort to rigorous theoretical basis have been developed as alternatives to probability in handling uncertainty in expert systems.

5.2   BAYESIAN APPROACH TO HANDLING UNCERTAINTY

By using probability, we can generalize observations about events to arrive at statements about a population of objects or conversely from the population to specific events. The Bayesian approach uses Bayes' theorem for handling uncertainty in the process of drawing inference about objects or events. Bayes' theorem states that:

Let:

$\{B_1, B_2, \ldots, B_n\}$ be a set of events forming a partition of the sample space S, where $P(B_i) \neq 0$, for $i = 1, 2, \ldots, n$.

Let:

A be any event of S such that $P(A) \neq 0$. Then, for $k = 1, 2, \ldots, n$, we have

$$P(B_k/A) = \frac{P(B_k \cap A)}{\sum_{i=1}^{n} P(B_i \cap A)}$$

$$= \frac{P(B_k)P(A|B_k)}{\sum_{i=1}^{n} P(B_i)P(A|B_i)}$$

Referring to Figure 5.1, the shaded area is the event A that we are given and the events labeled B_i are the events about which inferences are to be drawn. Bayes' theorem allows us to calculate the probability of having an event B_i given that the event A has occurred. Bayes' theorem can be restated in terms of objects and parameters in a knowledge base, as discussed earlier under the concepts of knowledge sets.

For example, if it is known that 2% of a population have tuberculosis (T), then we can define the following [60];

Fact: $P(T) = 0.02$

If $P(X|T)$ = probability that an X-ray of a tubercular person is positive

and $P(X|\text{Not-}T)$ = probability that an X-ray of a healthy person is positive

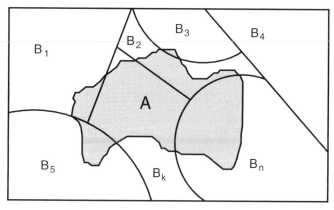

Figure 5.1. Events in a sample space.

Then $P(T|X)$ = probability that a person with a positive X-ray has tuberculosis

Data: $P(X|T) = 0.90$
$P(X|\text{Not-}T) = 0.01$

Using Bayes' rule, we can calculate $P(T|X)$ as follows:

$$P(T|X) = \frac{P(T)P(X|T)}{P(T)P(X|T) + P(\text{Not-}T)P(X|\text{Not-}T)}$$

$$= \frac{(0.02)(0.90)}{(0.02)\,(0.90) + (0.98)\,(0.01)}$$

$$= 0.648$$

While the techniques for applying the probability approach are well developed, there are many reasons why conventional probabilistic analysis has not been very popular in expert systems, including:

1. The events that partition the sample space (knowledge base) must be disjoint. This, of course, is not necessarily the case in the reasoning approach that humans use in solving practical problems.
2. The prior probabilities, $P(A|B_i)$, must be known. Since most heuristic problem-solving methods rely on expert judgment rather than mathematical facts, these prior probabilities are usually not available. Even when they are available, they are often unreliable.
3. Bayesian reasoning could lead to combinatorial explosion of the analysis. Since the boundaries of the events leading to a problem solution

are usually indeterminate or ambiguous, there is a tendency to overpartition the sample space. This subsequently leads to large data requirements and analysis.

4. Users not familiar with probabilistic statements are likely to misinterpret the results of a probability analysis.
5. New users are likely to find probability analysis intimidating.

The statistical approach to reasoning can be optimal from a theoretical perspective. However, practicality often precludes their implementation in expert systems. The probability approach has been used only in a few expert systems. In many cases, simplifying assumptions are often made in an attempt to achieve practicality. Unfortunately, such assumptions reduce or nullify the power of the probability approach. Presented below are some important relations defined for parameters and assertions in handling uncertainty in expert systems.

5.2.1 Logical Relations

With logical relations (like predicate calculus), the truthfulness of hypothesis is completely determined by the truthfulness of the assertions defining it. The relations include primitive logical operations conjunction (AND), disjunction (OR), and negation (NOT). The logical AND is the minimum of the probability values of the component assertions, and the logical OR is the maximum of the probability values of the component assertions.

5.2.2 Plausible Relations

Each assertion contributes "votes" for or against the truthfulness of an hypothesis. Each rule has a rule strength associated with it that defines the degree to which a change in the probability of the evidence changes the probability of the hypothesis. The change can be positive or negative, to favor or disfavor the hypothesis.

5.2.3 Contextual Relations

This relation expresses a condition that must be established before an assertion can be brought into the reasoning process. This is an example of the goal-driven approach of backward chaining.

5.3 DECISION TABLES AND TREES

Decision tree analysis is used to evaluate sequential decision problems. In engineering analysis, a decision tree may be useful in evaluating sequential

TABLE 5.1. Decision Table for Task Selection

	Actions								
	Task 1			Task 2			Task 3		
Event	Long	Medium	Short	Long	Medium	Short	Long	Medium	Short
Rain	I	I	U	I	U	D	I	I	U
No Rain	I	D	D	U	D	D	U	U	U

I = Increased duration; D = Decreased duration; U = Unchanged duration

project events. A decision problem under certainty has two elements: *action* and *consequence.* The decision maker's choices are the actions, while the results of those actions are the consequences. For example, in an activity network planning, the choice of one task among three potential tasks in a given time slot represents a potential action. The consequences of choosing one task over another may be characterized in terms of the slack time created in the network, the cost of performing the selected task, the resulting effect on the project completion time, or the degree to which a specified performance criterion is satisfied.

If the decision is made under uncertainty, as in stochastic network analysis, a third element, an *event,* is introduced into the decision problem. If we extend the deterministic task selection process to a stochastic process, the actions may be defined as Select Task 1, Select Task 2, and Select Task 3. The durations associated with the three possible actions can be categorized as Long task duration, medium task duration, and short task duration. The actual duration of each task is uncertain. Thus, each task has some probability of exhibiting long, medium, or short durations. The events can be identified as weather incidents: rain or no rain. The incidents of rain or no rain are uncertain. The consequences may be defined as Increased project completion time, Decreased project completion time, and Uunchanged project completion time. However, these consequences are uncertain due to the probabilistic durations of the tasks and the variable choices of the decision maker. That is, the consequences are determined partly by choice and partly by chance. The consequence is dependent on which event, rain or no rain, occurs.

To simplify the decision analysis, the decision elements may be summarized by using a decision table. A decision table indicates the relationship between pairs of decision elements. The decision table for the preceding example is presented in Table 5.1. In the table, each row corresponds to an event and each column corresponds to an action. The consequences appear as entries in the body of the table. The consequences have been coded as I (Increased), D (Decreased), or U (Unchanged). Each event-action combination has a specific consequence associated with it. In some decision problems, the consequences may not be unique. Thus, a consequence that is associated with a particular event-action pair may also be associated with another event-action pair. The actions included in the decision table are the only ones that the decision maker wishes to consider. For example, subcontracting or task elimination could be other possible choices for the decision maker. The actions included in the decision problem are mutually exclusive and collectively exhaustive, so that exactly one will be selected. The events are also mutually exclusive and collectively exhaustive.

The decision problem can also be conveniently represented as a decision tree, as shown in Figure 5.2. The tree representation is particularly convenient for decision problems with choices that must be made at different times over an extended period. For example, resource-allocation decisions must be made several times during the life cycle of an engineering project. The choice of actions is shown as a fork with a separate branch for each action. The events are also represented by branches in separate forks. To avoid confusion in very elaborate decision trees, the nodes for action forks are represented by squares while the nodes for event forks are represented by circles. The basic guideline for constructing a tree diagram is that the flow of events should be chronological from left to right. The actions are shown on the initial fork because the decision must be made before the actual event is known. The events are thus shown as branches in the third-stage forks. The consequence resulting from an event–action combination is shown as the end point of the corresponding path from the root of the tree.

Figure 5.2 reveals that there are six paths leading to an increase in the project duration, five paths leading to a decrease in project duration, and seven paths leading to an unchanged project duration. The total number of paths is given by:

$$P = \prod_{i=1}^{N} n_i$$

where

P = total number of paths in the decision tree
N = number of decision stages in the tree
n_i = number of branches emanating from each node in stage i

Thus, for the example in Figure 5.2, the number of paths is $P = (3)(3)(2) = 18$ paths. As mentioned previously, some of the paths, even though they are distinct, lead to identical consequences. Probability values can be incorporated into the decision structure as shown in Figure 5.3. Note that the selection of a task at the decision node is based on choice rather than probability. In this example, it is assumed that the probability of having a particular task duration is independent of whether or not it rains. In some cases, the weather sensitivity of a task may influence the duration of the task. Also, the probability of rain or no rain is independent of any other element in the decision structure.

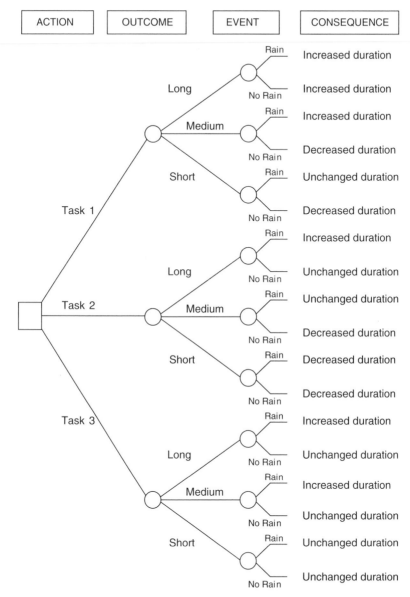

Figure 5.2. Decision tree for task selection.

If the items in the probability tree are interdependent, then the appropriate conditional probabilities will need to be computed. This will be the case if the duration of a task is influenced by the events Rain" and No-rain. In such a case, the probability tree should be redrawn as shown in Figure 5.4, which indicates that the weather event will need to be observed first before the task

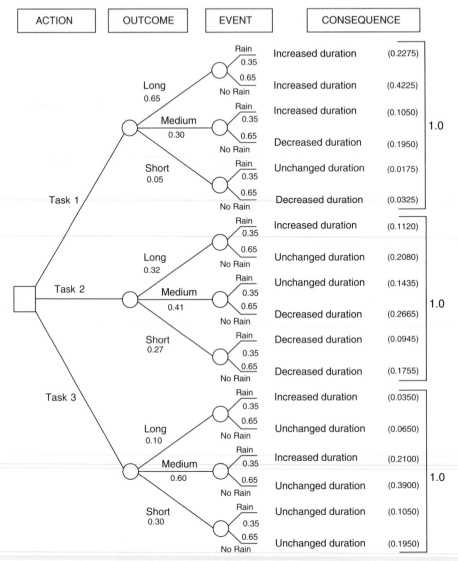

Figure 5.3. Decision tree with probability values.

duration event can be determined. For Figure 5.4, the conditional probability of each type of duration, given that it rains or it does not rain, will need to be calculated.

The respective probabilities of the three possible consequences are shown in Figure 5.3. The probability at the end of each path is computed by multiplying the individual probabilities along the path. For example, the probability of having an increased project completion time along the first path (Task 1, Long duration, and Rain) is calculated as:

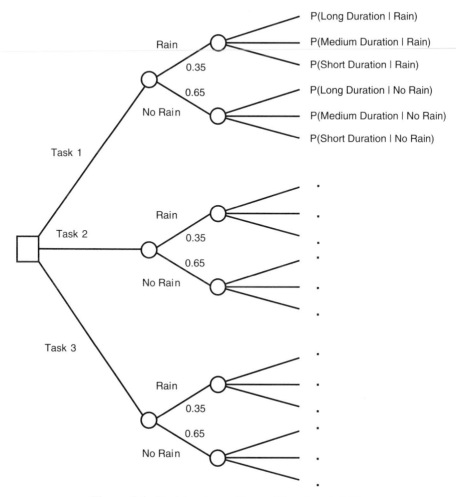

Figure 5.4. Decision tree with conditional probability.

$$(0.65)(0.35) = 0.2275$$

Similarly, the probability for the second path (Task 1, Long duration, and No-rain) is calculated as:

$$(0.65)(0.65) = 0.4225$$

The sum of the probabilities at the end of the paths associated with each action (choice) is equal to one, as expected. Table 5.2 presents a summary of the respective probabilities of the three consequences based on the selection of each task. For example, the probability of having an increased project duration when Task 1 is selected is calculated as:

TABLE 5.2. Probability Summary for Project Completion Time

	Selected Task		
Consequence	Task 1	Task 2	Task 3
Increased Duration	0.2275 + 0.4225 + 0.105 = 0.755	0.112	0.035 + 0.21 = 0.245
Decreased Duration	0.195 + 0.0325 = 0.2275	0.2665 + 0.0945 + 0.1755 = 0.5365	0.0
Unchanged Duration	0.0175	0.208 + 0.1435 = 0.3515	0.065 + 0.39 + 0.105 + 0.195 = 0.755
Column Sum	1.0	1.0	1.0

Probability $= 0.2275 + 0.4225 + 0.105 = 0.755$

Likewise, the probability of having an increased project duration when Task 3 is selected is calculated as:

Probability $= 0.035 + 0.21 = 0.245$

If the selection of tasks at the first node is probabilistic in nature, then the respective probabilities will be included in the calculation procedure. For example, Figure 5.5 shows a case where Task 1 is selected 25% of the time, Task 2 is selected 45% of the time, and Task 3 is selected 30% of the time. The resulting end probabilities for the three possible consequences have been revised accordingly. Note that all the probabilities at the end of all the paths add up to 1 in this case. Table 5.3 presents a summary of the probabilities of the three consequences for the case of weather-dependent task durations. The examples presented above can be extended to other decision problems in engineering and manufacturing that can be represented in terms of decision tables and trees.

5.4 DEMPSTER–SHAFER THEORY

Dempster–Shafer theory is another technique of handling uncertainty in expert systems. The theory attempts to distinguish between ignorance and uncertainty. Ignorance is definitely different from uncertainty and should be treated differently. Not knowing the specific value of a variable does not necessarily imply that the variable is subject to uncertainty. With classical probability theory, we are required to consider belief and disbelief as functional opposites. That is, if A, B, and C are the only three events in a sample space (S) and we know that $P(A) = 0.3$ and $P(B) = 0.6$, then classical probability theory would calculate 0.1 as the probability for the event C since $P(S) = 1.0$ and $P(A) + P(B) + P(C) = P(S)$. Unfortunately, this may not be accurate in representing human reasoning, since it is possible for a person to believe or disbelieve three different items with the same level of assurance (or probability). The "probability" of C may actually have nothing to do with uncertainty or probability. The fact may be that we are ignorant of the assurance level of C. Thus, knowing the probabilities of A and B does not necessarily imply that we can infer the probability of C.

In an attempt to overcome the shortcomings of classical probability in representing human reasoning, Dempster proposed a generalized theory of uncertainty versus ignorance [22]. The theory, which was later extended by Shafer [92], has come to be known as the Dempster–Shafer (D–S) theory of evidence. The theory is based on the notion that separate probability masses may be assigned to all subsets of a universe of discourse rather than just to

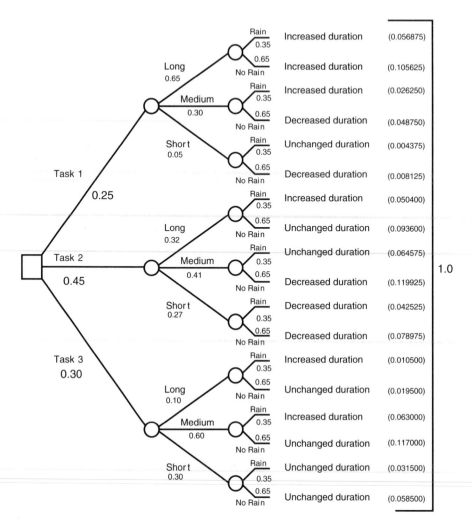

Figure 5.5. Probability distribution for task selection.

indivisible single members as required in traditional probability theory. As a result, D–S theory permits the following inequality:

$$P(A) + P(B) \leq 1.0$$

To illustrate the application of D–S theory, let us assume a universe of discourse representation **X** and a set corresponding to n propositions. We will assume that one and only one of the propositions is true. The propositions are assumed to be exhaustive and mutually exclusive. Define all the subsets of **X** as follows:

TABLE 5.3. Probability Summary for Weather-Dependent Task Durations

Consequence	Path Probabilities	Row Total
Increased Duration	0.056875 + 0.105625 + 0.02625 + 0.0504 + 0.0105 + 0.063	0.312650
Decreased Duration	0.04875 + 0.119925 + 0.042525 + 0.078975	0.290175
Unchanged Duration	0.004375 + 0.008125 + 0.0936 + 0.064575 + 0.0195 + 0.117 + 0.0315 + 0.0585	0.397175
	Column Total	1.0

$$\mathbf{H} = \{A\} \ni A \subseteq X$$

The set $\mathbf{H}$ contains 2^n elements, including the null set and $\mathbf{X}$ itself. Let the set function f, called the basic probability assignment, defined on $\mathbf{H}$ be a mapping to the interval $[0, 1]$. That is,

$$f:\mathbf{H} \rightarrow [0, 1] \ni \forall A \subseteq X, f(\phi) = 0 \quad \text{and} \quad \sum_{A \subseteq X} f(A) = 1$$

The function f defines a probability distribution on $\mathbf{H}$ as well as $\mathbf{X}$. This is in contrast to classical probability theory, where probability distribution is defined only on the individual elements of the sample space $\mathbf{X}$. The function f represents the measure of belief committed exactly to A. A belief function, *Bel*, corresponding to a specific f for the set A, is defined as the sum of beliefs committed to every subset of A by f. In other words, $Bel(A)$ is a measure of the total support or belief committed to the set A and establishes a minimum value for its likelihood. The belief function is defined in terms of all belief assigned to A as well as to all proper subsets of A. That is,

$$Bel(A) = \sum_{B \subseteq A} f(B)$$

For example, if $\mathbf{X}$ contains the mutually exclusive subsets P, Q, U, V, and W and we are interested in the particular subset $A = \{P, Q, W\}$, then we will have:

$$Bel(\{P, Q, W\}) = f(\{P, Q, W\}) + f(\{P, Q\}) + f(\{Q, W\}) + f(\{P, W\})$$
$$+ f(\{P\}) + f(\{Q\}) + f(\{W\})$$

Some important definitions related to D–S theory are presented below:

5.4.1   Support Function

The support function of the subset A is defined as $Bel(A)$.

5.4.2   Plausibility

The plausibility of A is defined as:

$$PL(A) = 1 - Bel(A^c)$$

5.4.3   Uncertainty of A

The uncertainty of a subset A of $\mathbf{X}$ is defined as

$$U(A) = PL(A) - Bel(A)$$

5.4.4   Belief Interval

The belief interval for a subset A (i.e., *the confidence* in A) is defined as the subinterval

$$[Bel(A), PL(A)] \text{ of the interval } [0, 1]$$

5.4.5   Focal Elements

The subsets A of **X** are called *focal elements* of the support function *Bel* when $f(A) > 0$.

We further define the following:

$$Bel(\phi) = 0$$

This indicates that no belief should be assigned to the null set.

$$Bel(X) = 1$$

This indicates that the "truth" is contained within **X.**

5.4.6   Doubt Function

The doubt of A is defined as:

$$D(A) = Bel(A^c)$$

This is a measure of the extent to which one believes in the complement of A, that is, the level of doubt associated with A.

Some of the most common operational properties of belief and plausibility functions are presented below:

$$PL(\phi) = 0$$
$$PL(X) = 1$$
$$PL(A) \geq Bel(A), \forall \, A$$
$$Bel(A) + Bel(A^c) \geq 1, \forall \, A$$
$$Bel(A) \leq Bel(B), \forall \, A \subseteq B$$
$$PL(A) \leq PL(B), \forall \, A \subseteq B$$

Some examples of belief intervals and their explanations are presented below:

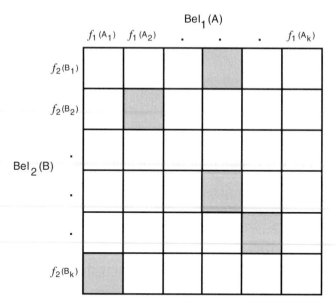

Figure 5.6. Combination of belief functions.

$[Bel(A), PL(A)] = [0, 0]$ Denotes belief that the proposition is false

$[Bel(A), PL(A)] = [1, 1]$ Denotes belief that the proposition is true

$[Bel(A), PL(A)] = [0, 1]$ Denotes no belief that supports the proposition

$[Bel(A), PL(A)] = [1, 0]$ Denotes belief that supports the proposition

$[Bel(A), PL(A)] = [0, 0.9]$ Denotes partial disbelief in the proposition

$[Bel(A), PL(A)] = [0.4, 1]$ Denotes partial belief in the proposition

$[Bel(A), PL(A)] = [0.4, 0.8]$ Partial belief and disbelief in the proposition

A consolidation function is used in D–S theory to combine evidence available from multiple knowledge sources to reduce uncertainty. The combining function is defined as $Bel_1 \odot Bel_1$. Given two probability assignment functions f_1 and f_2, corresponding to the belief functions Bel_1 and Bel_2, let $A_1, \ldots, A_k$ be the focal elements for Bel_1 and let $B_1, \ldots, B_p$ be the focal elements for Bel_2. Then $f_1(A_i)$ and $f_2(B_j)$ each assign probability masses on the unit interval $[0, 1]$. The probability masses are combined orthogonally as shown in Figure 5.6.

The unit square in the figure represents the total probability mass assigned by both f_1 and f_2 for all their common subsets. A particular cell within the square, shown shaded in the figure, has an assigned value depicted as $f_1(A_i)$ $f_2(B_j)$. Any subset C of **X** may have one or more of the cells committed to it. Consequently, the total probability mass committed to C is defined as:

$$f(C) = \sum_{i,j} f_1(A_i)f_2(B_j), \quad \forall\, i, j \ni A_i \cap B_j = C$$

The sum in the above equation must be normalized to account for the null intersections that have positive probabilities. These null intersections $A_i \cap B_j = \phi$ must be disregarded in the combination of the belief functions. Thus, the general form of Dempster's rule of combination is given by:

$$m_1 \odot m_2 = \frac{\displaystyle\sum_{A_i \cap B_j} f_1(A_i)f_2(B_j)}{\displaystyle\sum_{A_i \cap B_j \neq \phi} f_1(A_i)f_2(B_j)}, \quad \forall\, i, j$$

5.5   CERTAINTY FACTORS

Most heuristic methods use some sort of quasiprobabilistic technique to handle uncertainty. Two of these techniques are *certainty factors* and *fuzzy logic*. The most common representation of heuristic weights is the use of *certainty factors* (or confidence factors). In this approach, numbers greater than 0 are used for positive evidence and numbers less than 0 are used for negative evidence (e.g., -1 to 1, -100 to 100). These numbers are used merely as heuristics, and no criterion of theoretical correctness is associated with them.

The popular MYCIN expert system uses certainty factors in handling uncertainties. MYCIN was developed to diagnose and recommend therapies for bacterial infections in blood. It associates a certainty factor (CF) with each of its production rules. The certainty factor indicates the degree of certainty with which each fact or rule is believed to hold and is a number between -1 and 1. In MYCIN consultation, a frequently fatal cause of a disease would be assigned a higher certainty than another one that is more likely, but rarely fatal. To evaluate MYCIN's production rules, the following steps are followed [8]:

1. The CF of a conjunction of several facts is taken to be the minimum of the CF's of the individual facts. This is analogous to the view that "the weakest link in a chain determines the strength of the chain."
2. The CF of a disjunction of several facts is taken to be the maximum of the CF's of the individual facts.
3. The CF for the conclusion produced by a rule is the CF of its premise multiplied by the CF of the rule.
4. The CF for a fact produced as the conclusion of one or more rules is the maximum of the CF's produced by the rules yielding that conclusion.

Most of the procedures for manipulating certainty factors follow what are known as *ad hoc* techniques. These techniques typically have intuitive appeal but with no rigorous theoretical backing. They are used in place of the more formal methods as a practical approach to dealing with uncertainty. The formal theoretical approaches often pose difficulties in implementation. Several ad hoc procedures have been used with acceptable results in expert systems. The example below illustrates one ad hoc technique for combining certainty factors. Suppose we want to establish fact D, and the only rules available are the following:

Rule 1: **If** A and B and C, **then** CONCLUDE D (CF = 0.8)

Rule 2: **If** H and I and J, **then** CONCLUDE D (CF = 0.7)

If facts A, B, C, H, I, and J are known with the respective CF's of 0.7, 0.3, 0.5, 0.8, 0.7, and 0.9, then the following computations would produce a CF of 0.49 for D.

From Rule 1:

$$\text{min } \{CF(A), CF(B), CF(C)\} = \text{min } \{0.7, 0.3, 0.5\}$$
$$= 0.3$$
$$CF(D) \text{ based on Rule } 1 = 0.3(0.8)$$
$$= 0.24$$

From Rule 2:

$$\text{min } \{CF(H), CF(I), CF(J)\} = \text{min } \{0.8, 0.7, 0.9\}$$
$$= 0.7$$
$$CF(D) \text{ based on Rule } 2 = 0.7(0.7)$$
$$= 0.49$$

Rule combination:

$$CF(D) = \text{max } \{CF(D)_1, CF(D)_2\}$$
$$= \text{max } \{0.24, 0.49\}$$
$$= 0.49$$

This method of handling uncertainty has been used quite extensively in many expert systems. However, it does have some flaws. For example, it is not suitable for situations involving high levels of interaction between goals. Several variations of the mathematical approach to combining certainty factors have been proposed and used in many systems.

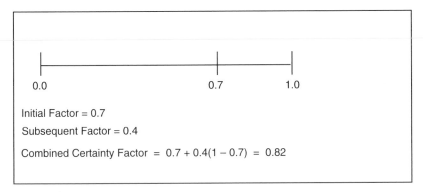

Figure 5.7. Combination of certainty factors.

Figure 5.7 shows an example of combining a series of certainty factors for one parameter. The method illustrated in the figure uses certainty levels between 0 and 1 (or between 0% and 100%). This method may be suitable for systems using nonmonotonic reasoning, in which case parameter instantiations may vary based on subsequent levels of certainty. The combined certainty factor is calculated by the formula below:

$$CCF = (\text{initial CF}) + (\text{subsequent CF})(1 - \text{initial CF})$$

The formula is applied repeatedly in case of more than two certainty factors in series. The flaw in this method, though, is that if the very first certainty factor encountered for the parameter is 1, then all subsequent certainty values for the parameter would not have any effect on the prior instantiation. The method then regresses to monotonic logic.

Figure 5.8 shows how the certainty level of a premise induces a certainty level on the conclusion of a rule. Figure 5.9 shows the effect of combining an uncertain premise and an uncertain rule. Researchers and developers of

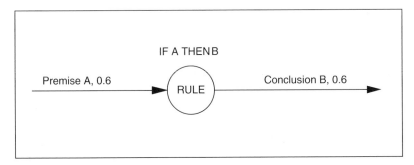

Figure 5.8. Premise certainty factor induced on conclusion.

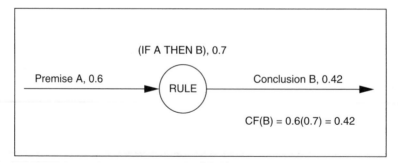

Figure 5.9. Conclusion certainty factor.

expert systems continue to investigate mechanisms that could more accurately reflect the reasoning process of humans when dealing with uncertain information. Despite their deficiencies, ad hoc methods for combining certainty factors have been used more extensively than the more formal approaches. This is because the formal approaches are difficult to implement, particularly if certain assumptions must be met for them to be valid. Sensitivity analysis conducted by Buchanan and Shortliffe shows that the ad hoc approaches, while not optimal, satisfy the basic needs in most problem scenarios [8]. However, much more research is needed before a standard approach can be developed.

5.6   FUZZY LOGIC

Another approach to managing uncertainty is the concept of fuzzy sets, first introduced by Zadeh in 1965 [107]. The objective of fuzzy sets was to generalize the notions of a set and propositions to accommodate the type of fuzziness or vagueness in many decision problems. Since their introduction, fuzzy sets have attracted much attention. The emergence of practical applications of artificial intelligence has intensified the interest and research in fuzzy sets. Recently, fuzzy logic has found a wide variety of applications ranging from industrial process control and consumer electronics to medical diagnosis and investment management [108]. In contrast to classical logic, fuzzy logic is aimed at providing a body of concepts and techniques for dealing with modes of reasoning that are approximate rather than exact. Extensions of fuzzy sets now include concepts such as *fuzzy arithmetic, possibility distributions, fuzzy statistics, fuzzy random variables,* and *fuzzy set functions.* Among the derived concepts is the concept of fuzzification, which permits the incorporation of fuzzy reasoning into any normal set.

In formal truth logic, it is required that every proposition be either true (1) or false (0). While "0" or "1" treatment fits conventional computer processing perfectly, it can impose serious restrictions on machine reasoning intended

TABLE 5.4. Degree of Membership for Fuzzy Set

Average Points	Grade of Membership (Possibility Value)
2.00	0.00
2.25	0.12
2.50	0.25
. . .	. . .
3.50	0.82
3.60	0.90
4.00	1.00

to duplicate the imprecise aspects of human reasoning. Fuzzy logic is a technique for dealing with sources of imprecision and uncertainty that are nonstatistical in nature.

Fuzzy logic uses a multivalued membership function to denote membership of an object in a class rather than the classical binary true or false values used to denote membership. In fuzzy logic, the source of imprecision is the absence of sharply defined criteria for class membership rather than the presence of random variables. Each class contains a continuum of grades of membership. Thus, a product will not be considered to be either good or bad. Depending on the product's actual quality level, it will have a certain degree of being good or being bad. A question of interest is to determine when a product makes the transition from being a bad product to being a good product.

In many practical real-world problems, the transition point is not clearly defined. It is fuzzy! The degree of membership in one category or another will depend on the membership functions that users or producers define to convey the varying levels of quality of the product. A fuzzy set is described by a membership function that maps a set of objects onto the interval of real numbers between 0 and 1. In standard set theory, an object is either a member of a set or not a member of the set. In fuzzy set, the transition from membership to nonmembership is gradual rather than abrupt because there are no distinguishable boundaries.

To illustrate the concept of fuzzy sets, we define set **A** to be the class of "high" academic grade point averages. Because the definition of "high" is subjective, we assign a range of average points and corresponding possibility values to the set **A** as shown in Table 5.4.

The term *high* can be modified with linguistic hedges such as "quite," "very," and "somewhat." Figure 5.10 shows a distribution of grade points based on linguistic hedges. Given a particular specification of grade point level, the distribution can be used to determine an appropriate classification of the grade point level. For example, a grade point of 3.6 may have a classification of "very high" with fuzzy confidence of 0.7, a classification of

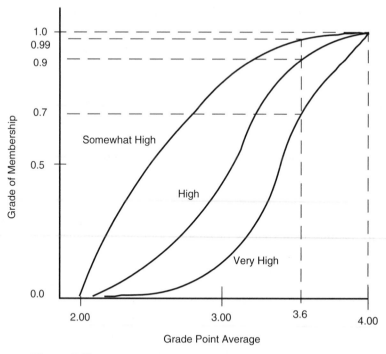

Figure 5.10. Example of fuzzy set distribution with modifiers.

"high" with confidence of 0.9, or a classification of "quite high" with a fuzzy confidence of 0.99.

With the use of fuzzy sets, the imprecise aspects of human reasoning can be captured in machine reasoning. Though the theory of fuzzy logic has been around for quite a while, it is just becoming popular for knowledge-based systems applications.

5.6.1   Definition of Fuzzy Set

Let A be a set of objects defined over a sample space **X.** For a finite set defined as

$$\mathbf{X} = x_1, x_2, \ldots, x_n$$

we can represent **A** as a fuzzy set with the linear combination below:

$$\mathbf{A} = u_i(x_1), u_2(x_2), \ldots, u_n(x_n)$$

where u_i is the grade of membership of x_i in **A.** In general, for a sample space of objects defined as $\mathbf{X} = \{x\}$, the fuzzy set $\mathbf{A}$ in $\mathbf{X}$ is a set of ordered pairs defined as:

$$\mathbf{A} = \{x, u_a(x)\}, \quad x \in \mathbf{A}$$

A value of $u_a(x) = 0$ indicates that x is not a member of $\mathbf{A}$, while $u_a(x) = 1$ implies that x is completely contained in $\mathbf{A}$. Values of $u_a(x)$ between 0 and 1 indicate that x is a partial member of $\mathbf{A}$. Characteristic membership functions for fuzzy sets are different from probabilities and should not be confused with probabilities. Probability is a measure of the degree of uncertainty based on the frequency or proportion of occurrence of an event. By contrast, a fuzzy characteristic function relates to the degree of vagueness which measures the ease with which an event can be attained.

With the definition of fuzzy set, we have a means of expressing a function $\mathbf{GOOD}(x)$ to convey the information about the quality level of the manufactured product mentioned earlier. The fuzzy set $\mathbf{A}$ can be defined as:

$$\mathbf{A} = \{good\}$$

That is, $\mathbf{A}$ is the set containing those items that can be classified as "good." Obviously, some items will be stronger members of the set than other items. There will be some items at the low end of good and some items at the high end of good.

For this example, we can define x as a quantitative measure of a particular quality characteristic of the product. An example is the measure of the surface finish or surface roughness of the product. If the measures of surface roughness range from, say, 1 to 50, then we might assign the membership values shown in Table 5.5. A surface roughness of 1 is the most desirable, while a surface roughness of 50 is the least desirable in this particular example. Note that Table 5.5 indicates that the highest degree of membership is 0.95 (less than 1). This is logical since it may be impossible to obtain a perfect surface finish without any roughness at all. A fuzzy set is said to be normal if its highest degree of membership is one.

Figure 5.11 presents what the author calls a fuzzy set grid. The grid shows the gradual change in the degree of membership from one level to another. Even though discrete lines are used to depict the grid in the figure, the changes in membership grade are, in fact, so gradual that the changes do not follow a discrete pattern. The figure represents a bivariate set whereby an item is classified as "good" based on two quality characteristics: surface roughness and porosity. Items with low values of surface roughness (i.e., high surface finish) and low values of porosity have the strongest degree of membership in the fuzzy set $\mathbf{A}$, which is defined as $\mathbf{A} = \{good\}$. That is, $\mathbf{A}$ is the set of good products. The degree of membership in $\mathbf{A}$ slowly decreases as surface roughness and porosity increase.

TABLE 5.5. Product Quality Classification Using Fuzzy Set

Surface Roughness (x)	Degree of Membership in the GOOD set $u_a(x)$
1.00	0.95
5.20	0.88
10.50	0.70
. . .	. . .
35.00	0.10
45.00	0.05
50.00	0.00

An item located in the upper left-hand corner of the grid has the highest degree of membership in **A.** That is, it is the best of the good items. An item located in the lower right-hand corner of the grid has the lowest degree of membership in **A.** That is, it is the worst of the good items. The bivariate fuzzy set grid may be extended to a trivariate (three-factors) case. In that case, the grid would be represented as a solid box with nonhomogeneous density. The density of the box would change gradually in different directions to indicate varying degrees of membership in the trivariate fuzzy set.

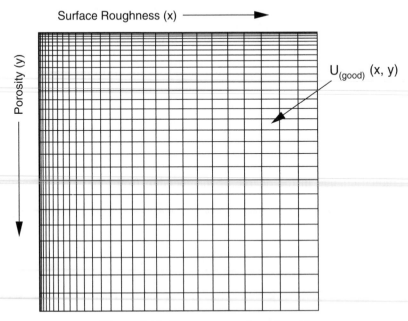

Figure 5.11. Fuzzy set membership grid.

Operations on fuzzy sets are similar, in some respects, to the operations on conventional sets. The standard operations and characteristics of fuzzy sets are presented below. Let **A, B, C, D,** . . . be fuzzy sets defined on the universal set **X.** Then we have the following:

Equality: $\mathbf{A} = \mathbf{B}$ if and only if $u_A(x) = u_B(x)$, $\forall\, x \in X$

Containment: $\mathbf{A} \subseteq \mathbf{B}$ if and only if $u_A(x) \leq u_B(x)$, $\forall\, x \in X$

Intersection: $u_{A \cap B}(x) = \min_x\{u_A(x),\, u_B(x)\}$

Union: $u_{a \cap B}(x) = \max_x\{u_A(x),\, u_B(x)\}$

Complement: $u_{A'}(x) = 1 - u_A(x)$

The intersection of two fuzzy sets **A** and **B** is the largest fuzzy subset that is a subset of both. Similarly, the union of two fuzzy sets **A** and **B** is the smallest fuzzy subset having both **A** and **B** as subsets. Note that in the properties defined above, the min and max operators are applied to the membership values $u_A(x)$ and $u_B(x)$ and not the fuzzy sets themselves. Thus, the min and max operators should not be confused with the largest and smallest fuzzy subsets explained above. Operational properties that hold for fuzzy sets are presented below:

Distributive property:
$\mathbf{A} \cup (\mathbf{B} \cap \mathbf{C}) = (\mathbf{A} \cup \mathbf{B}) \cap (\mathbf{A} \cup \mathbf{C})$

$\mathbf{A} \cap \mathbf{C}) = (\mathbf{A} \cap \mathbf{B}) \cup (\mathbf{A} \cap \mathbf{C})$

Associative property:
$(\mathbf{A} \cup \mathbf{B}) \cup \mathbf{C} = \mathbf{A} \cup (\mathbf{B} \cup \mathbf{C})$

$(\mathbf{A} \cap \mathbf{B}) \cap \mathbf{C} = \mathbf{A} \cap (\mathbf{B} \cap \mathbf{C})$

Commutative property:
$\mathbf{A} \cap \mathbf{B} = \mathbf{B} \cap \mathbf{A}$

$\mathbf{A} \cup \mathbf{B} = \mathbf{B} \cup \mathbf{A}$

Idempotence property:
$\mathbf{A} \cap \mathbf{A} = \mathbf{A}$

$\mathbf{A} \cup \mathbf{A} = \mathbf{A}$

DeMorgan's Law:
$$u_{(A \cap B)'}(x) = u_{A' \cup B'}(x)$$

$$u_{(A \cup B)'}(x) = u_{A' \cap B'}(x)$$

The following relationships should also be noted:

$$A \cap A' \neq \phi$$

$$A \cup A' \neq X$$

$$A \cap \phi = \phi$$

$$A \cup \phi = A$$

$$A \cap X = A$$

$$A \cup X = X$$

The first two expressions above hold because for $u_A(x) = a$, where $0 < a < 1$, we have:

$$u_{A \cup A'}(x) = \max\{a, 1 - w\}$$

$$\neq 1$$

$$u_{A \cap A'}(x) = \min\{a, 1 - a\}$$

$$\neq 0$$

Referring to our earlier example, Table 5.5 gives the membership values for the set GOOD based on the observed surface finish of the product. Such membership values may be obtained through empirical studies or subjective experimentations. In some cases, it is possible to define a function that generates the membership values directly. Such a function might be of the form presented below. Figure 5.12 presents a plot of the function $u_A(x)$.

$$u_A(x) = \begin{cases} \sqrt{x - 1}, & \text{if } 1 \leq x \leq 2 \\ 0, & \text{otherwise} \end{cases}$$

The functional form of the membership function may be based on characteristics relating to the utility of the item with respect to its various quality levels or some other criterion of interest.

Certain operations that are unique to fuzzy sets are presented below.

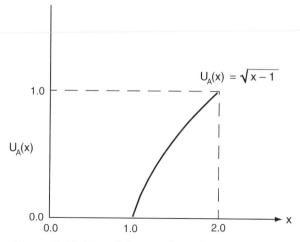

Figure 5.12. Plot of degree of membership function.

Dilation: The dilation of *A* is defined as:

$$DIL(A) = \sqrt{u_A(x)}, \quad \forall \, x \in X$$

Concentration: The concentration of *A* is defined as:

$$CON(A) = [u_A(x)]^2, \quad \forall \, x \in X$$

Normalization: The normalization of *A* is defined as:

$$NORM(A) = \frac{u_A(x)}{\max_x\{u_A(x)\}}, \quad \forall \, x \in X$$

For the function presented in Figure 5.12, DIL(*A*), CON(*A*), and NORM(*A*) are shown in Figure 5.13. Dilation tends to increase the degree of membership of all partial members. Concentration is the opposite of dilation. It tends to decrease the degree of membership of all partial members. Normalization performs the function of normalizing the membership function.

Fuzzy membership functions can be used to generate confidence factors in *modus ponens* reasoning as an alternative to probability and certainty factors. For example, referring to the product quality example presented earlier, we may have the following rule:

If surface-roughness is-less-than 10, **then** product-quality is good

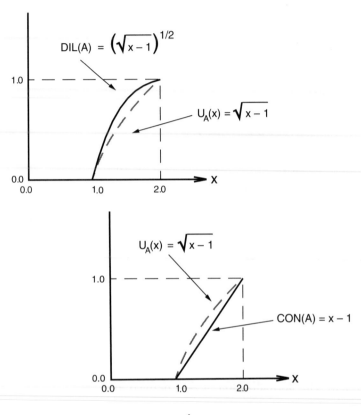

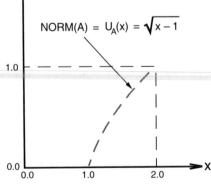

Figure 5.13. Unique operations on membership functions.

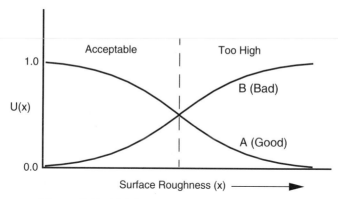

Figure 5.14. Unidirectional membership functions.

Now suppose we are given the following premise:

Surface-roughness is 10.5

Our conclusion would be that the product is good but with a certain level of fuzzy membership level (FML). That is,

Product-quality is *good* (FML = 0.70)

where FML = $U_A(10.5)$ = 0.70 as presented in Table 5.5.

Figure 5.14 presents two unidirectional membership functions. Curve A is defined for the set of good products based on the surface roughness. Note that as surface roughness increases, the degree of membership in the GOOD set decreases. Curve B is defined for the set of bad products. As the surface roughness increases, the degree of membership in the BAD set increases. Under fuzzy set reasoning, a product can be classified as being both *good* and *bad*. It is the degree of membership in the specific fuzzy set that makes a difference. Note that an item with a surface roughness located at the intersection of curves A and B has equivalent degrees of membership in either of the two sets GOOD and BAD. At this point, we would be indifferent to classifying the item as either good or bad.

Figure 5.15 presents two bidirectional membership functions. A bidirectional function is defined as one that starts at one end, reaches a peak or valley, and then changes direction. Curve B may be suitable for applications dealing with parameters, such as temperature, where both the low end and high end of the function are desirable. As shown in Figure 5.15, temperatures at the low end and at the high end have lower degrees of membership in the set of ACCEPTABLE-TEMPERATURE, while temperature values in the middle range have higher degrees of membership. This, for example, may be the

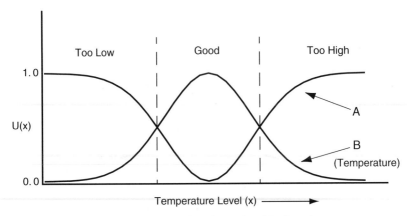

Figure 5.15. Bidirectional membership functions.

case when monitoring the ambient temperature of a work station. Temperatures that are too low are not desirable, as are temperatures that are too high. Curve *A* in Figure 5.15 presents a situation that is opposite to the temperature example. Curve *A* indicates that both the values at the low and high ends are more desirable than those in the middle range. Examples for this case are left as an exercise for the reader.

6

FUZZY SYSTEMS

While neural networks are an excellent tool for modeling unknown systems and solving optimization problems, fuzzy systems provide an alternative approach to representing problems and processing information. While there are many computational algorithms developed to process numerical data, fuzzy systems provide an alternative way to manipulate information, not just data.

In neural networks, data reduction is obtained by building a model out of the given data. When a model adequately predicts the output of an unknown input, the network is said to model the underlying dynamics of the system. Knowledge is therefore encapsulated in the derived model. In fuzzy logic, knowledge can be captured in terms of rules and linguistic variables. When the rule set adequately process the fuzzy inputs to produce an adequate response, the rule set and the associated definition of the linguistic variables are said to have modeled the underlying structure of the system.

6.1 CRISP LOGIC VERSUS FUZZY LOGIC

Much of the foundation of fuzzy logic stems from the roots of classical logic. Hence before the formal introduction of fuzzy sets is presented, a brief review of classical logic is given to highlight the parallel and the differences between the two approaches.

6.1.1 Crisp Sets

In classical set theory, a set is a collection of objects. For example, a class is a collection of students. A set of positive numbers is a collection of all numbers that are positive. There are many commonly used sets, as defined below.

$Z = \{\ldots -2, -1, 0, 1, 2, \ldots\}$, set of all integers

$N = \{1, 2, 3, \ldots\}$, set of all positive integers

$N_0 = \{0, 1, 2, 3, \ldots\}$, set of all nonnegative integers

$N_n = \{1, 2, 3, \ldots, n\}$

$N_{0,n} = \{0, 1, 2, 3, \ldots, n\}$

$\mathfrak{R}$: set of all real numbers

$\mathfrak{R}^+$: set of all positive real numbers

Participation in the set is all or nothing. In other words, either an object is part of the set or it is not. On one hand, if an object x is a member of the set A, then it is written $x \in A$. On the other hand, if the object x is not a member of the set A, then it is written as $x \notin A$.

There are primarily three ways to define a set. The first way is to enumerate all the members of the set. For example, $N = \{1, 2, 3, \ldots\}$ is the set of all positive integers and the set is defined by enumerating all the elements in N. When there are too many items to enumerate, it is sometimes easier to identify the elements by specifying the properties of the set. For the set of all positive integers, the set can also be defined as $N(x) = \{x \mid x > 0, x \text{ an integer}\}$. Here, the symbolism said the set N is composed of all numbers x where x is greater than 0 and x is an integer. This definition is equivalent to the first definition by enumeration. A third way to define a set is to specify the degree of participation in the set for each element of interest. This is called the characteristic function, $\chi_A\colon X \to \{0, 1\}$. For classical set theory, the characteristic function maps onto a set of two elements, 0 and 1. Thus, the characteristic function for $x = 0$ for set N is 0, i.e., $\chi_N(0) = 0$, while the characteristic function for $x = 1$ for set N is 1, i.e., $\chi_N(1) = 1$. In summary, the three ways to define a set are.

Enumeration: $\qquad\qquad\qquad A = \{a_1, a_2, a_3\}$

Rule property: $\qquad\qquad\qquad A = \{x \mid p(x)\}$

Characteristic function: $\qquad \chi_A(x) = 1$ if $x \in A$

$\qquad\qquad\qquad\qquad\qquad\quad \chi_A(x) = 0$ if $x \in A$

A set with no elements is called an empty set and is written as $\emptyset$. A universal set is one that contains all elements of interest. A finite set is a set with a finite number of elements. An infinite set is a set with an infinite number of elements. The set A defined above is a finite set, while the set N is an infinite set. The cardinality of a set, indicated by two vertical bars ($|.|$), is the number of elements in the set. The cardinality of N is infinite, $|N| = \infty$, while the cardinality of A is 3, i.e., $|A| = 3$. A power set is a new set consisting of all possible ways of combining various elements in the old set. The power set of A consists of $2^{|A|} + 1$ elements: $P(A) = \{\emptyset, a_1, a_2, a_3, a_1a_2, a_1a_3, a_2a_3, a_1a_3, a_1a_2a_3\}$.

Two sets are equal ($=$) if both sets have identical elements; otherwise they are not equal ($\neq$). If $A = \{a_1, a_2, a_3\}$ and $B = \{a_1, a_2, a_3\}$, then $A = B$. If $C = \{a_1, a_2\}$, then $A \neq C$. A subset ($\subseteq$) is a set that contains some or all of the elements that are in the original set. A proper subset ($\subset$) is a set that contains strictly some of the elements that are in the original set. Hence $A \subseteq B$ and $A \not\subset C$ but $C \subset A$.

There are three commonly used operators related to sets. The COMPLE-MENT ($\sim$) operation is an operator that produces a set containing elements that are not in the original set. A relative complement is the complement of a set with respect to another set. Hence the relative complement of A with respect to set B is $B - A = \{x \mid x \in B \text{ and } x \notin A\}$. The absolute complement is the complement of a set with respect to the universal set. Hence the absolute complement of A is $\sim A = \{x \mid x \notin A\}$. Assume that there is a class with five students. The universal set in this case is the set of all five students, $U = \{\text{Adam, Beverly, Charlie, David, Eponine}\}$. Let the set of males be $M = \{\text{Adam, Charlie, David}\}$ and the set of females be $F = \{\text{Beverly, Eponine}\}$. The absolute complement or complement for short of the set of males is the set of females, $\sim M = F$.

The UNION and INTERSECTION operation are called binary operators because they operate on two sets, producing a third set. The union ($\cup$) of two sets is a new set composed of elements that are in either or both of the original sets, i.e., $A \cup B(x) = \{x \mid x \in A \text{ or } x \in B\}$. For example, the union of the set of males and females is the entire universal set. Likewise, the intersection ($\cap$) of two sets is a new set composing of elements that must exist in both of the original sets, i.e., $A \cap B(x) = \{x \mid x \in A \text{ and } x \in B\}$.

There are many well-established properties related to three set operators. We will state without proof some of these properties. Let U be the universal set.

Identity:	$A \cup \emptyset = A$	$A \cap U = A$
Idempotency:	$A \cup U = U$	$A \cap \emptyset = \emptyset$
Involution:	$A\backslash\backslash = A$	
Commutativity:	$A \cup B = B \cup A$	$A \cap B = B \cap A$
Associativity:	$A \cup (B \cup C) = (A \cup B) \cup C$	$A \cap (B \cap C) = (A \cap B) \cap C$

Distributivity: $A \cap (B \cup C) = (A \cap B) \cup$ $A \cup (B \cap C) = (A \cup B) \cap$

$(A \cap C)$ $(A \cup C)$

Absorption $A \cup (A \cap B) = A$ $A \cap (A \cup B) = A$

Three special properties are noteworthy. In classical set theory, the law of contradiction says that the intersection between a set and its complement produces an empty set:

$$A \cap A\backslash = \emptyset$$

In other words, there is nothing in common between the set and its complement; that is an element cannot be in the set and in its complement at the same time. The law of excluded middle says that the union of a set and its complement yields the universal set:

$$A \cup A\backslash = U$$

This means that an element must either belongs to a particular set or to its complement. There is no middle ground. Finally, DeMorgan's law relates the union and the intersection operator.

$$(A \cap B)\backslash = A\backslash \cup B\backslash$$

$$(A \cup B)\backslash = A\backslash \cap B\backslash$$

DeMorgan's law says that the complement of the intersection of two sets is the union of the complement of each individual set. Likewise, the complement of the union of two sets is the intersection of the complement of each individual set.

Disjoint sets are sets that do not intersect with one another, i.e., $A \cap B = \emptyset$. Nested sets are sets that are successively subsets of the previous set. Any set that is defined by a single interval of real numbers is called a convex set. Any set that is defined by more than one interval is not a convex set. The upper bound of a finite set is the maximum element of the set. For an infinite set, the supremum is the largest value of the infinite set. Likewise, the lower bound of a finite set is the minimum element of the set. For an infinite set, the infimum is the smallest value of the infinite set.

6.1.2   Fuzzy Sets

In classical set theory, participation of an element in a set is either all or nothing. Hence the characteristic function maps an element into either 0 (not in the set) or 1 (in the set):

$$\chi_A: x \rightarrow \{0,1\}$$

In fuzzy set theory, the participation of an element in a set is a matter of degree from all to nothing. In other words,

$$\mu_A: x \rightarrow [0,1] \text{ or } A: x \rightarrow [0,1]$$

where μ_A is called the membership function for the set A. Here, μ_A and A are synonymous since each set A is uniquely defined by a membership function.

In real life, there are many occasions where the participation of an element in a set is not all or nothing. A tall person is generally accepted to be someone whose height is more than 6 ft. However, if we line up 10 persons whose height ranges from 5 ft to 7 ft, then the concept of tallness begins to be less precise. Those towards the 7-ft end are generally considered to be tall, while those towards the 5-ft end are generally considered to be not tall. But it is harder to determine if those in the middle are tall or not. To a somewhat tall person, those who are taller are tall. To someone who is 4 ft tall, even 5 ft, 6 in. is tall. This shows that the concept of tallness is really a matter of degree and not a matter of all or nothing.

In speaking about height, giving a numerical value may seem to convey a precise data value, but it speaks nothing of the connotation regarding the data point. But in everyday language one speaks of a person as kind of tall, very tall, not tall, etc. Consider the height of an adult: the range possibly goes from 1 ft to 7 ft. Description of height can include short, medium, or tall. These descriptions can be defined as in Figure 6.1.

A short person can be anyone less than 3 ft tall. This person has full participation in the set of short people and has no participation in the set of medium-height or tall persons. When a person's height is more than 3 ft, this person begins to have less participation in the set of short persons but at the same time has more participation in the set of medium height persons. In contrast, Figure 6.1 also shows the membership functions for crisp sets. A person with a height less than 4 ft belongs to the set of short persons. Then a person with a height of 4 ft, 1 in. belongs to the set of medium-height persons. Likewise, a person whose height is 5 ft, 11 in., belongs to the set of medium-height persons (similar to the one whose is 4 ft, 1 in.), but the person who is 1 in. taller, belongs to the set of tall persons. This clearly shows that the boundaries of crisp sets are sharp while the boundaries of fuzzy sets are not sharp at all. Thus the labels "crisp" and "fuzzy."

In crisp logic, for a single variable such as height, the linguistic variable, such as tall and short, describing the variable height is nonintersecting and disjoint. A person is either short or medium height. In fuzzy logic, an object may have participation in more than one set at the same time. Hence, a person who is 4 ft, 6 in. may participate in both the sets for short people and the set

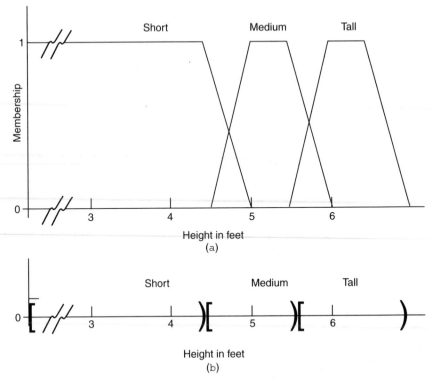

Figure 6.1. Membership functions: (a) fuzzy sets and (b) crisp intervals.

for medium-height people. As this person grows taller, the participation in the set of short people decreases and the participation in the set of medium-height people increases.

A fuzzy set corresponding to a particular linguistic variable is defined by the membership function. In general, a membership function can take on any shape. A number of shapes have been commonly used.

Triangular shape: $(1/a)(x - r) + 1, x \in [r - a, r]$

$(1/b)(r - x) + 1, x \in [r, r + b]$

0, otherwise

Trapezoidal shape: $(1/a)(x - r) + 1, x \in [r - a, r]$

$1, x \in [r, s]$

$(1/b)(s - x) + 1, x \in [s, s + b]$

0, otherwise

Exponential shape: $A(x) = 1/(1+(1/a)(x - r)^2), x \in [r - a, r + a]$

0, otherwise

Gaussian shape: $A(x) = \exp(-|a(x - r)|)$

Cosine shape: $A(x) = (1 + \cos((1/a)\pi(x - b))/2, x \in [r - a,$
$r + a]$

0, otherwise

Most membership functions have a number of common characteristics. The membership values are nonnegative and range between 0 and 1. If the membership function rises to 1, the fuzzy set is called a normal set; otherwise it is subnormal. In general, the membership decreases monotonically on the left side and on the right side. A membership function can be decomposed into a number of components. The base consists of the range that is nonzero membership values. The core consists of the range with nonzero membership values. The height is the maximum value of the membership function.

$$h(A) = \sup_x A(x)$$

When the height of the fuzzy set is one ($h(A) = 1$), the fuzzy set is normal, when the height ($h(A) < 1$) is less than 1.

A membership function can be defined in a number of ways. Just like crisp sets, a fuzzy set can be defined by its property or by the characteristic function. First, a membership function can be defined by its property either graphically through a plot as shown in Figures 6.1 and 6.2 or through actual descriptions through equations. Alternatively, a membership function can also be defined by the characteristic function for each element in the range. Hence the set of the medium-height people can also be defined as

$$M(x) = \{0/1, 0/2, 0.5/3, 1/4, 1/5, 0.5/6, 0/7\}$$

The slash symbol does not refer to an arithmetic division operation; rather, the "numerator" refers to the membership degree while the "denominator" refers to the corresponding element.

It is important to note that a crisp set is a special case of a fuzzy set. When the boundary of a fuzzy set is sharp, the membership values will only take on 0 and 1 values, thus yielding a crisp set. This means that all fuzzy operations must also satisfy the requirement of their crisp operation counterparts. In fact, the crisp characteristics can be considered as the boundary conditions for the fuzzy operations.

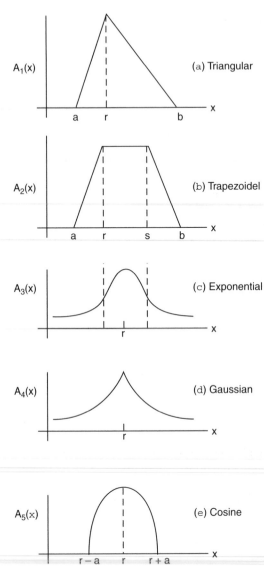

Figure 6.2. Membership function shapes.

6.1.3   Fuzzy Set Construction

The definition of a fuzzy set lies in the shape of the membership function. A number of methods have been proposed in the literature for determining the membership shape. The simplest method is a direct method with one expert. The membership function is drawn in a way closely resembling the underlying meaning of the fuzzy set for the linguistic variable. For example, given the crisp interval for the high and low values, the boundaries are made unsharp to approximate the meaning more closely.

Another direct method is based on inputs from multiple experts. Multiple experts are asked to determine the characteristics of the linguistic variables. These inputs are then averaged to form the shape of each membership function. This is a common way to obtain a membership function from a population of inputs.

Unweighted average: $A(x) = (1/n) \sum_{i=1}^{n} a_i(x)$

Weighted average: $A(x) = \sum_{i=1}^{n} c_i a_i(x)$ when $\sum_{i=1}^{n} c_i = 1$

An alternative to obtaining the membership function shape from experts is indirectly by pairwise comparison. Experts are presented with two samples from the linguistic variable and the experts are asked to compare the degree of participation for the two given samples. At the end, the results of the comparisons are compiled to form the shape of the membership functions.

6.1.4   Fuzzy Set Operations

Similar to crisp set theory, there are three basic operations for fuzzy sets: complement, union, and intersection. Recall that the characteristic function for elements in a crisp set is either 0 or 1, while that for a fuzzy set is between 0 and 1. Therefore the complement can be defined as

$$A\backslash(x) = 1 - A(x)$$

This is called the standard complement. Note that if $A(x)$ is crisp, then the complement of 0 is 1 and the complement of 1 is 0.

An extension of the crisp intersection operation is the standard intersection operation for fuzzy sets. The intersection of two sets gives what is common between the two sets. Hence the standard intersection is defined as

$$(A \cap B)(x) = \min[A(x), B(x)]$$

In some literature the intersection is called a meet operation. An extension of the crisp union operation is the standard union operation for fuzzy sets and is defined as

$$(A \cup B)(x) = \max[A(x), B(x)]$$

The definitions of standard complement, standard intersection and standard union lead to a set of properties that is similar to that for the crisp set case. However, it is important to note that for fuzzy sets, the operation does not obey the law of contradiction or the law of the excluded middle. This is

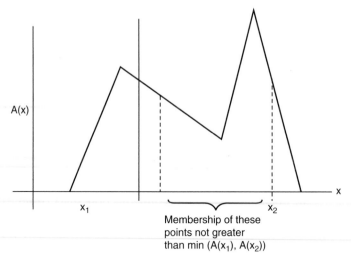

Figure 6.3. An example of a nonconvex set.

obvious because the characteristic function does not take on values of 0 and
1 only. Figure 6.3 shows an example of a nonconvex set.

A fuzzy set is convex if for any $\lambda \in [0,1]$, the following condition is
satisfied.

$$A(\lambda x_1 + (1 - \lambda)x_2) \geq \min[A(x_1),A(x_2)]$$

The rules for one fuzzy set being a subset of another fuzzy set can be
directly extended from the crisp case. In crisp set, the measure of the number
of elements in a set is called the set cardinality. For fuzzy sets, this concept
of set cardinality is extended to indicate the "size" of the fuzzy set. Scalar
cardinality is defined as

$$|A| = \Sigma_x A(x)$$

This is also called the sigma count.

There is another way to relate two fuzzy sets together, called a subsethood
measure. It measures the degree of one fuzzy set (B) being included in another
fuzzy set (A).

$$S(A,B) = |A \cap B|/|A|$$

Or alternatively,

$$S(A,B) = 1/|A| (|A| - \Sigma_x \max(0,A(x) - B(x)))$$

Note that the subsethood of $S(A,B)$ is different from $S(B,A)$. While the nu-

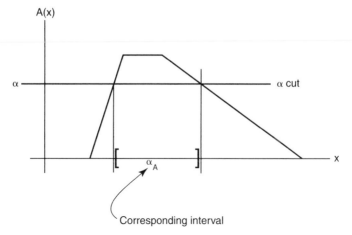

Figure 6.4. Example of α-cuts.

merator is the same, the intersection of the two sets, the denominator is not the same. For $S(A,B)$, the subsethood indicates the degree of B in A, while for $S(B,A)$ the subsethood indicates the degree of A in B.

Another concept for comparing two sets is the Hamming distance, which measures the number of disparate elements in the two sets. Since the participation is not whole, the distance between two fuzzy sets must be modified to measure the distance between each element of the two sets.

$$d(A,B) = \Sigma_x \,|A(x) - B(x)|$$

It is evident from this section that most of the crisp concepts can be directly extended for fuzzy sets. The operations are extended because the definition for the extension degenerates back to the original definition when a fuzzy set degenerates into a crisp set.

6.1.5 α-Cuts

The principle of an α-cut, as shown in Figure 6.4, is fundamental to the understanding of a fuzzy set. While a regularly shaped membership function can be described by lines or curves, the equations describing the shapes are rather complicated when the membership function becomes irregular. Another way to view a membership function is to see the function as a stack of pancakes or horizontal cuts. Each horizontal cut through the membership creates a range with the same membership value. As these horizontal cuts are placed one on top of another, the original membership is recovered. By definition, an α-cut is a crisp set:

$$^{\alpha}A = \{x|A(x) \geq \alpha\}$$

and correspondingly a strong α-cut:

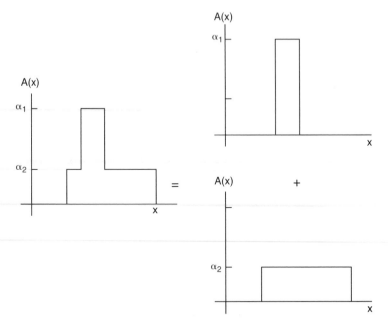

Figure 6.5. Fuzzy set decomposition.

$$^{\alpha+}A = \{x|A(x) > \alpha\}$$

Consider the example of height again. Assume that the range of the height variable is an integer and goes from 1 ft to 7 ft. Assume that the set of medium-height people can be defined as shown in Figure 6.5. The membership function for a person who is medium height can be defined by enumeration as $M(x) = \{0/1, 0/2, 0.5/3, 0.5/4, 1.0/5, 0.5/6, 0/7\}$. This means that the α-cut for the various α values are ranges given below.

$$\alpha = 0: \quad [3,6]$$
$$\alpha = 1: \quad [5,5]$$

Note that the ranges form nested sets. Each range represents a pancake. When the pancakes are placed one on top of another, the original membership function is recovered. Since each cut gives a crisp set, the entire membership function can immediately be recovered by the union of the properly scaled crisp sets. This is the decomposition theorem.

$$A = \cup_\alpha \alpha \, (^\alpha A)$$

$$A = \cup_\alpha \alpha \, (^{\alpha+}A)$$

α-cuts have a number of interesting properties. The definitions of core and support can be succinctly defined by α-cuts.

$$\text{Core}(A) = {}^1A$$

$$\text{Support}(A) = {}^{0+}A$$

If $\alpha_1 < \alpha_1$, then the relationship between different α-cuts is shown below.

$${}^{\alpha 1}A \supseteq {}^{\alpha 2}A$$

$${}^{\alpha 1+}A \supseteq {}^{\alpha 2+}A$$

Other properties are also given below.

$${}^{\alpha}(A \cap B) = {}^{\alpha}A \cap {}^{\alpha}B$$

$${}^{\alpha}(A \cup B) = {}^{\alpha}A \cup {}^{\alpha}B$$

$${}^{\alpha}(A\backslash) = {}^{(1-\alpha)+}(A\backslash)$$

The concept of the α-cut is used to generalize operations or properties on crisp sets into operations or properties of fuzzy sets. Any operation or property that is thus generalized from classical set theory into fuzzy set theory is called cutworthy if the properties of the α-cuts are preserved. Likewise, any operation or property that preserves the strong α-cut property is called strong cutworthy.

6.1.6 Extension Principle

Given a crisp variable, a crisp function maps the values of the original variable to another crisp variable. The function f represents a curve drawn on the plot with x as the range and y as the domain (see Figure 6.6). It is also possible to define the inverse function f^{-1} relating y to x.

$$f: x \rightarrow y$$

$$f^{-1}: y \rightarrow x$$

It is of interest to find out what happens to a fuzzy set defined on the original crisp variable and how this fuzzy set shape would be changed on the data space of the new variable.

$$f: A(x) \rightarrow B(y)$$

The extension principle states that the new fuzzy set $B(y)$ is related to the original fuzzy set $A(x)$ as follows:

$$B(y) = \sup_{x|y=f(x)} A(x)$$

Likewise, the inverse of the function on fuzzy sets can also be defined:

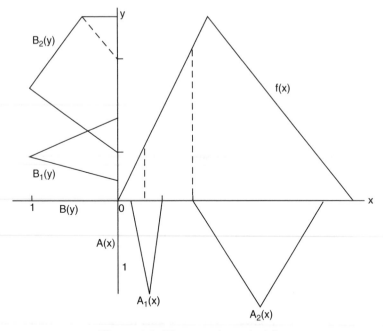

Figure 6.6. The extension principle.

$$A(x) = B(f(x))$$

Note that the inverse does not necessarily recover the original function. This is because the mapping function f is not always uniquely invertible. The inverse may not be a function at all. An example of the extension principle is shown below.

Note that the membership function shape is not necessarily preserved after the mapping. While the functional mapping may not have preserved the shape of the membership function, the properties of the α-cut are nevertheless preserved. This means that given an α-cut through the original fuzzy set, the mapping of this α-cut will yield the same α-cut on the transformed fuzzy set.

6.2 FUZZY OPERATIONS

In the previous section, the operation for complement, union, and intersection was defined. In reality, there are infinite ways to define each of these operations. In this section we will consider the definition and behavior of fuzzy operators. The varieties allow a more appropriate capture of the underlying connotation indicated by the operator.

6.2.1 Fuzzy Complement

The basic definition of the complement of a fuzzy set is the opposite of what is defined in the original set. If the fuzzy set points to what is certain, then the complement points to what is not certain. If the original fuzzy set points to the degree of the participation in the set of interest, the complement points to the degree of nonparticipation in the set of interest.

$$c: [0,1] \rightarrow [0,1]$$

A number of properties define an operation as a complement operation. The defining conditions are the boundary conditions obtained from crisp logic. This is always the case because the fuzzy definition must necessarily degenerate to the crisp definition.

Boundary conditions: $c(0) = 1$

Monotonicity: $c(1) = 0$

$$c(a) \geq c(b) \text{ if } a \leq b$$

Other optional properties are nice to have but not always necessary.

Continuity: c is a continuous function

Involutability: $c(c(A)) = A$

Some examples of fuzzy complements are shown below.

Threshold complement: $c(a) = 1$ for $a \leq t$

$c(a) = 0$ for $a > t$

Standard complement: $c(a) = 1 - a$

Cosine complement: $c(a) = 0.5(1 + \cos \pi a)$

Sugeno class complement: $c_\lambda(a) = (1 - a)/(1 + \lambda a)$

Yeager class complement: $c_w(a) = (1 - a^w)^{1/w}$

In general, a fuzzy complement can be defined by any strictly increasing or strictly decreasing functions. If g is a strictly increasing function, then a complement can be derived from the following formulation:

$$c(a) = g^{-1}(g(1) - g(a))$$

The function g is called an increasing function generator. Likewise, if f is a strictly decreasing function, then the complement function can also be derived.

$$c(a) = f^{-1}(f(0) - f(a))$$

In this case, the function f is called a decreasing function generator.

There is an intrinsic relationship between the increasing generators and the decreasing generators. Given an increasing generator g, it is possible to obtain a corresponding decreasing generator f and its pseudoinverse f^{-1}.

$$f(a) = g(1) - g(a)$$
$$f^{-1}(a) = g^{-1}(g(1) - a)$$

Likewise, given a decreasing generator f, it is possible to obtain a corresponding increasing generator g and its pseudoinverse g^{-1}.

$$g(a) = f(0) - f(a)$$
$$g^{-1}(a) = f^{-1}(f(0) - a)$$

An interesting property related to the fuzzy complement operation is that every fuzzy complement has an equilibrium point where the fuzzy complement is itself.

The wide range of definitions for fuzzy complement allows for different interpretations or usage of the complement operation. As an example, suppose the evidence points to the fact that the accused is a murderer with a certainty of 0.8, i.e., the fuzzy value that the accused is a murderer is 0.8. The audience's view that the accused is not a murderer is probably 0.2. However, from the prosecutor's viewpoint the certainty that the accused is not a murderer is only 0.1, while in the defense attorney's view the certainty that accused is not a murderer has a fuzzy value of 0.9. All three viewpoints relate to the accused being NOT a murderer, hence the complement is based on the fact that the accused IS a murderer with certainty of 0.8.

6.2.2   Fuzzy Intersection

The intersection of two fuzzy sets results in a third fuzzy set that contains the elements common to the two original sets.

$$i: [0,1] \times [0,1] \rightarrow [0,1]$$

The defining conditions for a fuzzy intersection, also called the t-norm or triangular norm, are the boundary conditions obtained from crisp logic. In addition, the properties of monotonicity, commutativity, and associativity are also needed.

$$\text{Boundary conditions:} \quad i(a,1) = 1$$
$$\text{Monotonicity:} \quad b \leq c \rightarrow i(a,b) \leq i(a,c)$$
$$\text{Commutativity:} \quad i(a,b) = i(b,a)$$
$$\text{Associativity:} \quad i(a,i(b,c)) = i(i(a,b),c)$$

Other optional properties that are nice to have but are not always necessary are listed below.

$$\text{Continuity:} \quad i \text{ is a continuous function}$$
$$\text{Idempotency:} \quad i(a,a) = a$$
$$\text{Subidempotency:} \quad i(a,a) < a$$
$$\text{Strict monotonicity:} \quad b < c \rightarrow i(a,b) < i(a,c)$$

This definition of a fuzzy intersection operation must degenerate to the usual understanding of set intersection for crisp logic. So, if $a,b \in \{0,1\}$, then the boundary condition $i(a,1) = a$ implies

$$i(0,1) = 0$$
$$i(1,1) = 1$$

Now the commutativity property $i(a,b) = i(b,a)$ provides another combination:

$$i(1,0) = i(0,1) = 0$$

Finally, the monotonicity property: $b \leq c \rightarrow i(a,b) \leq i(a,c)$

$$0 \leq 1 \rightarrow i(0,0) \leq i(0,1) = 0$$

Some examples of fuzzy intersections are given below.

Standard intersection:	$i(a,b) = \min(a,b)$
Drastic intersection:	$i(a,b) = a$ if $b = 1$
	$i(a,b) = b$ if $a = 1$
	0 otherwise
Algebraic product intersection:	$i(a,b) = ab$
Bounded difference intersection:	$i(a,b) = \max(0, a + b - 1)$
Yeager class intersection:	$i(a,b) = 1 - \min\{1,[(1 - a)^w +$
Schweizer and Sklar:	$(1 - b)^w]^{1/w}\}$
	$i(a,b) = [\max(0, a^p + b^p - 1)]^{1/p}$

There are many other examples of fuzzy intersections (see Klir and Yuan).

It can be shown that there is an ordering to many of these fuzzy intersections:

$$i_{di}(a,b) \leq i_{bd}(a,b) \leq i_{ap}(a,b) \leq i_{si}(a,b)$$

In general, the drastic intersection provides the lower bound for all intersections and the standard intersection provides the upper bound for all intersections.

In general, a fuzzy intersection can be obtained from any strictly decreasing functions. If f is a strictly decreasing function, then the intersection function can also be derived.

$$i(a,b) = f^{-1}(f(a) + f(b))$$

Another method of obtaining a new fuzzy intersection operation is in terms of an existing fuzzy intersection operation. If g is a strictly increasing and continuous function between 0 and 1, then

$$i(a,b) = g^{-1}(i(g(a),g(b)))$$

The wide range of definitions for the fuzzy intersection operation allows for different interpretations or usage of the intersection operation. Continuing from the example of the accused, suppose the accused has been seen in the crime scene with a fuzzy value of 0.6 and the accused also has a weapon with a fuzzy value of 0.7. The question is to ascertain the truth value of the accused using the weapon at the crime scene. The audience's view that the accused is a murderer because he was seen in the crime scene AND using his weapon at the crime scene would most likely be a fuzzy value around 0.42 (algebraic product). The prosecutor's view that the accused is a murderer would likely to be a fuzzy value of 0.6 (standard intersection), while the jury's view that the accused is a murderer might have a fuzzy value of 0.3 (bounded difference). On the other hand, the defense attorney's view that the accused is a murderer has a fuzzy value of 0.0 (drastic intersection).

6.2.3 Fuzzy Union

The union of two fuzzy sets results in a third fuzzy set that contains the elements that may be included in either of the two original sets.

$$u: [0,1] \times [0,1] \rightarrow [0,1]$$

As usual, the defining conditions for a fuzzy union, also called the *t*-conorm, are the boundary conditions obtained from crisp logic. In addition, the properties of monotonicity, commutativity, and associativity are also needed.

Boundary conditions:	$u(a,0) = a$
Monotonicity:	$b \leq c \rightarrow u(a,b) \leq u(a,c)$
Commutativity:	$u(a,b) = u(b,a)$
Associativity:	$u(a,u(b,c)) = u(u(a,b),c)$

Other optional properties that are nice to have but are not always necessary are listed below.

Continuity:	u is a continuous function
Idempotency:	$u(a,a) = a$
Superidempotency:	$u(a,a) > a$
Strict monotonicity:	$b < c \rightarrow u(a,b) < u(a,c)$

This definition of a fuzzy union operation must degenerate to the usual understanding of set union for crisp logic. So, if $a,b \in \{0,1\}$, then the boundary condition $u(a,0) = a$ implies

$$u(0,0) = 0$$
$$u(1,0) = 1$$

Now the commutativity property $u(a,b) = u(b,a)$ provides another combination:

$$u(0,1) = u(1,0) = 1$$

Finally, the monotonicity property:

$$b \leq c \rightarrow u(a,b) \leq u(a,c)$$
$$0 \leq 1 \rightarrow u(0,1) \leq u(1,1) = 1$$

Some examples of fuzzy unions are given below.

Standard union: $u(a,b) = \max(a,b)$

Drastic union: $u(a,b) = a$ if $b = 0$

                            $u(a,b) = b$ if $a = 0$

                            $u(a,b) = 1$ otherwise

Algebraic sum union: $u(a,b) = a + b - ab$

Bounded sum union: $u(a,b) = \min(1,a + b)$

Sugeno class union: $u(a,b) =$

Yeager class union: $u_w(a,b) = \min(1,(a^w + b^w)^{1/w})$

Schweizer and Sklar: $u_p(a,b) = 1 - [\max(0,(1 - a)^p$

                            $+ (1 - b)^p - 1)]^{1/p}$

Other examples of fuzzy unions are presented in Klir and Bo.

It can be shown that there is an ordering to many of these fuzzy intersections:

$$U_{su}(a,b) \leq u_{as}(a,b) \leq u_{bs}(a,b) \leq u_{du}(a,b)$$

In general, the drastic union provides the upper bound for all unions and the standard union provides the lower bound for all unions.

In general, a fuzzy union can be obtained from any strictly increasing functions. If g is a strictly increasing function, then the union function can also be derived.

$$u(a,b) = g^{-1}(g(a) + g(b))$$

Another method of obtaining a new fuzzy intersection operation is in terms of an existing fuzzy intersection operation. If g is a strictly increasing and continuous function between 0 and 1, then

$$u(a,b) = g^{-1}(u(g(a),g(b)))$$

The wide range of definitions for the fuzzy union operation allows for different interpretations or usage of the union operation. Continuing from the example of the accused, suppose the accused has been seen at the crime scene with a fuzzy value of 0.6 and the murder weapon also belongs to the accused with a fuzzy value of 0.7. The question is to ascertain the truth value of the accused being the murderer. The audience's view that the accused is involved in the murder based on the two evidences has a fuzzy value of 0.88 (algebraic sum). The prosecutor's view that the accused is involved in the murder is likely to be a fuzzy value of 1.0 (drastic union). However, the jury's view that the accused is a murderer has a fuzzy value of 1.0 (bounded sum), while the defense attorney's view that the accused is involved in the murder has a fuzzy value of 0.7 (standard union).

6.2.4 Duality

A duality property exists in crisp logic regarding the intersection and the union operation based on the standard definition of a complement operation. The duality property can be expressed in terms of DeMorgan's law.

$$(A \cap B)\backslash = A\backslash \cup B\backslash$$

$$(A \cup B)\backslash = A\backslash \cap B\backslash$$

The same properties also exist for fuzzy operators. DeMorgan's law can be extended using fuzzy operators.

$$i(a,b) = c(u(c(a),c(b))) \text{ if } c \text{ is involutive}$$

$$u(a,b) = c(i(c(a),c(b))) \text{ if } c \text{ is involutive}$$

However, not all definitions of intersections, union, and complement operations satisfy the above two conditions. The three operations forming a triple $<i, u, c>$ that does satisfy the two conditions above are called a dual triple. Some common triples are:

$$<i_{si}, u_{su}, c_s>$$

$$<i_{ap}, u_{as}, c_s>$$

$$<i_{bd}, u_{bs}, c_s>$$

$$<i_{di}, u_{du}, c_s>$$

Other examples of intersection, union, and complement operations are also possible.

If the intersection, union, and complement operations do form a dual triple, then it can be shown that the associated operations do satisfy the law of the excluded middle:

$$u(a,c(a)) = 1,$$

and the law of contradiction:

$$i(a,c(a)) = 0$$

6.2.5 Fuzzy Implication

Another operator often-used in expressing rules in fuzzy systems is the implication operator. A rule often takes the following form:

$$\text{Implication}(A,B) = \textbf{if } A, \textbf{ then } B$$

The if–then rule is sometimes also written as $A \rightarrow B$, thus giving rise to the implication operator. In crisp logic, implication is defined by the following truth table:

A	B	$A \rightarrow B$
0	0	1
0	1	1
1	0	0
1	1	1

If A is not true, there is nothing that can be inferred about B. Hence, regardless of the value of B the implication is true. If A is true, then B must be true for the implication to be true.

In crisp logic, the implication operator can be implemented with the elementary operators: AND, OR, and NOT. Since the realization of an arbitrary function in combinational logic is not unique, there are a number of ways to realize the implication operator. Three of these realizations are listed below.

$$\text{Implication}_1(a,b) = \sim\! a \cup b$$

$$\text{Implication}_2(a,b) = \max\{x \in \{0,1\} \mid a \cap x \le b)$$

$$\text{Implication}_3(a,b) = \sim\! a \cup (a \cap b)$$

$$\text{Implication}_4(a,b) = (\sim\! a \cap \sim\! b) \cup b$$

The implication of two fuzzy sets results in a third fuzzy set that conveys the meaning of the first set implying for the second set.

$$u: [0,1] \times [0,1] \rightarrow [0,1]$$

As usual, the defining conditions for a fuzzy implication are the boundary conditions obtained from crisp logic. In addition, the properties of monotonicity are also needed.

Boundary conditions: Implication(a,b) = 1 iff (if and only if) $a \leq b$

Monotonicity: $b \leq c \rightarrow$ Implication(a,b) $\leq$ implication(a,c)

                         $b \leq c \rightarrow$ Implication(b,a) $\geq$ implication(c,a)

Other desirable properties of implications are listed below.

Continuity: i and u are continuous functions

Identity: Implication(a,a) = 1

Dominance of falsity: Implication($0,1$) = 1

Dominance of truth: Implication($1,b$) = b

Contraposition: Implication(a,b) = implication($c(a),c(b)$)

Exchange: Implication(a, implication(b,c))

                         = implication(b, implication(a,c))

Using the above four definitions as a start, a fuzzy implication can be derived using the fuzzy definitions as a counterpart for the crisp operators.

$$\text{Implication}_1(a,b) = u(c(a), b)$$

$$\text{Implication}_2(a,b) = \max\{x([0,1] \mid i(a, x) \leq (b)$$

$$\text{Implication}_3(a,b) = u(c(a), i((a,b))$$

$$\text{Implication}_4(a,b) = u(i(c(a) \ c(b)),b)$$

While all of the four definitions above degenerate into the crisp boundary conditions, their fuzzy counterparts do not always yield the same values. This difference gives the user a variety of operators to choose from.

From the first definition of implication, there are many implications that can be derived using various forms of fuzzy union and fuzzy complement: Implication$_1(a,b)$ = $u(c(a), b)$. These are generally called the S-implications.

Kleene–Dienes implication: Implication(a,b) = $\max(1 - a,b)$

Lukasiewicz implication: Implication(a,b) = $\min(1,1 - a + b)$

From the second definition of implication, there are many implications that can be derived using various forms of fuzzy union and fuzzy complement: Implication$_2(a,b)$ = max$\{x\in[0,1] \mid i(a, x) \leq (b)$. These are generally called the R-implications.

Godel implication: Implication(a,b) = sup$\{x \mid \min(a,x) \leq (b)$

Lukasiewicz implication: Implication(a,b) = min$(1,1 - a + b)$

LR implication: Implication$_{LR}(a,b)$ = b if $a = 1$

                                            Implication$_{LR}$ (a,b) = 1 otherwise

From the third definition of implication, there are many implications that can be derived using various forms of fuzzy union and fuzzy complement: implication$_3(a,b)$ = $u(c(a), i((a,b)))$. These are generally called the QL-implications.

Zadeh implication: Implication$_{st}(a,b)$ = max$[1 - a,\min(a,b)]$

Kleene–Dienes implication: Implication(a,b) = max$(1 - a,b)$

It can be shown that there is an ordering to many of these fuzzy implications:

$$\text{Implication}_{LR}(a,b) \leq \text{implication}_{st}(a,b)$$

In general, implication$_{LR}$ provides the lower bound for all implications and the standard implication provides the upper bound for all implications.

In general, a fuzzy implication can be obtained from any strictly increasing continuous functions. If g is a strictly increasing function, then the implication function can also be derived.

$$\text{Implication}(a,b) = g^{-1}(g(1) - g(a) + g(b))$$

6.2.6 Fuzzy Aggregation

The fuzzy intersection and fuzzy union operations can be repeatedly applied when there are more than two variables. However, the lower and upper bounds for the intersection and union operations still hold. Note that the intersection operation produces a value that is between 0 and the minimum value of the input values. Likewise, the union operation produces a value that is between the maximum value of the input values and 1. In other words, the intersection covers the lower range of the possible values while the union covers the upper range of the possible values. An operation that produces a value in the middle range between these two extremes is called an aggregation operation. An example of an aggregation operation is the averaging operation.

An aggregation operation is an operation that produces a value in the middle range between the intersection and union operations.

$$h: [0,1]^n \to [0,1]$$

The boundary condition is very general for an aggregation operation.

$$h(0, \ldots, 0) = 0$$

$$h(1, \ldots, 1) = 1$$

The monotonicity property is

$$a_i \le b_i \to h(a_1, \ldots, a_n) \le h(b_1, \ldots, b_n)$$

Some examples of an aggregation operation are listed below.

Generalized means: $h_\alpha(a_1, \ldots, a_n) = [(a_1^\alpha + \ldots + a_n^\alpha)/n]^{(1/\alpha)}$

Harmonic mean: $h_{-1}(a_1, \ldots, a_n) = n/(1/a_1 + \ldots$

$+ 1/a_n), \alpha = -1$

Arithmetic mean: $h_1(a_1, \ldots, a_n) = (a_1 + \ldots + a_n)/n, \alpha = 1$

Ordered weighted average

(OWA): $h_w(a_1, \ldots, a_n) = w_1 a_1 + \ldots + w_n a_n$

6.3 FUZZY NUMBERS

An application of fuzzy concepts is fuzzy numbers. Quite often a measurement is not known precisely, but rather with some amount of uncertainty. Hence if one speaks of one's height as 5 ft, then it can be taken as 60 in. in a crisp sense. However, if one speaks of one's height as around 5 ft, then it can be taken as some number around 60 in. or in the vicinity of 60 in. This is a fuzzy concept and can be considered as a fuzzy 60 in.

6.3.1 Fuzzy Number Representation

A fuzzy number is a fuzzy set that conveys the meaning of a fuzzy value around the identified crisp number. In other words, a fuzzy 3 is a fuzzy set *around* the number 3. In general, a fuzzy number takes on a trapezoidal membership format, though this is not a requirement. The membership function for a fuzzy number is composed of a left side, a central interval (the core), and the right side. For most applications, a fuzzy number usually has a finite support and symmetric left and right side as shown in Figure 6.7.

Note that for all the representations above, Figure 6.7(a) shows a crisp 5. Figure 6.7(b) shows a crisp interval. Note that a crisp number has no width and has sharp boundaries on both sides. Likewise, a crisp set or interval has width but also has sharp boundaries. A fuzzy number that is triangular or trapezoidal in shape has width and unsharp boundaries. Figures 6.7(c)–(e) all convey the idea of a fuzzy 5. This is evident since all the membership functions are at maximum and are at 1 when the number is 5. The exact shape of the membership function expresses the idea to be conveyed. If Figure 6.7(c) is a fuzzy 5 representing the concept of 5, then Figure 6.7(d) also represents a fuzzy 5 with the meaning of very much 5 and Figure 6.7(e) also represents a fuzzy 5 with the meaning of around 5.

6.3.2   Fuzzy Number Operation

Like crisp numbers, fuzzy numbers can be added, subtracted, multiplied, and divided. Other operations are also possible. One approach to deal with fuzzy numbers comes from the concept of α-cuts. From the principle of decomposition, any membership function can be decomposed and recovered into a set of crisp intervals. Fuzzy arithmetic can then be performed by first decomposing the membership functions into sets of crisp intervals using α-cuts, performing the arithmetic on the intervals, and then recovering the membership function of the result by putting the intervals back together.

Arithmetic of fuzzy numbers using α-cuts depends on interval arithmetic. A summary of the interval arithmetic is well established and is summarized below.

Addition:	$[a,b] + [d,e] = [a + d, b + e]$
Subtraction:	$[a,b] - [d,e] = [a - e, b - d]$
Multiplication:	$[a,b]*[d,e] = [\min(ad,ae,bd,be),$
	$\max(ad,ae,bd,be)]$
Division:	$[a,b]/[d,e] = [\min(a/d,a/e,b/d,b/e),$
	$\max(a/d,a/e,b/d,b/e)]$

Using the interval logic formulas, arithmetic of fuzzy numbers can be accomplished using the idea of α-cuts. Let OP be a general operator for addition, subtraction, multiplication, or division, then:

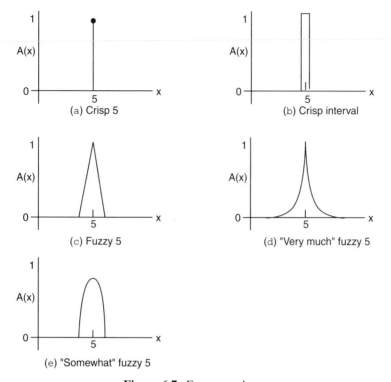

Figure 6.7. Fuzzy numbers.

$$OP \in \{+, -, *, /\}$$

$$^\alpha(A \text{ OP } B) = {}^\alpha A \text{ OP } {}^\alpha B$$

$$A \text{ OP } B = \cup_\alpha \alpha \, {}^\alpha(A \text{ OP } B)$$

As an example, let $A(x)$ and $B(x)$ be defined below.

$$A(x) = (x - 3) + 1, \ x \in [2,3]$$

$$A(x) = (3 - x) + 1, \ x \in [3,4]$$

$$B(x) = (x - 5) + 1, \ x \in [4,5]$$

$$B(x) = (5 - x) + 1, \ x \in [5,6]$$

The α-cuts for $A(x)$ and $B(x)$ can be described in a closed-form solution.

$$^\alpha A(x) = [2 + \alpha, 4 - \alpha]$$

$$^\alpha B(x) = [4 + \alpha, 6 - \alpha]$$

Hence,

$$^\alpha(A + B)(x) = [6 + 2\alpha, 10 - \alpha]$$

Unraveling the equations yield the resultant membership function

$$(A + B)(x) = (x - 8)/2 + 1, \ x \in [6,8]$$
$$(A + B)(x) = (8 - x)/2 + 1, \ x \in [8,10]$$

In a more general setting, the extension principle can be used for any arbitrary single-variable or multiple-variable functions. Application of the extension principle for arithmetic operations on fuzzy sets yields the following.

$$(A + B)(z) = \sup_{z=x+y} \min[A(x), B(y)]$$

$$(A - B)(z) = \sup_{z=x-y} \min[A(x), B(y)]$$

$$(A * B)(z) = \sup_{z=x*y} \min[A(x), B(y)]$$

$$(A/B)(z) = \sup_{z=x/y} \min[A(x), B(y)]$$

In general, the extension principle is simpler and more versatile to apply than the approach based on interval logic.

Note that while fuzzy numbers can be added, subtracted, multiplied, or divided similarly to crisp numbers, whenever fuzzy numbers are used, the fuzziness of a number always increases. Hence, when fuzzy numbers are involved in an equation, the solution is not as simple as the crisp counterpart. For example, for crisp numbers, if $A + X = B$, then $X = B - A$. However, the above equations are not applicable for fuzzy numbers because in general, $A + X = A + (B - A) \neq B$. Therefore, the solution for the arithmetic problem can be obtained by unraveling the equations for the interval logic. Let $^\alpha A = [^\alpha a_1, {}^\alpha a_2]$, $^\alpha B = [^\alpha b_1, {}^\alpha b_2]$, and $^\alpha X = [^\alpha x_1, {}^\alpha x_2]$. Then the α-cut for the equation $A + X = B$ is

$$[^\alpha a_1, {}^\alpha a_2] + [^\alpha x_1, {}^\alpha x_2] = [^\alpha b_1, {}^\alpha b_2]$$

or in other words,

$$^\alpha X = [^\alpha b_1 - {}^\alpha a_1, {}^\alpha b_2 - {}^\alpha a_2]$$

The solution X can now be put together:

$$X = \bigcup_\alpha \alpha \, {}^\alpha X$$

While the formula may seem simple to apply, it is not apparent from the formula that a solution may not exist. Note that the solution X is constructed by piecing together the intervals with the respective proper α values. This implies that each individual $^\alpha X$ must be a valid interval. It is quite possible that the $^\alpha X$ interval does not exist and the upper limit is less than the lower limit, thus making an invalid interval. This often occurs when the fuzzy number B is less fuzzy than A.

6.3.3   Fuzzy Ordering

In addition to arithmetic operations, crisp numbers can also be compared in terms of their position on the number line. This is usually referred to as ordering. For crisp numbers, the comparison is straightforward, e.g., $3 < 5$ and $5 < 7$, etc. The idea of fuzzy ordering can also be extended to fuzzy numbers.

One method of comparing two fuzzy numbers is by means of the minimum and maximum operations for crisp numbers. The minimum of two crisp numbers yields the smaller of the two, while the maximum of two crisp numbers yields the bigger of the two. The same concept can be extended to fuzzy numbers by means of the extension principle.

$$\text{Min}(A, B)(z) = \sup_{z=\min(x,y)} \min[A(x),B(y)]$$

$$\text{Max}(A, B)(z) = \sup_{z=\max(x,y)} \min[A(x),B(y)]$$

6.4   FUZZY RELATION

A relation provides a weaker connection between two variables than a function. In a functional relationship, one variable (x) is an independent variable and the other (y) is a dependent variable. While more than one independent variable can take on the same value for the dependent variable, it is not permissible for an independent variable to take on more than one value for the dependent variable. Hence, there are many functions that are not invertible. If y is a function of x, that does not imply that x is a function of y. For example, there are many independent variables in a sine function that have the same dependent value, hence the function is not invertible unless the interval of the dependent variable is limited.

6.4.1   Definition of a Fuzzy Relation

A relation on the other hand provides a connection that is much less restricted that a function. If x is related to y, then y is related to x. It is also possible that some values of the variables are related to one another while other values of the variables are not. In the most general case, a crisp relation is defined below.

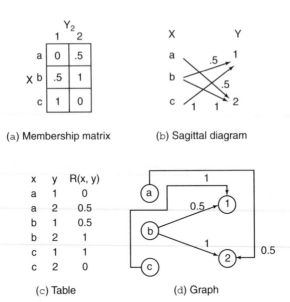

(a) Membership matrix   (b) Sagittal diagram

(c) Table   (d) Graph

Figure 6.8. A relation defined by a membership matrix.

$$R(x_1, \ldots, x_n) = 1 \text{ if } <x_1, \ldots, x_n> \in R$$

$$R(x_1, \ldots, x_n) = 0 \text{ otherwise}$$

A relation is commonly defined in one of two ways: a membership matrix or a sagittal diagram. A membership matrix lists the set values of one variable on one side and maps the set values of the variable in the other side.

For crisp relations, if there is a relation, then the corresponding matrix element is 1; otherwise the matrix element is 0. The membership matrix clearly identifies all possible values of x and y and enumerates which element in x is related to which element in y. For fuzzy relations, the relation can also be defined by the membership matrix method, except the element values in the matrix need not be 0 or 1, but rather between 0 and 1.

A second method to define a relation is by means of a Sagittal Diagram, where a line is drawn between the elements of the sets whenever a relation exists. For crisp relation, a line indicates there is a relation while no line indicates that no relation exists. For fuzzy relation, the degree or strength of the relation is indicated in the line. Figure 6.8 shows examples of relations.

6.4.2 Binary Relation

A binary relation $R(X, Y)$ is a relation of two sets: X and Y. Similar to a function, the domain of a relation shows the maximum Y values of the relation for the corresponding x values.

$$\text{dom } R(x) = \max_y R(x,y)$$

Likewise, the range of a relation shows the maximum X values of the relation for the corresponding y values.

$$\text{range } R(y) = \max_x R(x,y)$$

The height of a relation is the maximum value in the relation.

$$H(R) = \max_x \max_y R(x,y)$$

The inverse of a relation is to access the relation from the opposite direction.

$$R^{-1}(y,x) = R(x,y)$$

In a relation, the inverse is simply the transpose of the membership matrix.

A binary relation on a single set is a relation giving the connection of the elements in the same set. Three properties are typically used to describe a fuzzy relation: reflexivity, symmetry, and transitivity. Reflexivity refers to the property in a relation that an element is related to itself, i.e., the relation of x with x is itself. Symmetry is a property that the relation is bidirectional, i.e., if x is related to y, then y is related to x. Transitivity indicates that the relational property is transferable, i.e., if x is related to y and y is related to z, then x is related to z.

There are two specific relations that are noteworthy: *equivalence* and *compatibility*. The equivalence relation shows that the elements of a set are equivalent to one another. This relation is reflexive, symmetric, and transitive. Clearly, an element is equivalent to itself, hence the relation is reflexive. If an element x is equivalent to another element y, then the element y is also equivalent to element x by definition, hence the relation is symmetric. Furthermore, if an element x is equivalent to y and y is equivalent to z, then x is equivalent to z, hence the relation is also transitive.

For a crisp definition of equivalence, the elements of the membership matrix are either 0 or 1. For a fuzzy definition of equivalence, two elements are similar if the relation between the two elements yields a value higher than some specified degree. This is called a similarity relation. The similarity relation partitions the entire set into a number of sets where all equivalent states are equivalent to one another within the set.

Another relation that is like the equivalence relation is the compatibility relation. While the equivalence concept conveys the idea that the two specified elements are exactly identical to one another, the compatibility concept conveys the idea that the two specified elements are close to one another. Hence the latter is also called a proximity relation or a tolerance relation. The compatibility equation is reflexive and symmetric but not transitive. An element is surely close to itself, hence the relation is reflexive. If an element x is close to y, then y must also be close to x, hence the relation is also symmetric. However, if an element x is not close to y, and another element z is also not close to y, the relation is not symmetric.

6.4.3 Operations with Relations

Information in a relation can be retrieved and manipulated just like a fuzzy set. The most common usage is to use the relation to find the value of a resultant fuzzy set given the value of an initial fuzzy set. This operation is called the max–min composition.

The problem can be stated as follows. Given a relation $P(X,Y)$ between $X(x)$ and $Y(y)$ and a fuzzy set X', what is Y' as suggested by the relation.

$$Y(y)' = X(x)' \; o \; P(X,Y)$$

$$Y(y)' = \max_x \; \min \; [X(x),P(x,y)]$$

It is clear from the definition that the operation is called the max–min composition. In general, the max-min composition can be used to relate two relations. Given two relations $P(X,Y)$ between X and Y and $Q(Y,Z)$ between Y and Z, what is the relation between X and Z, i.e., find $R(X,Z)$?

$$R(x,z) = [P(x,y) \; o \; Q(y,z)]$$

$$R(x,z) = \max_y \; \min \; [P(x,y),Q(y,z)]$$

The max–min composition operation is also known as the standard composition. Properties of the standard composition are listed below.

Associativity:	$[P(x,y) \; o \; Q(y,z)] \; o \; R(z,w) = P(x,y) \; o$
	$[Q(y,z) \; o \; R(z,w)]$
Inverse or reverse	
composition:	$[P(x,y) \; o \; Q(y,z)]^{-1} = Q^{-1}(z,y) \; o \; P^{-1}(y,x)$
NOT commutative:	$P(x,y) \; o \; Q(y,z) \neq Q(z,y) \; o \; P(y,x)$

Since one of the definitions of the fuzzy intersection operation is the min operation, the standard max-min composition can immediately be generalized using the fuzzy intersection instead of the min operation. The resultant operation is called the sup-i composition where the supremum is used instead of the max operation and the intersection operation used instead of the min operation.

$$[P \; o^i \; Q](x,z) = \sup_y i[P(x,y), \; Q(y,z)]$$

Clearly, if the intersection operation is chosen to be the min operator, then $P \; o^i \; Q \Rightarrow P \; o \; Q$. Properties of the sup-$i$ composition are similar to the standard composition.

There is another variation to the standard composition based on the implication operator. This is called the inf-ω_i operation.

$$(P \; o_{\omega i} \; Q)(x,z) = \inf_y \omega_i[P(x,y), Q(y,z)]$$

It is possible to use different definitions of implication for this operation. Properties of this operation are listed below.

Commutativity: $P \; o_{\omega i} \; (Q \; o_{\omega i} \; S) = (P \; o^i \; Q) \; o_{\omega i} \; S$

Other properties: $P^{-1} \; o^i \; (P \; o_{\omega i} \; Q) \subseteq Q$

$$R \subseteq (R \; o_{\omega i} \; Q^{-1}) \; o_{\omega i} \; Q$$

From the equations above, it can be inferred that the sup-i composition o^i and the inf-ω_i operation $o_{\omega i}$ are somewhat inverse to one another.

6.5   EVIDENCE THEORY

In evidence theory, a belief measure is the degree of belief based on available evidence that a given element belongs to the set A. The basic principle of the believe measure is that the sum is greater than the parts. When evidences are put together, the degree of belief can likewise be accumulated. Note that probability is a special case of a belief measure. While the belief measure deals with hard evidence, the plausibility measure deals with what can be implied or inferred from the evidence.

6.5.1   Believability and Plausibility

The basic definition of a belief measure, the degree of belief, $Bel(x) \rightarrow [0,1]$, based on the available evidence that a given element of x belongs to set A, is:

$$Bel(A_1 \cup \ldots (A_n)) \geq \Sigma_j \; Bel(A_j) - \Sigma_{j<k} \; Bel(A_j \cap A_k)$$

$$+ \ldots + (-1)^{n+1} \; Bel(A_1 \cap \ldots (A_n))$$

In other words, the belief measure is superadditive. As an example, for three sets of evidence,

$$Bel(A \cup B \cup C) \geq Bel(A) + Bel(B) + Bel(C) - Bel(A \cap B)$$
$$- Bel(A \cap C) - Bel(B \cap C) + Bel(A \cap B \cap C)$$

Properties of the belief measure are listed below:

Boundary conditions:	$Bel(\emptyset) = 0$
	$Bel(X) = 1$
Monotonicity:	$Bel(A) \leq Bel(B)$ if $A \subseteq B$
Superadditive:	$Bel(A \cup B) \geq Bel(A) + Bel(B) - Bel(A \cap B)$
Continuous from above:	$Bel(A) + Bel(A\backslash) \leq 1$

For the plausibility measure, the degree of plausibility, $Pl(x) \rightarrow [0,1]$, based on the available evidence that a given element of x belongs to set A, is:

$$A_1 \cap \ldots \cap A_n) \leq \Sigma_j Pl(A_j) - \Sigma_{j<k} Pl(A_j \cup A_k)$$
$$+ \ldots + (-1)^{n+1} Pl(A_1 \cup \ldots \cup A_n)$$

In other words, the plausibility measure is subadditive. For three sets of evidence,

$$Pl(A \cap B \cap C) \leq Pl(A) + Pl(B) + Pl(C) - Pl(A \cup B)$$
$$- Pl(A \cup C) - Pl(B \cup C) + Pl(A \cup B \cup C)$$

Properties of the plausibility measure are listed below:

Boundary conditions:	$Pl(\emptyset) = 0$
	$Pl(X) = 1$
Subadditive:	$Pl(A \cap B) \leq Pl(A) + Pl(B) - Pl(A \cup B)$
Continuous from below:	$Pl(A) + Pl(A\backslash) \geq 1$

Similar to the union and intersection operations, there is also a duality relationship between believability and plausibility.

$$Pl(A) = 1 - Bel(A\backslash)$$
$$Bel(A) = 1 - Pl(A\backslash)$$

The degree of belief is usually derived from the basic probability assignment (BPA), which measures the probability that a set element belongs to the set. In other words, it is the probability density function for the elements of the set. Note that the basic probability assignment is defined on the power set of x. Since the BPA is a probability measure, the sum of all the BPA's for the entire power set must necessarily be summed to 1. The properties of a BPA are given below.

$$\text{Boundary conditions:} \qquad m(\emptyset) = 0$$

$$\Sigma_A \, m(A) = 1$$

Note that there is no relation between the BPA of the elements or its inverse. Hence, $m(X) = 1$ is not required.

The believability and plausibility measures can be derived directly from the basic probability assignment.

$$Bel(A) = \Sigma_{B|B \subseteq A} \, m(B) \; \forall \; A \in \{\text{power set of } X\}$$

$$Pl(A) = \Sigma_{B|B \cap A \neq 0} \, m(B) \; \forall \; A \in \{\text{power set of } X\}$$

Likewise, the basic probability assignment can also be obtained from the believability measure.

$$m(A) = \Sigma_{B|B \subseteq A} \, (-1)^{|A-B|} \, Bel(B)$$

In summary, the basic probability assignment, $m(A)$, measures the degree of evidence or belief that the element in question belongs to set A alone. On the other hand, the believability measure, $Bel(A)$, is the total evidence or belief that the element belongs to A and all special subsets of A. The plausibility measure, $Pl(A)$, is the total evidence or belief that the element belongs to A and subsets, and also the additional evidence or belief associated with sets that overlap with A.

Since believability measures deal with the hard evidence while the plausibility measures deal with what can be inferred,

$$Pl(A) \geq Bel(A), \; \forall \; A \in \{\text{power set of } X\}$$

A special case called total ignorance occurs when there is evidence that the element is in the universal set, but there is no evidence about its location in any subset of X.

$$m(X) = 1 \text{ and } m(A) = 0 \; \forall \; A \neq X$$

$$Bel(X) = 1 \text{ and } Bel(A) = 0 \; \forall \; A \neq X$$

$$Pl(\emptyset) = 0 \text{ and } PL(A) = 1 \; \forall \; A \neq \emptyset$$

A believability measure not only describes the degree of belief for the elements of a set, it also allows evidence to be combined from different experts into a cohesive picture. This is called the Dempster rule of combination:

$$m_{1,2}(A) = (\Sigma_{B \cap C = A} \, m_1(B) \, m_2(C))/(1 - K)$$

where

$$K = \Sigma_{B \cap C = \emptyset} \, m_1(B) \, m_2(C)$$

6.5.2 Uncertainty

In crisp sets, one possible measure of uncertainty is the number of alternatives available. When there are no alternatives, there is no uncertainty. The more alternatives there are, the larger the uncertainty. Hartley has proposed a class of functions that can be used to measure the uncertainty of a nonempty but finite set.

$$U(A) = c \, \log_b |A|$$

If the set is infinite, then a modified form of the Hartley function is used.

$$U(A) = \log(1 + \mu(A))$$

In particular, when $c == 1$ and $b == 2$, then $U(A) = \log_2 |A|$ and is called the Hartley function. The resultant measure is called bits.

Extending the same idea to fuzzy sets, the nonspecificity or imprecision of a fuzzy set can be measured in terms of the size of alternatives. For finite sets, the generalized Hartley function is:

$$U(A) = (1/h(A)) \int_0^{h(A)} \log_2 |^\alpha A| \, d\alpha$$

As an example, consider the two membership functions $A_1(x)$ and $A_2(x)$, as shown in Figure 6.9. Note that the core of the two sets is the same, but the support of $A_1(x)$ is much wider than $A_2(x)$. Consequently, the nonspecificity of $A_1(x)$, $U(A_1)$ is and is much greater than that of $A_2(x)$ or $U(A_2)$.

6.5.3 Fuzziness

Another uncertainty measure is the fuzziness measure, which is a measure of a lack of distinction between the set and its complement. The less a set differs from its complement, the fuzzier it is. This is a measure that makes a dis-

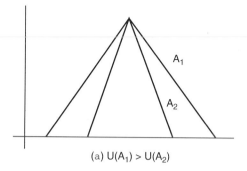

(a) $U(A_1) > U(A_2)$

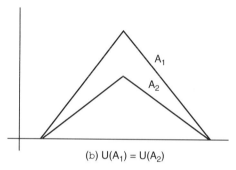

(b) $U(A_1) = U(A_2)$

Figure 6.9. Nonspecificity of fuzzy sets.

tinction between a crisp set and a fuzzy set. The fuzziness measure can be defined by the following.

Boundary condition: $f(A) = 0$ if A is a crisp set

                               $f(A)$ is maximum if and only if

                               (iff) $A(x) = 0.5 \ \forall \ x \in X$

Monotonicity: $f(A) \leq f(B)$ when A is sharper than B

                               $A(x) \leq B(x)$ when $B(x) \leq 0.5$

                               $A(x) \geq B(x)$ when $B(x) \geq 0.5$

One formulation for the fuzziness measure is given below.

$$f(A) = \Sigma_x \left(1 - |2A(x) - 1|\right)$$

Figure 6.10 shows a number of fuzzy sets and its corresponding fuzziness

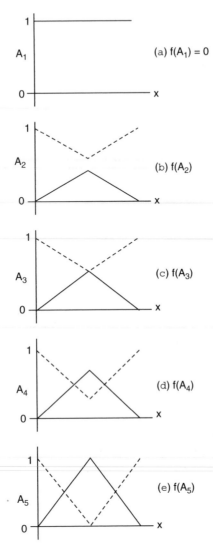

Figure 6.10. Fuzziness measure of fuzzy sets.

measure. The complement of the fuzzy set is also given to highlight the comparison with the complement.

As a comparison between nonspecificity and fuzziness, note that a gain in information always reduces the nonspecificity, but a reduction in fuzziness does not necessarily imply a gain in information.

6.5.4 Nonspecificity

Hartley's function has been generalized to provide a measure of nonspecificity. The concept can be further extended for application in evidence theory. The nonspecificity measure is defined as below:

$$N(m) = \Sigma_A\ m(A)\ \log_2 |A|$$

The nonspecificity function is a weighted Hartley function of the focal elements in the body of evidence. When there is no uncertainty in the body of evidence, then $N(m) = 0$. On the other hand, when there is total ignorance, then $N(m) = \log_2|x|$. Conflict, $Con(\{x\})$ is the sum of all evidential claims that conflict with x. $H(m)$ is the expected value of conflict among all evidential claims within a given probabilistic body of evidence.

It is of interest to compare the concept of nonspecificity fuzzy sets with the equivalent for probability theory. In probability theory, the disorderliness is measured by the Shannon entropy.

$$H(m) = -\Sigma_x\ m(x)\ \log_2 m(x)$$

For fuzzy sets, the concept of entropy can be extended, leading to two entropy-like measures, dissonance and confusion, which are defined below.

$$\text{Dissonance} = -\Sigma_A\ m(A)\ \log_2 Pl(A)$$

$$\text{Confusion} = -\Sigma_A\ m(A)\ \log_2 Bel(A)$$

Dissonance is the total value of the conflict with the given evidence. Confusion is the total value of the conflict with the given evidence but does not scale each particular conflict of $m(B)$ with respect to $m(A)$ according to the degree of violation in the subsethood. A direct measure of conflict expressing the individual degree of conflicts is defined as follows.

$$\text{Conflict } (A) = \Sigma_B\ m(B)\ |B - A|/|B|$$

An extension of this is called strife and discord.

$$\text{Strife} = -\Sigma_A\ m(A)\ \log_2 \Sigma_B\ m(B)\ |A \cap B|/|A|$$

$$\text{Discord} = -\Sigma_A\ m(A)\ \log_2 \Sigma_B\ m(B)\ |A \cap B|/|B|$$

Discord is the mean value of the conflict with the given evidence. Strife is the mean value of the conflict with the given evidence but does not scale each particular conflict of $m(B)$ with respect to $m(A)$ according to the degree of violation in the subsethood.

6.6   FUZZY LOGIC

The field of expert systems grew out of classical logic. Significant parallelism can be seen among set theory, Boolean algebra, and proportional logic.

6.6.1   Multivalued Logic

In Boolean algebra, a variable x can take on only two values: $x \in \{0,1\}$. Much research has been done on extending the possible values of x beyond two values. If x can take on three values, this is called a three-value logic. If x can take on three or more values, this is called multivalued logic. If x takes on n values, this is called an n-value logic. In general, the values of x take on values between 0 and 1.

$$T_n = \{0, 1/(n-1), 2/(n-1), \ldots, (n-2)/(n-1), 1\}$$

The Boolean operations of complement, union, and intersection can be extended into an n-valued logic system.

Note that a variable in Boolean algebra takes on only two values: $x \in \{0,1\}$. Likewise, a variable in an n-value logic takes on only n values: $x \in \{0, 1/(n-1), 2/(n-1), \ldots, (n-2)/(n-1), 1\}$. However, a variable in a fuzzy system takes on values between 0 and 1: $x \in [0,1]$. A fuzzy system is therefore sometimes referred to as an infinite value logic system.

6.6.2   Unconditional Fuzzy Propositions

In classical logic, there are two types of propositions: conditional and unconditional. An unconditional proposition such as "The ball is red" is composed of a subject "the ball" and a predicate "is red." On the other hand, a conditional proposition takes on the form "If A then B." A conditional proposition is simply the implication relation. These propositions can be directly extended to the fuzzy case. The primary difference is that in classical logic, the ball is either red or it is not red. However, in the fuzzy case, there are many degrees of truth regarding the ball being red. Likewise for conditional propositions, there can be many degrees of truth related to the implication.

For an unconditional proposition, the truth value of the proposition is simply the degree of participation of the predicate in the set related to the subject. Hence, if the ball is red, then the truth value of the proportion is simply the degree of redness.

Proposition: Subject is predicate

Truth(Proposition) = predicate(subject)

For example, if the proposition is "The ball is red," then the truth value of the proposition is Red(ball).

If the proposition is further qualified regarding the degree of truth, then the original truth value must be further mapped by a transformation function to reflect the specified qualification.

Proposition: (Subject is predicate) is qualified

Truth(Proposition) = Qualified(predicate(subject))

For example, if the proposition is "The ball is red is very true," then the truth value of the proposition is Very(Red(ball)).

If, instead of a single predicate, the subject is related to a set of predicates through a probability distribution function, the truth of the proposition can also be obtained.

Proposition: Subject is p_1 with probability p_1

Proposition: Subject is p_2 with probability p_2

Proposition: Subject is p_3 with probability p_3

Truth(Proposition) = Σ_i predicate$_i$(subject) * p_i

It is also possible to have quantitative propositions, i.e., propositions that relate to quantity information. For example, saying that there are 10 balls in the basket is a quantitative proposition. For crisp set, the quantity is merely the cardinality of the set. The same also applies to fuzzy set.

Proposition: There are quantity balls in the basket

Truth(Proposition) = Quantity($|$Basket$|$)

where $|.|$ represents the cardinality of the set. Hence, if the proposition is "There are about 10 red balls in the basket," then the truth of the proposition is About_10($|$Red$|$).

6.6.3 Conditional Fuzzy Propositions

For a conditional proposition, the truth value of the proposition is denoted by the fuzzy implication of the relation.

Proposition: **If** x is A, **then** y is B

A conditional proposition is also commonly known as a rule. The implication conveyed by the rule yields a relation

$$R(x,y) = \text{Implication}(A(x),B(y))$$

Based on how much x belongs to A and y belongs to B, the truth value of the proposition is simply the corresponding value of the relation.

In classical logic, three primary principles are used to combine propositions to make new inferences:

Modus ponens:	$(a \wedge (a \Rightarrow b)) \Rightarrow b$
Modus tollens:	$(b \vee \wedge (a \Rightarrow b)) \Rightarrow a \backslash$
Hypothetical syllogism:	$((a \Rightarrow b) \wedge (b \Rightarrow c)) \Rightarrow (a \Rightarrow c)$

The same three principles can directly be extended to fuzzy sets also.

In *modus ponens*, a rule with an antecedent and a consequent is given. When a simple unconditional proposition is given, it is matched with antecedent of the rule. If the proposition matches the antecedent, then the rule fires or is applied and the proposition in the consequent is added to the knowledge base. In crisp logic, the antecedent must match the given unconditional proposition exactly before the rule can be applied.

Rule:	**If** x is A, **then** y is B
Fact:	x is A
Conclusion:	y is B

For fuzzy logic, the *modus ponens* is extended for approximate matches. This is called the generalized *modus ponens*. The given unconditional proposition and the antecedent of the rule do not have to match exactly. Rather, the degree of the match is the degree that the rule can be applied.

Rule:	**If** x is A, **then** y is B
Fact:	x is A'
Conclusion:	y is B'

The conclusion B' is found by the max–min composition operation.

$$B' = A' \ o \ R(x,y)$$

In *modus tollens*, a rule with an antecedent and a consequent is given. When a simple unconditional proposition is given, the complement of the proposition is matched with the complement of the consequent of the rule. If the two complements match, then the rule fires or is applied and the complement of the antecedent is added to the knowledge base. In crisp logic, the complement of the consequent must match the complement of the given unconditional proposition exactly before the rule can be applied.

Rule:	**If** x is A, **then** y is B
Fact:	y is $B\backslash$
Conclusion:	x is $A\backslash$

For fuzzy logic, the *modus tollens* is extended for approximate matches. This is called the generalized *modus tollens*. The given unconditional proposition and the consequent of the rule do not have to match exactly. Rather, the degree of the match is the degree that the rule can be applied.

Rule:	**If** x is A, **then** y is B
Fact:	y is B'
Conclusion:	x is A'

The conclusion A' is found by the max–min composition operation.

$$A' = R(x,y) \ o \ B'$$

In hypothetical syllogism, a rule with an antecedent and a consequent is given. A second rule with another antecedent and consequent is also given. The proposition in the consequent of the first rule is matched with the antecedent of the second rule. If the two propositions match, then both rules can be applied and the antecedent of the first rule is matched to the consequent of the second rule. In crisp logic, the match must be exact before the rules can be applied.

Rule:	If x is A, then y is B
Rule:	If y is B, then z is C
Conclusion:	If x is A, then z is C

For fuzzy logic, the hypothetical syllogism can also be extended for approximate matches. This is called the generalized hypothetical syllogism. The consequent of the first rule does not have to match exactly with the antecedent of the second rule. Rather, the degree of the match is the degree that the rules can be applied.

Rule:	If x is A, then y is B
Rule:	If y is B, then z is C
Conclusion:	If x is A, then z is C

The conclusion A' is found by the max–min composition operation.

$$R(x,z) = R(x,y) \ o \ R(y,z)$$

6.6.4   Selection of Implication Operator

One of the primary uses of the fuzzy implication operator is to define the implication relation in rules. Since there are many ways to form an implication operation, it is crucial to determine which implication definition should be used and which one should not be used. Since the implication operator is the central operation used in the generalized *modus ponens,* generalized *modus tollens,* and hypothetical syllogism, it is required that when an implication operator is used, the three principles must be satisfied. This requires that for generalized *modus ponens*:

Rule:	**If** x is A, **then** y is B
Fact:	x is A
Conclusion:	y is B

In other words, if the fact matches the antecedent exactly, we require that the implication operator give the consequent exactly.

$$B = A \ o \ R(x,y)$$

If the implication operator is to be used for the generalized *modus tollens* case, then given the consequent of the rule, it is expected that the antecedent be obtained exactly.

Rule:	**If** x is A, **then** y is B
Fact:	y is B
Conclusion:	x is A

or

$$A = R(x,y) \ o \ B$$

Similarly, if the implication operator is to be used for the hypothetical syllogism case, then if the consequent of the first rule matches the antecedent of the second rule, it is expected that a resultant rule is obtained with the antecedent from the antecedent of the first rule and the consequent from the consequent of the second rule.

Rule:	If x is A, then y is B
Rule:	If y is B, then z is C
Conclusion:	If x is A, then z is C

Or

$$R(x,z) = R(x,y) \ o \ R(y,z)$$

6.6.5 Multiconditional Reasoning

In most expert systems, typically more than a single rule is given. A set of rules is called a rule set. When a proposition is made, the proposition is compared to the entire rule set. The result is then compiled form the entire set of matching rules.

Rules:	p_1: If x is A_1, then y is B_1
	p_n: If x is A_n, then y is B_n
Fact:	x is A'
Conclusion:	y is B'

In crisp logic, all consequents from matching rules are added to the knowledge base. When there are a lot of rules, it is easy to have contradicting results.

In fuzzy logic, since an exact match is not required, almost every rule in the rule set may be activated, albeit to a different degree. For some rules, there is a good match between the given proposition and the antecedent. The influence of these consequents should be weighted more heavily than other consequents coming from rules with a lesser match between the proposition and the antecedents. The method is called the method of interpolation. The first step is to compute the degree of compatibility of the rule based on the compatibility of the proposition and the antecedent of the rules.

$$r_j(A') = h(A' \cap A_j) = \sup_x \min(A'(x), A_j(x))$$

where j is the index of the rule. The second step is to compute the compilation of all the consequents weighted by the degree of compatibility of the corresponding rule.

$$B'(y) = \sup_j \min(r_j(A'), B_j(y))$$

A graphical interpretation of the method of interpolation is given in Figure

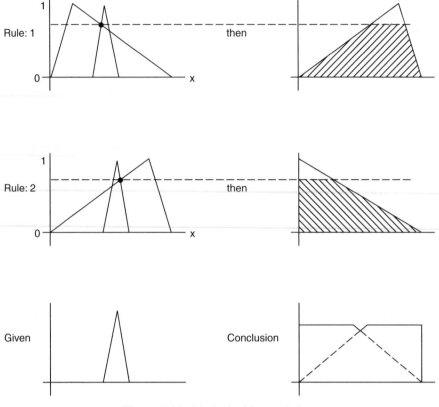

Figure 6.11. Method of interpolation.

6.11. It can be shown that for standard max-min composition, the above procedure is equivalent to the standard compositional rule of inference

$$B'(y) = A'(x) \, o \, R(x,y)$$

where

$$R(x,y) = \sup_j \min[A_j(x), B_j(y)]$$

The result of the method of interpolation gives a fuzzy set. In many applications, it is of interest to convert the fuzzy set into a crisp value. This process is called defuzzification. There are three popular ways to defuzzify a fuzzy set into a crisp number: the center of area method, the center of maxima method, and the mean of maxima method.

The center of area method is also called the center of gravity method. The crisp value is simply the centroid of the resultant membership function.

$$d_{CA}(A) = (\int A(z)z\,dz)/(\int A(z)\,dz)$$

and in the discrete case

$$d_{CA}(A) = (\Sigma_{k=1}^{n} A(z_k)z_k)/(\Sigma_{k=1}^{n} A(z_k))$$

This is the most common method used, and every part of the membership function contributes to the final answer. In the second method, the center of maxima method, the crisp value is the midpoint between the largest and the smallest values with maximum membership.

$$d_{CM}(A) = (\inf Z + \sup Z)/2, \ Z = \{z|A(z) = h(A)\}$$

and in the discrete case

$$d_{CM}(A) = [\min(z_k|A(z_k) = h(A)) + \min(z_k|A(z_k) = h(A))]/2$$

In the third method, the mean of maxima method, the crisp value is computed to be the arithmetic mean of all values with maximum membership. In the discrete case,

$$d_{MM}(A) = \Sigma A(z_k)/|Z|$$

The advantage of this method is that the resultant crisp value is less affected by outliers. It is also possible to weight the various contributions in the summation for $d_{MM}(A)$.

6.7 SUMMARY

Fuzzy systems provide a more general way to represent concepts, ideas, and propositions. In fuzzy systems, the distinction between one number and the next, between one interval and the next, between one concept and the next, is unsharp, i.e., the transition is not abrupt. Hence, a crisp variable becomes a special case of a fuzzy variable. By means of the extension principle, most crisp operations and functions can be directly extended to fuzzy sets. Such is the case for Boolean algebra and crisp arithmetic.

Another distinct advantage of fuzzy sets is that many of the concepts in expert systems can also be incorporated in fuzzy systems. Rules in expert systems can readily be implemented in the implication operator in fuzzy systems. Hence, knowledge processing with rules is natural in fuzzy systems and knowledge inference actually reduces into manipulation of the implication operator.

7

NEURAL NETWORKS

7.1 INTRODUCTION

Many complex systems are built from simple foundational elements. The field of Boolean algebra came into existence due to the selection of simple elements that can only take on two values: 0 and 1. These elements are combined by three basic operations: AND, OR, and NOT. From these simple elements and operations, complex combinational circuits and sequential circuits can be constructed, eventually culminating in today's computers. Mathematicians also have long worked with set theory, an extension where a set may consists of more than 0 and 1 values. The Boolean operations AND, OR, and NOT have been extended for set theory to UNION, INTERSECTION, and COMPLEMENT. More recently, the concept of fuzzy logic has been introduced by Zadeh. In fuzzy logic, the participation of an element's membership in a set is not binary, that is, none or all, but rather in degrees between none and all.

In the field of signal processing, many modeling techniques are based on a simple linear model: the linear combiner, where the output is a linear combination of the weighted inputs. Much study has been devoted to finding the best techniques for estimating the parameters of a linear model. Statistical techniques have long been developed for linear regression that is a form of a linear combiner. Deterministic signal-processing techniques for linear models have been well developed in recent decades. Adaptive signal-processing techniques provide a means to obtain model parameters iteratively, thus simplifying the application of many computationally intensive approaches.

The original motivation for studying neural networks stems from the desire to perform with machines complex and intelligent tasks that only the human brain is now capable of. It is commonly accepted that while the response time of a nerve cell is on the order of milliseconds, the collective intelligence of billions of billions of nerve cells in the human brain is staggering. A human brain is able to recall images and events that occurred decades ago and can recognize a single face out of the millions of faces and images seen before.

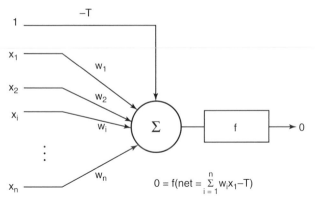

Figure 7.1. A neurode.

Yet the study of anatomy has shown that on the surface the operation of a single brain cell is extremely limited. It is indeed intriguing to see that the totality of these simple nerve cells can achieve the wonders of modern technology. Hence, there is tremendous interest by researchers in recent decades in studying the biological neural networks in an attempt to construct artificial neural networks from simple artificial neurons that would equally achieve what two and a half pounds of a typical human brain can attain.

7.1.1 Definition of a Neurode

A biological nerve cell is composed of a cell body. A large number of tree-like incoming branches called dendrites collect sensory inputs to the cell body. The dendrites make "contact" with other nerve cells through a synapse. When a nerve cell is put into an active state, it fires, that is, an electrical impulse is generated and sent along a conduit called an axon. When the electrical impulse passes through a synapse, a number of chemical reactions are evoked, causing specific chemicals to be released and collected by the dendrites. When enough sensory inputs have been collected by the dendrites of the receiving nerve cell, it in turn fires. The efficacy of the electrical stimulation from an impulse on an axon passing through a synapse is variable dependent on a large number of parameters, such as the availability of ions and the general health of the body.

An artificial neuron or neurode is a simple processing element patterned after the biological model. A neurode, as shown in Figure 7.1, is composed of a number of inputs and a single output. Each synapse of a biological neuron represents an input of the neurode. The efficacy of the synaptic junction is represented by a multiplicative weight associated with that neurode input. The coincidence of the synaptic stimulation is modeled by a simple summation. The activation of the neurode is defined by an activation of the weighted sum of the input. In equation format, the output, o, of a neurode can be expressed as:

$$o = f(\text{net})$$

$$\text{net} = \Sigma_{i=1}^{N} w_i \, x_i$$

where x_i are the inputs, w_i are the weights associated with the inputs, and f is a nonlinear function. There are a total of N inputs. The same equation can also be expressed in matrix form:

$$o = f(W^T X)$$

where $W = [w_0, w_1, \ldots, w_N]$ and $X = [1, x_1, \ldots, x_N]$. Note that the constant threshold has been defined as x_0 and is set to 1.

The above definition immediately highlights the similarity between a neurode and a linear combiner. In fact, the net parameter is precisely a linear combiner. The primary difference between a neurode and a linear combiner is that for a neurode, there is an additional nonlinear transformation, f, following the linear combiner. In most cases, this transformation or activation function is taken to be nonlinear. In the extreme case when the activation is taken as a linear function, and more specifically a linear ramp function, then a neurode is the same as a linear combiner. In other words, a neurode is a linear combiner and more.

7.1.2   Variations of a Neurode

There are a number of variations on the format of a neurode. Most of the variations stem from the different definitions of the input range for x and in the choice of the activation functions f. If the $x \in \{0,1\}$ or $x \in \{-1,1\}$, then the input is discrete. If $x \in \{0,1\}$, then the input is called unipolar. If $x \in \{-1,1\}$, then the input is bipolar. If $x \in \mathcal{R}^1$, then the input is continuous. The weights of the neurode are usually represented as real numbers. If the activation function produces only discrete values due to a threshold function, the output is said to be discrete. Most other activation functions produce continuous outputs. The activation can be a simple linear function, though most of the time the activation function is taken to be a nonlinear function. Following are a number of commonly used activation functions:

Discrete output
  Unipolar outputs
    Threshold function (or hardlimiter or heaviside function)
    Stochastic function
  Bipolar outputs
    Sign(net)
    Stochastic function

Continuous output
    Unipolar outputs
        Linear function
        Piecewise function
        Sigmoidal function
    Bipolar outputs
        Signum function
        Linear function
        Piecewise function
        Hyperbolic tangent function

The use of different activation functions produces different results. While there have been reports of special activation functions with special characteristics, e.g., periodic, most activation functions are monotonically increasing. The hyperbolic tangent function is of particular interest because the steepness of the curve can be adjusted with different values of the λ parameter. When λ increases, the transition becomes steep. It is worth noting that when λ approaches infinity, the hyperbolic tangent function approaches the sign function. The same observation can be made about to the sigmoidal function. As the λ parameter of the sigmoidal function approaches infinity, the sigmoidal function approaches the hardlimiter function.

7.2 SINGLE NEURODE

7.2.1 The McCulloch–Pitts Neurode

One of the early studies of the behavior of a neurode is the McCulloch–Pitts neurode. The input is discrete $x \in \{0,1\}$ and the output is also discrete $o \in \{0,1\}$. The activation function is a simple threshold function:

$$o = 1 \text{ if net} \geq 0$$

$$o = 0 \text{ if net} < 0$$

where net $= W^T X$. Note that a nonzero threshold is automatically accounted for as w_0 in the above formulation. Figure 7.2 shows a McCulloch–Pitts neurode.

7.2.2 McCulloch–Pitts Neurodes as Boolean Components

There are many uses for McCulloch–Pitts neurodes. One notable observation is that one or more neurodes can be arranged to function as simple Boolean elements: an AND, OR, or NOT gate. For example, if a McCulloch–Pitts neurode takes on a single input, and let the weights $W = [-1.001,1]$, then

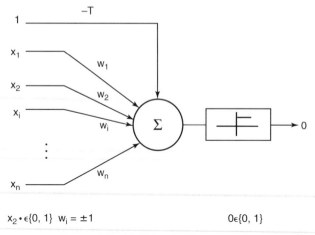

$x_2 \cdot \epsilon\{0, 1\}$ $w_i = \pm 1$ $0 \epsilon \{0, 1\}$

Figure 7.2. McCulloch–Pitts neurode.

the neurode functions as a NOT gate. However, given a two-input McCulloch–Pitts neurode, if $W = [0.001,1,1]$, then the neurode functions as an OR gate. If $W = [1,1,1]$, then the neurode functions as an AND gate. This implies that all combinational circuits composed of AND, OR, and NOT components can be directly replaced by McCulloch–Pitts neurodes, and hence a neural network.

Using the basic principle of a McCulloch–Pitts neurode, more complex and useful structures can be built. For example, McCulloch–Pitts neurodes can be connected to produce an analog-digital converter using the successive comparison approach [Zurada]. The single input x is a continuous parameter between 0 and 1. The output o_1 to o_4 represents four binary bits. Each of the binary bits is produced by a single McColloch–Pitts neurode. The first neurode compares with half of the dynamic range and reports whether the input x is above or below the half way mark. This determines the most significant bit. If this bit is 1, then half of the dynamic range is subtracted from the input, otherwise the input is left alone. The comparison continues in like manner with the next significant bit until the desired resolution is reached.

7.2.3   Single Neurode as Binary Classifier

A McCulloch–Pitts neurode can also be used as a binary classifier that separates the input into two classes. This is done by examining or unraveling the equation for the output. Assume that the neurode has two inputs x_1 and x_2. Then the output can be expressed as:

$$net = w_0 + w_1x_1 + w_2x_2$$

$$o = 1 \text{ if net} \geq 0$$

$$o = 0 \text{ if net} < 0$$

Clearly, the output separates the entire input space into two classes represented by $o = 1$ and $o = 0$. The decision boundary is the hyperline that separates the input space into these two classes. The equation of this hyperline is given by:

$$w_0 + w_1x_1 + w_2x_2 = 0$$

The input space on one side of the hyperline belongs to one class, while the input space on the other side belongs to the other class. Hence a single neurode is a binary classifier.

Given two clusters of raw data, it is of interest to determine the parameters of the binary classifier, i.e., determine $W = [w_0, w_1, w_2]$. If the locations of the clusters are known, then the hyperline can be determined immediately by realizing that the equation of a line can also be written using the segment-bisector form:

$$(a - b)^T x + (1/2)(\|a\|^2 - \|b\|^2) = 0$$

where a and b are the locations of the clusters and $\|\cdot\|$ represents the Euclidean norm of the enclosed vector. Comparing the segment-bisector form with the equation of the hyperline, it is evident that:

$$w_0 = (1/2)(\|a\|^2 - \|b\|^2)$$

$$[w_1, w_2] = (a - b)^T$$

The same technique can be derived using the principle of minimum distance, hence the above equation is also called the minimum-distance classifier. If the locations of the two clusters are not known and only the original data points are given, then an iterative technique can be applied to determine the weights of the neurode.

A special case of the general binary classifier is the Bayesian classifier, where the decision boundary is drawn according to the maximum likelihood function. Assume that the elements of the two classes have a Gaussian distribution with different means (μ_1 and μ_2). Let C be the covariance matrix of the combined distribution. Then the log-likelihood function is the log of the likelihood ratio.

$$\Lambda(x) = \log f_1 - \log f_2$$

If the classes are assumed to behave like a Gaussian distribution, the log-likelihood function can be simplified to become:

$$\Lambda(x) = (\mu_1 - \mu_2)^T C^{-1} x + (1/2)(\mu_2^T C^{-1} \mu_2 - \mu_1^T C^{-1} \mu_1)$$

The above form is very similar to the minimum-distance classifier. In fact, the form can directly be mapped to the neurode equation. Define

$$W = (\mu_1 - \mu_2)^T C^{-1}$$

$$T = (1/2)(\mu_2^T C^{-1} \mu_2 - \mu_1^T C^{-1} \mu_1)$$

Then:

$$\Lambda(x) = Wx + T$$

As usual, the bias can also be wrapped as one of the weights and an augmented form for a neurode can immediately obtained:

$$\Lambda(x) = W'X'$$

where $W' = [T\ W]$ and $X' = [1\ x]^T$. So a McCulloch–Pitts neurode is also a Bayesian classifier.

7.2.4   Single-Neurode Perceptron

In general, the weights associated with a neurode with an arbitrarily chosen activation function can be determined, albeit iteratively. In some literature, a neurode is also called a perceptron. A single discrete perceptron can be trained to produce a particular desired output in response to a particular input. Given a set of input–output pairs $\langle X,d \rangle$ where $X \in \Re^N$ and $d \in \{0,1\}$, the goal is to determine the weights W such that the predicted output o is the same as the desired output d. The problem can be solved iteratively by minimizing the total prediction error:

$$E = \Sigma_{i=1}^{N} (1/2)(d_i - o)^2$$

Starting from random initial weights, each weight can be updated by the method of gradient descent.

$$\Delta w = (1/2)\eta(d_i - o)y_i$$

The adaptation equation is repeated applied for all input data points until the error is below the acceptable threshold.

The same procedure can also be applied to a continuous perceptron, i.e., a perceptron whose output is a real number. The problem can be restated as follows. Given a set of input–output pairs $\langle X, d \rangle$ where $X \in \Re^N$ and $d \in \Re$, the goal is to determine the weights W such that the predicted output o is the same as the desired output d. The problem can be solved iteratively by minimizing the total prediction error:

$$E = \Sigma_{i=1}^{N}(1/2)(d_i - o)^2$$

Starting from random initial weights, each weight can be updated by the method of gradient descent.

$$\Delta w = (1/2)\eta(d_i - o)f'(\text{net})y_i$$

$$\text{net} = W^T X$$

The factor $f'(\text{net})$ is the derivative of the activation function. Note that the adaptation equation includes this additional term because of the relationship between the neurode output and the activation function. The adaptation equation is repeated applied for all input data points until the error is below the acceptable threshold.

7.3   SINGLE-LAYER FEEDFORWARD NETWORK

7.3.1   Multicategory SLP

A single neurode or perceptron can function only as a dichotomizer partitioning the input space into two classes. Hence more than one perceptron is needed when there are more than two classes. This is called a multicategory single-layer perceptron (SLP). Putting together more than one perceptron results in a single-layer feedforward network, as shown in Figure 7.3. Since the output of each perceptron is independent of the others, the training procedures for a single discrete or continuous perceptron can be readily extended to the single-layer feedforward case.

7.3.2   Associative Memory

Looking from a broader perspective, a single-layer perceptron provides a transformation from a multidimensional input to a multidimensional output.

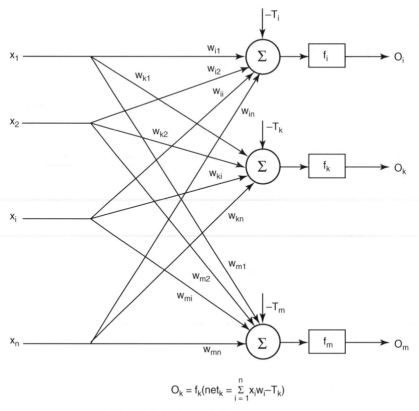

$$O_k = f_k(net_k = \sum_{i=1}^{n} x_i w_i - T_k)$$

Figure 7.3. A single-layer perceptron.

In other words, a single-layer perceptron provides a mapping from input to output such that $f: \Re^N \rightarrow \Re^M$, where N is the input dimension and M is the output dimension. This is commonly called an associative memory. In equation form, an associative memory can be described as follows:

$$O = f(W^T X)$$

where the dimension of the input X is N, the dimension of the output O is M, and the dimension of the weight matrix W is N by M. Note that the activation $f(.)$ is applied to every element of the output array.

A linear associator is obtained when the activation function is taken to be a ramp function, i.e., $f(z) = z$. In this case, the output is simply $O = W^T X$, i.e., the output is a linear combination of the input, hence the name. A linear associator is often used to map the input space to the output space. Given a set of input–output pairs $\langle X_i, D_i \rangle_{i=1}^{K}$ where K is the number of input–output pairs, X_i represents the ith pair of the given input vector, and D_i represents the corresponding output vector, the problem is to determine the weight matrix $W_{N \times M}$ such that the output of the linear associator is the same as the desired output.

7.3.3   Correlation Matrix Memory

Hebbian learning (also called correlation matrix memory) is an approach proposed by Hebb for determining the weights of a linear associator based on the principle of classical conditioning. In classical conditioning, an unconditioned stimulus (food) causes an unconditioned response (salivation) in a system (an animal). A conditioned stimulus (bell) originally causes no specific response. When the unconditioned stimulus and the conditioned stimulus are paired together, an association is made in the system such that after awhile the conditioned stimulus also elicits a conditioned response similar to the unconditioned response. Hebb postulated that the unconditioned response (neuronal output) causes an association (increases weights) to be formed with the input (unconditioned stimulus AND conditioned stimulus that was presented simultaneously). In other words, the excited output of a neurode strengthens the associated weights of the corresponding excited output. Mathematically speaking, this association can be written as the outer product of the input and output vector: $W = DX^T$. The correlation matrix memory can be summarized as follows:

Given $\langle X_i, D_i \rangle$

One-step training: $W = \Sigma_{i=1}^{K} DX^T$

One-step recall: $O = W^T X$

Hebbian learning provides a simple way to determine the weights. However it is of interest to find out how accurate is the prediction. The output O can be computed directly from the above equations.

$$O = W^T X = \Sigma_{i=1}^{K} DX^T X$$

$$= D(\Sigma_{i=1}^{2K} X^T X)$$

where the term in parentheses is simply a scalar. Clearly, the ability for perfect recall depends on the $\Sigma_{i=1}^{K} X^T X$ term. If this term yields the Kroneck delta, δ_{ij}, then the correct desired output vector D is fully recovered. If not, a residual results. In other words, the input vector X must be orthonormal. If X is orthogonal but is not of unit length, the output will be scaled. The correlation matrix approach is simple to apply, but perfect recall dictates that the input vectors must be orthonormal.

7.3.4   Pseudoinverse Memory

Another way to look at the problem is from the numerical analysis perspective. All the supplied input–output pairs can be written as a system of linear equations:

$$D_i = W^T X_i$$

There are $K \times M$ equations represented by the above matrix equations and $N \times M$ unknowns in the weight matrix. As long as K is larger than N, we have an overdetermined system of linear equations. In most cases, the number of given patterns is usually much greater than the dimension of the input vector. The application of the least-means-squares approach leads to the pseudoinverse solution of the above equation. Hence this is called the pseudoinverse approach. For this approach, define X as the input matrix and D as the desired output matrix. X and D are now in matrix form containing all the given data: $X \in \mathfrak{R}^{N \times K}$ and $D \in \mathfrak{R}^{M \times K}$.

Given $\langle X, D \rangle$

One-step training: $W = D(X^T X)^{-1} X^T$

One-step recall: $O = W^T X$

The pseudoinverse approach is also a single-step training procedure. While the approach seeks to minimize the total mean-square error, it does not allow the ability to fine tune the derived weight matrix.

7.3.5   Widrow–Hoff Approach

While the pseudoinverse approach is based on the mean-square-error principle, another approach, commonly known as the Widrow–Hoff equations, is based on the least-expected-error principle. Define the autocorrelation matrix R_{xx} and the crosscorrelation vector r_{xd} as below:

$$R_{xx} = E[XX^T]$$

$$R_{xd} = E[XD]$$

where $E[.]$ represents the expectation operator. By minimizing the expected square error, an expression for the weights can be found. The solution is commonly known as the Widrow–Hoff equation.

$$W = R_{xx}^{-1} r_{xd}$$

In summary,

Given $\langle X, D \rangle$

One-step training: $W = R_{xx}^{-1} r_{xd}$

One-step recall: $O = W^T X$

This approach is attractive because the weight matrix can be obtained in one step, similar to some of the other approaches discussed so far. Statistically speaking, the weight matrix thus obtained is optimal.

7.3.6   Least-Mean-Squares Approach

When the dimension of the input and output vectors become large, the dimension of the weight matrix also becomes corresponding large. Because of the matrix inversion operation, it becomes impractical to apply the Widrow–Hoff approach. Widrow has also developed an iterative method to adaptively determine the weight matrix using the principle of steepest descent. Instead of using the expected error, the algorithm uses the instantaneous error. Define the cost function to be the following:

$$\xi(W_t) = (1/2) (D_t - W_t O_t)^2$$

The weights can be determined by adjusting the weights in the direction of the negative gradient of the cost function.

Given $\langle X, D \rangle$

Initialization: W_0 = random

Multistep training: $\Delta W_t = \eta X_t \xi(W_t)^T$

One-step recall: $O = W^T X$

Note that while the training is multistep (iterative), the recall is still single-step. Widrow has shown that the LMS algorithm asymptotically converges to the Widrow–Hoff solution, i.e., the optimal solution. The LMS algorithm is attractive because it is simple to implement and is iterative. In some neural network literature, this approach is also known as the delta rule.

7.3.7   Adaptive Correlation Matrix Memory

Previously, it has been shown that the correlation matrix memory approach is a single-step training, single-step recall method and hence does not allow for fine tuning. This approach can be modified to so that the weights are adaptively obtained. The new approach is called the adaptive correlation matrix approach. The initial weights are set to zero at the beginning. Subsequent presentation of the input sample points causes the weights to settle adaptively on the best value for predicting the output.

Given $\langle X, D \rangle$

One-step initialization: $W_0 = 0$

Multistep training $\Delta W_t = \eta x_t d^T$

One-step recall: $O = W^T X$

This adaptive modification provides the ability for the algorithm to fine tune and obtain the best values for the weights according to the principle of Hebbian learning.

7.3.8   Error-Correcting Pseudoinverse Method

The same approach can also be applied to the pseudoinverse approach. Previously, it has been shown that the Correlation matrix memory approach is a single-step training, single-step recall method and hence does not allow for fine tuning. This approach has been further modified to allow fine tuning by adding an adaptive stage at the end. The new approach is called the error-correcting (or iterative) correlation matrix approach. After the initial weights are determined according to the correlation matrix approach, the weight matrix is further refined by iteratively correcting the parameters.

Given $\langle X, D \rangle$

One-step initialization: $W_0 = D(X^T X)^{-1} X^T$

Multistep training: $\Delta W_t = \eta X_t (O_t - W_t^T X)^T$

One-step recall: $O = W^T X$

The error-correcting pseudoinverse matrix approach allows the user a way to fine tune the weights so that the prediction can more closely approach the desired values.

7.4   SELF-ORGANIZING NETWORKS

In many practical applications, it is not unusual for the dimension of the input space to be large. Some parameters may be significant, while others may not. It is always of interest to determine which parameters play a more significant role than others in the input-output relationship. It is further of interest to find out if the given sample points can be modeled by a smaller number of parameters. In other words, the original space is called the data space and may be of high dimension composed of all the input parameters. We would like to find a mapping that would transform the sample points from the data space to the feature space. The feature space contains a small number of parameters, yet still contains all the essential characteristics originally contained in the data space. This is called data reduction.

Classification can be considered as data reduction. The original sample points in the data space are mapped into the feature space composed of the different classes. Regardless of the input dimension, the feature space is merely the class of the input space. The input space has been partitioned into distinct regions where each region represents one class. Specifying a data point to be in a particular class means that the data point possesses all the inherent characteristics related to that class as indicated by the centroid of the class. Deviations to the centroid are considered to be random perturbations and insignificant.

Modeling can also be thought of as data reduction. Given a set of sample points, the original data space is transformed into a set of parameters related to the underlying model. The parameters of the model summarize the characteristics of the underlying model dynamics. This approach is generally called parametric because, based on the specified functional form, the given sample points are modeled by specific values of the model parameters. In other words, the feature space is the collection of parameters. Parametric modeling has been widely used in many applications. The caveat in parametric modeling is that the specified functional form adequately describes the underlying model characteristics. For example, one can fit a straight line to data derived from a quadratic function. Likewise, the same data can also be fitted to a cubic. In general, the underlying model is unknown. The determination of the best model is a separate and nontrivial task in itself.

A more general approach than parametric modeling is nonparametric modeling. In the later case, no assumptions have been made regarding the functional form. An example of nonparametric modeling is the principal components approach.

7.4.1   Principal Components

Given a set of input sample points $x_i \in \Re^N$, the idea is to find a small set of exemplars that can be used to describe collectively most of the sample points. There are many numerical methods that can be used for this purpose. One such technique is the eigenvalue/eigenvector analysis. Define the input data matrix as $X = [x_1, x_2, \ldots, x_K]$ where $x_i \in \Re^N$. The dimension of X is therefore $N \times K$. Using the orthogonality transformation, the input matrix X can be decomposed into three matrices.

$$XU = U\Lambda$$

where U is an orthogonal matrix $U^{-1} = U^T$ and Λ is a diagonal matrix. The decomposition procedure is well understood and can be found in many numerical analysis texts.

The diagonal elements of the Λ matrix are called eigenvalues. Hence, $\Lambda = \text{diag}(\lambda_1, \lambda_2, \ldots \lambda_K)$. It is customary to arrange the eigenvalues in decreasing order $\lambda_1 > \lambda_2 > \ldots \lambda_K$. The eigenvalues in the Λ matrix are related to the variance or the "power" of the input data. The columns in the original U matrix are called eigenvectors: $U = [u_1, u_2, \ldots u_K]$ where $u_i \in \Re^N$. Eigenvectors are unit vectors that identify the basic characteristics of the input data in a nonparametric format. For this reason, eigenvectors are also called basis vectors.

From the U and Λ matrixes, the original matrix X can be fully recovered, rearranging the eigenvalue equation:

$$X = U\Lambda U^T$$

or written in terms of the eigenvalues and their corresponding eigenvectors:

$$X = \Sigma_{i=1}^K \lambda_i u_i u_i^T$$

In the above formulation, the eigenvectors form the basis of the feature space and the eigenvalues show the weightings of the individual contributions of the eigenvectors. Since the eigenvectors are unit vectors, their contribution is completely normalized. However, the relative importance of the eigenvectors is indicated by the corresponding eigenvalues. The larger the eigenvalue, the more the associated eigenvector contributes to explaining the variance of the input data. On the other hand, if the eigenvalue is small, then the corresponding eigenvector most likely models the random perturbations that exist in the input data.

Data reduction is achieved by realizing that not all the eigenvectors are needed in reconstructing the input data matrix. Only the significant eigenvectors with large eigenvalues are used. Define P as the number of significant eigenvalues to be used. Then the original data matrix can be recovered as follows:

$$X = \Sigma_{i=1}^P \lambda_i u_i u_i^T$$

The significant eigenvalues and their associated eigenvector is called principal components. Since each eigenvector is orthogonal to all the others, the principal components are independent of one another. Hence the principal components show the degree of independent processes that exist in the underlying model dynamics.

7.4.2   Clustering by Hebbian Learning

Suppose a set of input sample points is given. Note that no output values are given or needed at this point. It is of interest to define a model that would adequately describe the input data space. This is in essence the clustering problem. Without explicitly indicating which sample point belongs to which class, the problem at hand is to find out the number of clusters and the corresponding centroid locations of the clusters.

In the study of linear associators, the method of adaptive Hebbian learning has been presented as an effective way to determine the weights in an iterative manner. Consider a single neurode with input vector x_t, scalar output y, and time index t. Repeating the update equation for the weight vector W_t at time index t for the adaptive correlational matrix memory approach for a single neurode, it is reasoned that the same process can be used to form clusters. This is done by replacing the desired output with the actual neurode output.

$$W_{t+1} = W_t + \eta x_t y^T$$

Beginning with initial random weights, the update equations iteratively enforce those weights that produce an output.

One major problem with the above update equation is that the weights can grow unchecked and unbounded. The more the input patterns are presented, the more the outer product adds to the weights. For this reason, this approach has not been in widespread use.

7.4.3   Clustering by Oja's Normalization

In an effort to curb the unboundedness of the weights, Oja proposed to normalize the weights after each weight update. In other words, the relative importance of each weight is redistributed among all the weights.

$$W_{t+1} = (W_t + \eta x_t y)/\text{sqrt}(\Sigma(W_t + \eta x_t y)^2)$$

The summation term gives the power (squared value) of all the weights. The weights are therefore normalized by the square root of the total weight power. This in essence causes the weights to be bounded in magnitude.

A first-order approximation of Oja's normalization is obtained by replacing the square root operation with the first-order series expression for a square root.

$$W_{t+1} = W_t + \eta y(x_t - yW_t) + O(\eta^2)$$

Notice that in the above equation there is positive feedback to increase the weights for self-amplification. However, at the same time, there is also negative feedback to control the growth of the weights.

Oja's extension to the weight update equation results in some very interesting properties. Taking expectations on both sides of the equation, convergence is obtained when the update is zero, i.e., $\lim(t \to \infty) E[W_{t+1}] = E[W_t]$. When convergence condition is reached, it can be shown that W_t converges to the largest eigenvector of data-correlation matrix.

$$\lim_{t \to \infty} E[W_t] = u_1$$

where u_1 is the largest eigenvector of $R = E[XX^T]$. This implies that repeated presentation to a neural network that updates according to Oja's extension eventually causes the weights to converge automatically to the largest eigenvector.

The other eigenvector can be obtained by Hotelling's deflation. By deleting the contribution of the most significant eigenvector, a new data set can be formed so that the same technique can again be applied, thus causing the algorithm to converge subsequently to the next-largest eigenvector. If the first neurode has already converged to the largest eigenvector, then based on the Hotelling's deflation principle, a new data set can be formed by subtracting the effects of this eigenvector. In summary, the generalized Hebbian algorithm (GHA) is given below.

Neurode output:	$y = W^T x$
Weight update:	$W_{t+1} = W_t + \eta y(x_t' - yW_t)$
For the first neurode:	$x' = x$
For the second neurode:	$x' = x - w_1 y_1$
For the third neurode:	$x' = x - w_1 y_1 - w_2 y_2$

Note that for the first neurode, the input is the same as the original data input $x_1 = x$. For the second neurode, the modified input is

$$x_2 = x - w_1 y_1$$

$$y_2 = w_2 x_2 = w_2(x - w_1 y_1)$$

$$= w_2 x - w_2 w_1 y_1$$

The first term in the above expression is simply the weights of the second neurode applied to the original input. The second term in the above expression is an added term stemming from the output (y_1) of the first neurode. This can be implemented by a direct lateral connection from the output of the first neurode to the input of the second neurode. Likewise for the third neurode, rearranging the modified input of the third neurode means there is a lateral connection from the output of the first and second neurode to the input of the third neurode. Architecturally speaking, this is shown in Figure 7.4.

Oja's extension shows that a two-layer network can be used to classify the input data space automatically into distinct clusters merely by presentation of the input patterns themselves. This is done by the addition of lateral connections at the output layer. In addition, for the algorithm to work, the convergence of the second and subsequent neurodes should be withheld until the

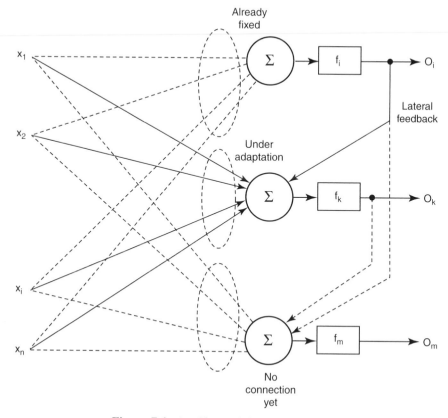

Figure 7.4. A self-organizing PCA network.

first neurode has converged. Then the weights for the second neurode are allowed to converge, and likewise for the subsequent neurodes in order.

7.4.4 Competitive Learning Network

The architecture for a competitive learning network, shown in Figure 7.5, is similar to that of an SLP. There are no explicit connections between the neurodes at the output layer. However, the output of all the neurodes at the output layer must be considered together during the weight update process.

The operation of a competitive learning network is essentially the same as that of an SLP, with one important distinction: not all the weights are allowed to be updated. When a pattern is presented to the network, all output neurodes examine and process the input pattern. Each output neurode generates an output. All neurode outputs are then compared and a winner is selected based on the largest neurode output. The winning neurode is then allowed to update its weights, while the weights of all other neurodes remain the same. Hence

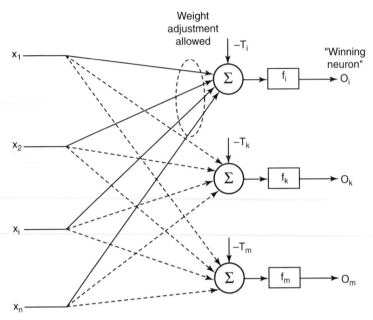

Figure 7.5. A competitive learning network.

this is called a winner-takes-all strategy. Only the winning neurode has the privilege of being updated. The competitive learning network is also called a Kohonen network.

Given the input sample points x_i, $i = 1, \ldots, p$ where each $x_i \in \mathfrak{R}^N$. The neurode output is as usual a nonlinear transformation of the linear combiner, $y = f[Wx]$.

Initial weights:	$w^0 = $ random
Training:	Select w_m such that $\| x - w_m \| \leq \| x - w_i \|$
	m is the winning neurode
Update weights:	$w_m^{t+1} = w_m^t + \alpha(x - w_m^t)$ for the winning neurode
	$w_i^{t+1} = w_i^t,\ i \neq m$ for other neurodes

The update equation causes the weight of the winning neurode to be more and more like the input pattern. If more than one sample point is selected by the neurode, the weights of the neurode tend to settle on the centroid of the sample points. In other words, the weights of the competitive networks yield the centroid location of the clusters. Each active neurode depicts a cluster and serves to represent the location of the associated cluster.

In summary, self-organizing networks such as PCA networks or competitive learning networks are SLPs with special training procedures. Because of

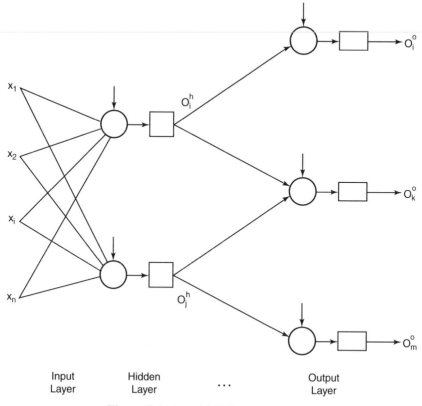

Figure 7.6. A multiple-layer perceptron.

the special process involved, these networks have been shown to be useful in automatically discovering clusters in the data space.

7.5   MULTIPLE-LAYER FEEDFORWARD NETWORK

7.5.1   Multiple-Layer Perceptron

While a single-layer feedforward network is able to map a multidimensional input space to a multidimensional output space, each output is basically independent of the others. A multiple-layer perceptron (MLP) is formed by putting more than one layer together. An MLP is particularly attractive because the additional layers allow the results of one layer to be further processed, arranged, and put together to make a complex system, as shown in Figure 7.6.

Recall that a single neurode basically creates a hyperline in the input space. An SLP therefore is equivalent to a set of hyperlines placed in the same input space working in parallel, each hyperline for a corresponding output neurode.

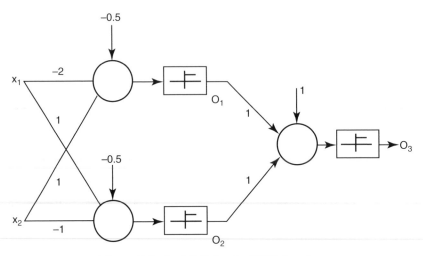

Figure 7.7. An MLP for the XOR function.

In order to correlate the different hyperlines together, thus creating multiple intersecting regions, additional layers are required. The first layer creates a set of hyperlines, and the second layer relates the hyperlines together to form a contiguous hyperregions. Since there can be any number of hyperlines, it is therefore possible to approximate the shape of any hyperregions in a piecewise manner.

While two layers are needed to join separate hyperlines together to form a hyperregion, another layer is needed to join multiple disparate hyperregions together into a single class. The third layer allows multiple hyperregions distributed anywhere in the input space to be related together. Hence it is commonly accepted that a three-layer feedforward neural network is capable of realizing any function for this reason.

7.5.2   XOR Example

As an example, consider a two-layer network for the exclusive-OR (XOR) function. An XOR function has two inputs, x and y, and a single output. The inputs and the outputs are discrete, taking on values of 0 and 1. When the inputs are distinct, the output is 1. When the input is the same, the output is 0. Figure 7.7 presents an MLP for the XOR function.

The XOR function can be solved using two McCulloch–Pitts neurodes in the first layer and a single McCulloch–Pitts neurode in the output. There are two input neurodes because there are two inputs. A single-output neurode suffices in the second layer since there is only a single-output variable. Each of the two neurodes in the first layer produces a line in the input space as shown. Note that the positive decision region for the first neurode is to the left of the line while that for the second neurode is to the right of the line. So doing means that the input for $\langle x,y \rangle = \langle 0,0 \rangle$ and $\langle 1,1 \rangle$ are left in the same region, hence producing the same output results.

7.5.3   Back-Error Propagation

While the MLP has the potential to approximate any function, the network can only be practically used if there exists a way to determine the weights that would approximate the desired function. Given a set of input–output pairs, it is highly desirable to be able to determine the weights directly from the given data. This problem has been solved using the generalized delta rule. The use of this rule has greatly enhanced the usage of neural networks, and there are many reports in the literature of the rule being applied successfully to solve many practical problems.

The basic idea of training a multiple-layer feedforward neural network is to generalize the delta rule for each weight. The delta rule requires the computation of the derivative of the error with respect to the weight of interest. This can be done by repeatedly applying the chain rule. In some literature, the generalized delta rule is also known as the back-error propagation method.

Given a set of input–output pairs $\langle X,D \rangle$ and a neural network with more than one layers, the problem at hand is to find the weights of the neurodes for each layer. In the previous section, the delta rule has been presented for a single-layer perceptron. The same notion can be extended to multiple layers. First, consider the output layer. Since each output neurode is independent of the others, the adaptation for each neurode in the output layer is the same. The output of the jth neurode in the output layer is obtained from the associated inputs to that neurode:

$$o_j^o = f(Wx)$$

The superscript o denotes the output layer. Since this is the output layer, the desired output is available and in fact given. Hence a cost function can be defined as the squared output error:

$$E = \Sigma(d - o_j^o)^2$$

The weights to the jth neurode can immediately be determined by finding the gradient of the squared error according to the weight of interest, denoted as:

$$\nabla w_{ij}(E)$$

The weight update equation is derived from the negative gradient and can be written as follows.

$$\Delta w_{ij}{}^o = -\eta \nabla w_{ij}(E)$$

where $\eta > 0$ is the step size or learning constant and is a small positive constant. If the "error" of the output neurodes is defined as

$$\delta_{oj} = (d_k - o_j{}^o)o_j{}^o \; f'(Wx)$$

the weight update equations for the output layer can be rewritten as:

$$\Delta w_i = \eta \; \delta_{oj} y_i$$

The update equation is obtained by repeatedly applying the chain rule to the cost function. Note that the update equation is applicable for an arbitrary activation function. The effects of the activation function is accounted for by the $f'(\text{net})$ term in the partial derivatives.

For neurodes in the hidden layer, the output of the neurodes is not directly given. However, with the use of the chain rule, the "desired" output can still be inferred. Beginning with the squared error at the output layer again, the weight update equation for the hidden layers can be rewritten as:

$$\Delta w_i = \eta \; \delta_{yj} z_i$$

In summary, the generalized delta rule can be extended to an arbitrary number of layers in the MLP. The activation function is arbitrary for any neurode in any layer. The connectivity pattern can also be arbitrary. In other words, the network designed can trim the network and specifically allow or disallow connections to be made. Furthermore, there can also be fixed weights in the connectivity pattern. Those weights that are supposed to be fixed are simply never updated. Those connections that are not supposed to exist simply take on zero weight values. The generalized delta rule is able to work with an arbitrary architecture of the neural network and under a variety of constraints. Because of such flexibility, the generalized delta rule has been commonly used for many neural network applications.

7.5.4   Variations in the Back-Error Propagation Algorithm

Because of its importance and widespread acceptance, the generalized delta rule has been a subject of intense study. There are many variations to the basic generalized delta rule reported in he literature. Some of these variations are presented here.

One variation deals with the definition of the error. The original definition is called the single-pattern error:

$$E = (1/2) \Sigma_{k=1}{}^K \{d_k - f[\text{net}(y_k)]\}^2$$

In this approach, the error is defined to be the error for each input pattern and to update the weight matrix after the presentation of each input pattern. This definition is straightforward but tends to be computationally intensive because all the weights have to be updated after each successive presentation of the input patterns. Due to the order of the presented patterns, it has been observed that sometimes the values of some of weights oscillate back and forth. Some patterns tend to pull the weights one way, while other patterns tend to pull the same weight in the opposite direction.

Since the oscillatory behavior partially comes from the order of the input patterns, one approach is to randomize the input pattern order. Define an epoch as a complete cycle of presenting all the input patterns once. The random approach dictates that the order of presenting the patterns is random in each epoch. This approach tends to minimize the oscillatory behavior, thus speeding up the convergence rate in many cases. However, this approach is still computationally intensive since the weights are still updated upon each presentation of the input pattern. In order to reduce the computational load, another approach is to eliminate the oscillatory behavior in the weight adaptation process. Hence, the weights are updated only after all the patterns are presented. This is called the cumulative error approach.

$$E = (1/2) \sum_{p=1}^{P} \sum_{k=1}^{K} (d_{pk} - o_{pk})^2$$

Instead of the error being used in one pattern and the weights updated immediately, all the patterns are presented first and the weights are updated according to the cumulative error.

The previous approach relies on the square of the error. This means that large errors tend to dominate the adaptation process. One proposal is to normalized the cumulative error so that the square root of the cumulative error is used.

$$E = (1/pk) \sqrt{\{\sum_{p=1}^{P} \sum_{k=1}^{K} (d_{pk} - o_{pk})^2\}}$$

Another approach is to simply used the absolute value of the error, commonly known as the L_1 norm instead of the Euclidean norm or the L_2 norm.

For classification, it is the number of wrong classifications that is important. Hence, this is called the classification approach.

$$E = N_{err}/pk$$

The actual deviations of the error values are of less importance. If the prediction is in error, then it is in error. How much in error is irrelevant.

7.5.5   Learning Rate and Momentum

The convergence rate of the update process is governed by the step size η, sometimes known as the learning constant. If η is small, then convergence is slow because the weights are updated by small increments. On the other hand, if η is large, then convergence is rapid because each update to the weight moves the weight a significant amount. However, if η is too large, then overshoot of the parameter values often, occurs causing oscillatory behavior. This leads to slow convergence again. In some cases, overshoots may also to divergence.

From the standpoint of accuracy in estimation of the weight values, if η is small, then more accurate estimation is obtained because each update can only move the weight a small amount, resulting in the weight not being able to wander around the target point. On the other hand, if η is large, then the weight estimation is less accurate because the weight value can wander farther from the ideal location.

The proper setting of the learning constant is very crucial. When the input data are known, it is possible to determine what the upper bound on η is. The optimal value must lie between 0 and the maximum value. Some researchers propose a learning schedule where the learning constant starts at a maximum value and gradually decreases in value as the iteration progresses.

In general, the convergence rate of the generalized delta rule is slow. To speed up the convergence, a momentum term is sometimes used.

$$\Delta w(t) = -\eta \, \nabla E(t) + \alpha \, \Delta w(t - 1)$$

The first term on the right-hand side is the usual gradient term controlled by the step size η. The second term on the right-hand side is called momentum term and is dependent on the previous change. If the current change in the specific weight in question has the same sign as the previous change, then the momentum term enhances the change. This extra enhancement can be exponentially increasing when the requested change in the gradient is the same sign for consecutive steps.

The inclusion of the momentum term in the update equation makes the update itself an autoregressive process. This process can be unraveled into a series representation.

$$\Delta w(t) = -\eta \, \Sigma_{n=0}^{N} \, \alpha^n \, \nabla E(t - n)$$

In other words, the momentum allows the gradient at a particular step to influence the updates for later steps. The use of the momentum generally increases the convergence rate of the adaptation. The amount of momentum to be added is controlled by a positive constant $\alpha > 0$. However, care should be exercised in setting the values for α because too large a value may cause unnecessary oscillations in the update process.

There is a delicate balance between the choice of η and α because the two parameters are not independent from one another. In many applications, even the momentum term is on a schedule.

7.5.6 Other Back-Error Propagation Issues

In the generalized delta rule, the algorithm has been shown to converge regardless of the initial values of the weights. However, the choice of the initial values of the weights does affect the convergence rate. It is obvious that if the values of the initial weights are close to the optimal values, the convergence will be rapid. On the other hand, if the initial weights are far from the optimal values, then the convergence depends on the value of the learning constant and the momentum constant.

While the back-error propagation algorithm is able to determine the values of the weights in a neural network, the algorithm does not leave any hints as to the proper architecture of the neural network. The architecture of the neural network must be determined *a priori*.

When speaking about the architecture of a neural network, a user must determine the number of layers, and the number of neurodes to use in each layer. In terms of the input layer, the input dimension is usually dictated by the application. Likewise for the output layer, the output dimension represents the number of categories or classifications required for the problem. Hence the output dimension is usually also dictated by the problem. As for the hidden layer, it is not easy to determine the appropriate number of neurodes. The general rule of thumb is to start with a large number and prune afterwards, or to start with a small number and slowly increase.

7.5.7 Counterpropagation Network

In previous sections, a single layer of competitive learning network was used to automatically "discover" the clusters inherent in the input data. Quite often it is highly desirable to label the classes or to combine the classes into a single class. This can be done by adding a special output layer after the competitive learning layer. An architecture of the combined network is shown in Figure 7.8.

There are two layers in the network. The first layer is the Kohonen network with competitive learning strategy. The purpose of this layer of the network is to automatically and adaptively locates the clusters in the input data space. The second layer is the counterpropagation network, sometimes called the outstar or the Grossberg layer. The purpose of this network is primarily to combine clusters found in the first layer and to label the clusters in the desired output.

The training of the first layer was presented in earlier sections. Once the clusters are found, one of the neurodes in the Kohonen layer will be active upon presentation of a particular input sample data. Since the initial weights are random, which neurode will respond to the particular input sample is also random even though only one of the neurodes will be active. Hence the output of the first layer can be considered as a permutation vector where all elements of the vector are zero except one.

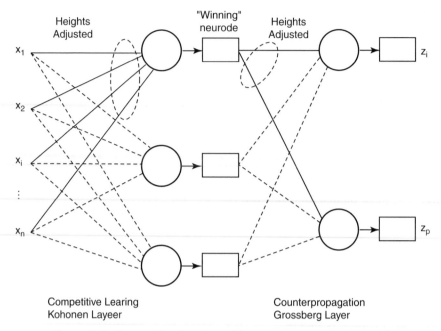

Figure 7.8. Competitive learning with counterpropagation network.

The addition of the second layer allows the network to manipulate the permutation vector. To combine clusters into a single class, a connection can be made from the output of the first layer to the input of the same neurode on the output layer. To label a particular class with a specific output pattern, simply use the weights of the second layer to generate the desired results. In other words, the weights of the second layer are trained according to the desired output. At this phase of the training, a sample pattern is presented to the first layer of the network. It is assumed that the Kohonen layer has already been trained. Therefore the weights are fixed. The presentation of a pattern causes one of the neurodes in the first layer to become active while all the outputs of all the rest of the neurodes are zero. The single activated neurode is connected to every neurode of the output layer in a star configuration. Hence it is called an outstar. Typically the activation function of the output layer is taken to be a linear ramp function. The weights of the activated neurode can now be trained. In fact, the weight is simply the desired output.

7.6   RADIAL BASIS NETWORKS

One of the primary uses of back-error propagation is modeling. Given samples of the input and output pairs, the neural network finds the proper transformation so that the input space can be properly and accurately mapped to the output space. The mapping can also be thought as function approximation. The transformation is the function that must be approximated from a set of given samples.

Function approximation can be accomplished in two ways: finding a suitable function or interpolating. In the first method, the goal is identify a function and estimate the parameters of that function so that the output of the function adequately produces the expected output values. Many techniques have been developed in this direction. Most involve the user finding the form of the function and the algorithm determining the best parameter values. Hence the problem becomes a parameter-estimation problem.

While interpolation is often less thought of as function approximation, from another perspective it is in fact a function used for approximation. The former method is called parametric approximation because the function is fixed, and only the parameters are varied to fit the application. The latter method is called nonparametric approximation because there is no specified form to the function and the form of the function varies with the number of data points used.

7.6.1 Interpolation

To highlight the similarity of neural networks with interpolating functions, this section reviews some of the interpolation methods, in particular the nearest neighbor interpolation, the Lagrange interpolation, and the spline interpolation.

In the nearest neighbor interpolation method, the closest neighbors to the unknown input point are selected. The function values of the unknown input point are then calculated in proportion to the selected points that are closest to the unknown point. Mathematically, the interpolated value is calculated as follows:

$$y = \Sigma_{j=0}^{n} d_j \, f_j(x, x_j)$$

The method works reasonably well and requires no training. However, the closest points must be determined before the interpolation formula is applied.

In the Lagrange interpolation, the interpolation is carried out by defining the Lagrange function. The form of the Lagrange function is predetermined and is formed from the given points. There is no need to select points for the interpolation as all sample points are used in the function.

$$L(x) = (\Pi_{l=0, i \neq j}^{n} (x - x_i)) / (\Pi_{l=0, i \neq j}^{n} (x_j - x_i))$$

$$y = \Sigma_{j=0}^{n} f(x_j) \, P_j(x)$$

In essence, the Lagrange function is the interpolating function used to approximate the model. What is so powerful about Lagrange interpolation is that the interpolating function changes according to the unknown input. This is in contrast to many function approximation methods including the MLP, where one function is used to approximate the entire range of the input data.

In the Lagrange interpolation, the interpolated values at the given sample points are guaranteed to take on the given function values. The interpolating function is therefore continuous. This is also the case for the nearest neighbor approach; however, the derivatives are not continuous for the sample points. In the spline interpolation approach, the algorithm is designed in such a way that the derivatives at the sample points are also continuous.

7.6.2   Radial Basis Network

The derivation of the radial basis network is based on the principle of a regularizing network. While for a typical neural network the goal is to minimize the cost function, here the cost function is usually taken to be the square error. For a regularizing network, an additional term, called the regularizing term, is added.

$$E(F) = (1/2) \sum_{i=1}^{N} (d_i - F(x_i))^2 + \lambda \xi(\|DF\|^2)$$

The object is to find a function (F) such that the cost function is minimized. The cost function is composed of two terms. The first term is the standard error term. The second term is the regularizing term, based on some operation (D) that is related to the derivative of the function sought. Note that when λ goes to zero, the cost function degenerates to the standard cost function. Including the regularizing term allows the smoothness of the interpolating function can be controlled because the regularizing term is related to the derivatives of the function.

Poggio has shown that the solution to minimizing such a cost function lies in the use of Green's functions. The form of the solution function can be shown to be:

$$F_\lambda(x) = (1/\lambda) \sum_{i=1}^{N} (d_i - F(x_i))G(x,x_i)$$

where $G(x,x_i)$ represents a properly chosen Green's function, x is the unknown input, and x_i is the given sample points. The Green's function is similar in function to the Lagrange interpolating functions. In both cases the function is dependent on the sample points. Also, the value of the Green's function is dependent on the distance measure between the unknown input point and the sample point, i.e., the L_2 norm: $\|x - x_i\|^2$.

Note that the left part of the above function is constant and is dependent only on the sample points. Define this part as w_i and rewriting the solution function, we have:

$$F_\lambda(x) = \Sigma_{i=1}^N w_i G(x, x_i)$$

The above formulation bears tremendous resemblance to the two-layer neural network presented so far. The first layer of the network implements the Green's function while the second layer of the network, the output layer, implements the above solution. In other words, w_i is the weights for the output neurode.

Formally, a radial basis function (RBF) network is a neural network composed of two layers, the RBF layer and the encoding layer. Each neurode in the RBF layer is formed from a given sample point. The output of the neurode in the RBG layer is the Green's function. The sample points acts as a center. The unknown point is compared to the center and the value of the neurode diminishes as the unknown point moves farther away from the center, the sample point. This behavior is similar to the inverse of the Euclidean distance. In most cases, the Euclidean distance is radially symmetric, hence the name. A number of Green's functions have been proposed in the literature. Some of the more commonly used Green's functions are:

Inverse quadrics: $f(x) = 1/(x^2 + \sigma^2)a,\, a > 0$

Quadrics: $f(x) = (x^2 + \sigma^2)b,\, 0 < b < 1$

Gaussian: $f(x) = \exp(-(x^2/2\sigma^2))$

Spline: $f(x) = x^2 \ln(x)$

Cubic: $f(x) = x^3$

The neurodes in the second layer simply serve to implement the weights needed to relate all the RBF outputs together. This is similar to the interpolating function, where the contribution of each of the centers is weighted. Compared to Lagrange interpolation, the Green's function is comparable to the Lagrange function and the weights are the function values of the sample points.

In summary, the neurodes in the two layers of a RBF network can be described as follows:

First layer: $G(\|x - x_i\|) = \exp(-\|x - x_i\|^2)$

Second layer: $y = \Sigma_{j=1}^m w_i\, G(\|x - x_i\|) + b$

The output neurode can be augmented to include the bias. Define $G' = [G\ 1]$ and $W' = [W\ b]^T$. Then

$$y = W^T G$$

Note that the second layer is merely a linear combiner. The first layer transforms the input into a different space analogous to the inverse distance measure.

From a slightly different perspective, the determination of the weights and other parameters of the RBFs is a parameter-estimation problem. The only difference between an RBF network and an MLP is that we are now stipulating specific functional characteristics for the neurodes in the first layer. Instead of using the typical neurode (a linear combiner with a non-linear transformation) as the first layer, we are now using the RBF neurodes. The second layer in both cases remains the same. For the MLP, the network parameters, namely the weights, are obtained by the generalized delta rule, which stems from the successive application of the chain rule. While the functional form for the first layer may have been changed, the same procedure can still be applied.

So far, the RBF network is constructed with each RBF neurode corresponding to each given sample point. When the number of given sample points is large, a large RBF network naturally results. It is of interest, of course, to trim the network to a smaller size than the original. One way to do so is to use representative sample points instead of all the sample points. In other words, if clusters can be found a priori, then the location of the center or centroid of the clusters can be used instead of all the sample points in the cluster. This approach, however, adds an additional step in the analysis as the user must first determine the number and location of the clusters before applying the RBF network for modeling.

Another approach is to apply the generalized delta rule to the RBF network. For the first layer, the parameters to be estimated are the location x_i and the spread of the centers C. For the output layer, the parameters are of course the weights.

First Layer: $\phi_C(\|x - x_i\|) = \exp(-(x - x_i)C^{-1}C(x - x_i))$

Second layer: $y = \Sigma_{j=0}^m w_i\, \phi_C(\|x - x_i\|)$

Using the method of steepest descent, the parameters of the RBF layer and the output layer can be found using the delta rule. The derivation has been omitted here but can be found in the references.

$$\Delta w_i = -\eta_1 \nabla_w E$$

$$\Delta t_i = -\eta_2 \nabla_t E$$

$$\Delta C_i^{-1} = -\eta_3 \nabla_\Sigma E$$

The adaptation process now carries out the two tasks: finding the clusters and estimating the parameters of the clusters.

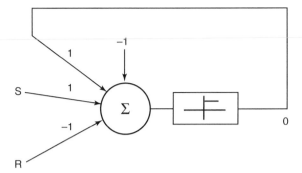

Figure 7.9. A McCulloch–Pitts neurode as an SR flip-flop.

For categorical data, the location of clusters provides an efficient way to summarize the data. For noncategorical data, a large number of clusters is required. For example, the approximation of a straight line will require a number of centers spaced throughout the line so that the approximation can be kept within the desired accuracy.

7.7   SINGLE-LAYER FEEDBACK NETWORK

In an earlier section, a single feedforward neurode has been shown to simulate the operation of many combination circuit components. In digital logic, combinational circuits are formed entirely from feedforward circuits. Another major area of digital logic is sequential circuit. The basic building block in sequential circuit is a flip-flop. A flip-flop is composed with all combinational circuit components but is connected together with feedback. The feedback allows the flip-flop to remember previous information. Using flip-flops and other combinational circuit components, a sequential circuit is built that can remember information. A flip-flop stores a single bit of information. A shift register remembers a word.

If the output of a McCulloch–Pitts neurode is fed back as one of the inputs, then the neurode behaves like a flip-flop. Let $X = [T,s,r,o]$, where o is the neuronal output fed back to itself after passing through a delay element, and let $W = [\ \ ]$, then the McCulloch–Pitts neurode behaves as an S-R flip-flop. Figure 7.9 shows a McCulloch–Pitts SR flip–flop. In other words, when SR = 00, the flip-flop output remains as is. If the previous output is 0, the next output is 0. If the previous output is 1, then the next output is 1. However, if the SR input is 10, then regardless of the previous output, the next output is 1. Likewise, if the SR input is 01, then regardless of the previous output, the next output is 0. This also implies that all sequential circuit elements can be replaced by McCulloch–Pitts neurodes, hence a neural network.

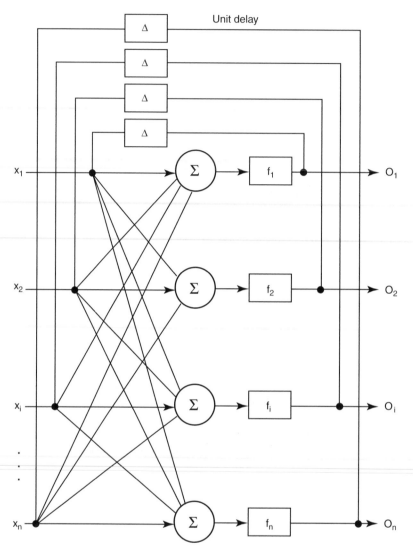

Figure 7.10. A single-layer feedback network.

7.7.1 Single-Layer Feedback Network

In a single-layer feedback network, the delayed output of each neurode is connected to the input of every other neurode except itself. In other words, there is no self-excitation. The architecture of such a network is shown in Figure 7.10.

The network is initialized by the input X producing an initial output. Once the network has been initialized, the network continues to update itself because the output is fed back to itself. The network will continue to change until the delayed output produces the exact same output. The network is then said to be in equilibrium.

A feedback network is called a dynamic system. For a feedforward network, the output is always just a combination of the inputs and does not change according to time as long as the input remains the same. For a feedback network, the input only initializes the network. Once initialized, the network output will continue to change. Depending on the system characteristics of the network, a dynamic system could continue to change or stabilize at an equilibrium point. In some cases, a dynamic system may diverge, causing the output to grow unbounded. This usually happens when there is positive feedback. It is also possible for the system output to oscillate. This is called a limit cycle. The system neither converges nor diverges. The desirable case occurs, of course, when the dynamical system converges to equilibrium, i.e., a stable point.

For a dynamic system, there is a notion of an energy state related to the state of the network. The motion of a dynamic system is always towards the low energy state.

7.7.2 A Discrete Single-Layer Feedback Network

A discrete feedback network is formed when the activation of the neurodes is discrete. The feedback network is shown with McCulloch–Pitts neurode. The network is initially started with the input i. This causes an initial output.

$$y_0 = \text{sgn}(Wi - b)$$

Note that the bias b can be incorporated as part of the input as before. After the initial presentation of the input, the pattern is then removed and the output of the network is fed back to the input after a unit time delay.

$$y_{t+1} = \text{sgn}(Wy_t - b)$$

The state of the network is indicated by the energy level of the network and is defined as follows:

$$E = (-1/2)y^T Wy - i^T y + b^T y$$

The energy level is a function of the current output of the neurodes and the weights. Hence there is an energy level associated with the network at any time.

Since the network is dynamic, the training procedure is not so easy. Given a set of P input data sample points $X = \{x_i\}$ where $i = 1, \ldots, P$. In the training process, the idea is to adjust the weights so that given one of the input sample point as input to the network, the network produces the same output as the input. This is done with no self-excitation. In other words, there are no inconsistencies between the input and the output, a condition for stability. During the training process, the input sample is left at the input. The weights are then adjusted until the output equals the input

$$W_0 = XX^T$$

$$W_{t+1} = W_t + \mu\Delta E$$

The weights are adjusted so that when the same pattern is presented at the input, there are no further inconsistencies in the network and the network gives the same pattern as output. At this point the network is said to have been trained for that pattern. It is possible for a network to be trained to remember more than one input pattern. This can be achieved by repeatedly training each pattern in turn.

It can be shown that for a dynamic system, as the network changes, each change tends to cause the network to settle towards a lower energy state than before.

net_i	v_I^k	v_I^{k+1}	Δv_i	$net_i\Delta v_i$
>0	1	1	0	0
	−1	1	2	>0
<0	1	−1	−2	>0
	−1	−1	0	0

The above table shows that each change in the network output will always cause the energy to decrease or remain as is. In other words, the energy is nonincreasing since the change in energy is always negative or zero.

During recall, the weights are fixed. When the network is initialized by an unknown input pattern, the initial output is fed back to the input and the network successively adjusts its output in response to changes in its own output.

$$y = f(W^T X)$$

In summary, both the training and the recall for a single-layer feedback network are multistep. This is characteristic of a feedback network.

> Given $\langle X \rangle$
>
> Multistep training: $W_{t+1} = W_t + \mu\Delta E$
>
> Multistep recall: $O = W^T X$

Once the network has been trained, the trained samples can be retrieved.

When a new pattern is introduced at the output, the network immediately attempts to produce an output. If the input pattern is one of the trained patterns, the trained weights cause the network to produce an output that is consistent with the network. No further changes are produced. If the input pattern is not one of the trained patterns, then the network output is fed back to the input, causing the network to change. Since every change of the network will cause the network state to go towards a low-energy state, the network will eventually settle on one of the trained patterns as each of the trained patterns represents a low-energy state. Hence, a discrete single-layer feedback network is sometimes called a content-addressable memory. This means that the stored memory can be retrieved by supplying part of the desired memory. To retrieve one of the stored patterns, only part of the stored patterns is required to initialize the network. Based on the partial input, the network proceeds to gravitate towards the lowest energy state of one of the stored patterns and thus regenerate in the process the complete stored pattern at its output.

Content addressable memory can be used in a number of ways. One possible application is pattern recognition. A stored pattern contains both the pattern and the key for the class of the pattern. When an unknown pattern is presented to the network, the corresponding key according to the stored pattern is retrieved or regenerated by the network. In other words, the pattern has been recognized. Another application is image restoration. When a noisy pattern is presented to the network, the noisy pattern is gradually replaced by the stored pattern, thus "cleaning up" or restoring the image.

7.7.3   Bidirectional Associative Memory

A bidirectional associative memory (BAM) is a special case of a feedback network. Normally, the output of a neurode is fed back to the input of every neurode. In a BAM network, the single layer of neurodes is divided into two sections, with the output of the neurodes form one section connected to all the neurode inputs in the other section and vice versa. In other words, instead of building the correlation through the weights between every input pixels with every other input pixels, the correlation here is built between the neurodes in one section with the neurodes from the other section. The architecture of a BAM network is shown in Figure 7.11.

As an associative memory, one section of the network can contain the data while the other section of the network contains the key of the associated data. When the data are presented to one section of the network, the key is regenerated by the other section of the network. Likewise, when the key is presented to the other side of the network, the data are regenerated by the key on the other side of the network. Likewise, the BAM network can also be used for pattern recognition. The network is initially trained with the patterns and the associated class label. When an unknown pattern is presented to the

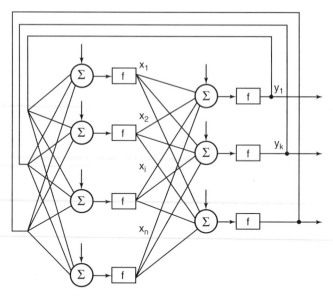

Figure 7.11. A bidirectional associative memory network.

network, the key associated with the closest stored pattern is regenerated on the other section.

7.7.4 Hopfield Network

Based on the properties of an electronic circuit arrangement, Hopfield proposed a feedback network as shown in Figure 7.12.

The Hopfield network is analogous to a single-layer feedback network. In Hopfield's original formulation, the network is composed of electronic components. A neurode is simulated by an operational amplifier. The input of the operational amplifier is a current sum. The currents are generated as a result of all the outputs of the amplifiers through current-limiting resistors. These resistors are analogous to the weights of a neural network. Hence the operational amplifier is in essence a linear combiner with input weights connected to the output of the other neurodes. Note that the input of the operational amplifier is also connected to a parallel resistive-capacitive network. The inclusion of the capacitor, a nonlinear component, provides the simulation of a nonlinear activation function.

The behavior of the circuit can be described according to the voltage and current relationship. With the components connected as shown, the nodal equation can be written at the input of the operational amplifier.

$$du_i/dt = (1/C_i) \, [\Sigma_{j=0}{}^n \, w_{ij}v_j - u_i(\Sigma_{j=0}{}^n \, w_{ij} + g_i) + i_i]$$

The nodal equation is called an equation of motion because it dictates how

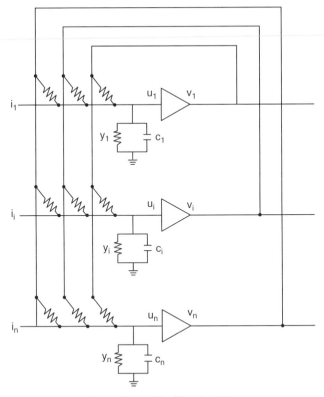

Figure 7.12. The Hopfield Net.

the neurode output, the voltage level, changes as a function of time. Hopfield has also shown that the energy function related to the network is a Lyapunov function and can be written as follows:

$$E(v) = (-1/2)v^T W v - I^T v + \Sigma_{i=0}^{n} (1/R_i) \int_0^{vi} f^{-1}(z)\, dz$$

The energy function defined above has been shown to be the Lyapunov function for the network. Note that the Lyapunov energy function and the equation of motion go in pairs because the Lyapunov function is not unique.

One of the major applications of the Hopfield net is optimization. Hopfield originally proposed the use of the network to solve the traveling salesman problem (TSP). The TSP is an NP-complete problem. It can be stated as follows: Given the location of N cities, find the shortest path that connects all the cities and returns to the originating city. All the cities must be visited once and once only.

The solution to the TSP and for any other optimization problems is first to define the objective function to be minimized. Since the Hopfield net tends to move towards a low-energy state as defined by the Lyapunov function, the Lyapunov function can be used as the objective function. The solution is then found by applying the corresponding equation of motion to the network output. When the network converges to a low energy state, a possible solution to the optimization problem is found.

In solving the TSP using a Hopfield net, the first step is to find a way to represent the solution space. Given N cities to be visited, an array of $N \times N$ neurodes can be used. Each row represents a city to be visited, and each column represents the order of the route. If the output of the neurodes represents a permutation matrix with one 1 in each row and one 1 in each column, then the permutation matrix represents a possible and legitimate route. For example, given 5 cities (A, B, C, D, E), then a 5×5 array of neurodes is used. If the array output is [0 1 0 0 0; 1 0 0 0 0; 0 0 0 0 1; 0 0 1 0 0; 0 0 0 1 0], then the route is B→A→D→C→E→B.

The next step in solving the TSP is to define the objective function. Since the energy function has a quadratic form, the objective function must also be in a quadratic form. The primary objective of the TSP is to minimize the path length. Hence the cost function is the path length.

$$E_1 = A\Sigma_X\Sigma_i\Sigma_j\, v_{Xi}\, v_{Xj}, i \neq j$$

In addition to the cost function, it is necessary to enforce further constraints to ensure that the solution is a legitimate route. Clearly, if the salesman does not go anywhere, the path length will be zero, and that is not an acceptable solution. Constraints are enforced by adding penalty to the cost function when the constraints are not satisfied. To enforce that each city is only visited once, each row of the permutation matrix must contain only a single one.

$$E_2 = B\Sigma_X\Sigma_i\Sigma_Y\, v_{Xi}\, v_{Yi}, X \neq Y$$

Likewise, to enforce that at each turn only one city is visited, each column of the permutation matrix must also contain only a single one.

$$E_3 = C(\Sigma_X\Sigma_i\, v_{Xi} - n)^2$$

The two constraints tend to discourage more than one 1 in each row or column but do not discourage (rather encourage) nothing in the rows or columns. Hence, an additional constraint is needed to ensure that there are exactly N 1's in the entire network. This is accomplished by another constraint.

$$E_4 = D\Sigma_X\Sigma_i\Sigma_Y\, d_{XY}\, (v_{Xi} + v_{Y,i-1}), X \neq Y$$

The final objective function is the weighted combination of the distance cost function and the three constraints formulated in quadratic forms.

With the desired objective function found, the next step is to cast the objective function in the form of the Lyapunov function for the Hopfield net.

Note that even though the formulation of the TSP problem indicates an array of neurodes, hence individually identified by a double index, in reality the neurodes are in a single layer because the output of any neurodes is fed back to the input of all other neurodes. Changing the energy function into a double index form and matching the objective function with the energy function, the weights of the neurodes can be found as follows:

$$W_{Xi,Yj} = -2A\delta_{XY}(1 - \delta_{ij}) - 2B\delta_{ij}(1 - \delta_{XY}) - 2C - 2Dd_{XY}(\delta_{j,I+1} + \delta_{j,i-1})$$

Note that there is no training of the weights here. Rather, the weights themselves represent the optimization problem to be solved. In fact, the weights encapsulate the problem itself. Thus, the problem is solved during the recall mode. The network is initialized with random weights and then let loose. As a dynamic system, the network output is constantly changed while the weights are fixed. Each change causes the energy function to decrease, thus accomplishing the objective of minimizing the objective function. Eventually, the output settles in a low-energy state representing a possible solution to the problem.

7.8 SUMMARY

A single neurode represents an elementary processing unit and can be used as a building block for a variety of systems and applications. The basic definition of a single neurode is a linear combiner followed by a nonlinear activation function. From such a simple processing element very complex systems can be built. With proper choice of the input weights, a neurode can function like any Boolean components. Hence, much as AND, OR, and NOT gates can be used to build powerful computers, collection of neurodes can be expected to perform complex tasks.

Collection of neurodes into a single layer in a feedforward manner provides powerful mapping abilities such as associative memory, modeling, function approximation, and classification. The power of the neural network lies not only in the fact that the network is capable of performing the above tasks, but even more in the fact that the network is able to learn how to perform the tasks from given examples. In fact, the network is able to learn on its own.

When additional layers are cascaded together into a multiple-layer network, it has been postulated that such a network is able to approximate an arbitrary function. The development of the generalized delta rule, more commonly known as the back-error propagation method, further enhances the use of multiple-layer perceptron. Complex and nonlinear models can now be modeled by the network.

When the output of the network is fed back to the input, a feedback network is obtained that functions like a dynamic system. A dynamic system is not only good for pattern recognition and image enhancement, but more importantly it can be used for solving optimization problems. Through taking advantage of the dynamics of the network, a solution to the optimization problem can be iteratively found.

7.9   REFERENCES

Fundamental concepts: [11–18, 61].
Feedforward networks: [10. 26, 49, 62, 75, 81, 94, 99].
Feedback networks: [3, 44, 82].
Reinforcement learning: [7].
Unsupervised training: [55].
Future directions: [2, 46, 104].
Reference textbooks: [39, 108].

8
NEURAL-FUZZY NETWORKS

The field of computational intelligence or soft computing encompasses three main research directions: artificial neural networks, fuzzy logic, and evolutionary algorithms. Each area is well suited to different aspects of the problem-solving process. In the first section below, these three technologies are compared.

8.1 TECHNOLOGY COMPARISONS

The strength of neural networks lies in their ability to model unknown systems easily. One of the most popular neural network models is based on a nonlinear transformation of a linear combiner. Using the backpropagation algorithm, the network can be trained with input data to model an arbitrary system, i.e., to approximate an arbitrary function. Other neural network models such as counterpropagation networks and radial basis function networks also provide function approximation using slightly different topology and training techniques. Furthermore, there is a whole set of other networks such as the Hopfield nets that are designed to solve open-ended optimization problems. A third type of neural networks, such as Karhonen's maps, can be used to discover clustering through a self-organizing weights update algorithm. With a slightly different training algorithm, a single-layer perceptron with added lateral connections can also be configured to do principal components analysis (PCA). PCA is another form of representing the input data with only the salient features with minimal dimensions.

While neural networks are ideal for modeling known or unknown associations that exist between the input and output data, significant data cleaning and preprocessing are usually needed. In other words, input data must be carefully coded and prepared for the network to process. Another difficulty with neural networks is that the network must first be trained. The more input data, the better the training results. The richer the input data, the more accurate the model. However, training requires substantial time and resources.

These difficulties restrict the widespread use of neural networks in many applications. In many decision-making systems, it is important to be able to explain the process by which the decision is made. It is not a simple matter to derive rules from neural networks.

The main concept in fuzzy logic is to use unsharp boundaries of membership functions to describe the implicitly imprecise concepts in data representation. From this perspective, fuzzy logic is ideally suited for user interactions and data representation. Since fuzzy logic is also numerical in nature, concepts can be expressed and manipulated as mathematical variables. Using the extension principle, most of the crisp operations can be readily adapted to fuzzy operations. In the crisp domain, models are made using regression or autoregressive-moving average representations, Likewise in the fuzzy domain, fuzzy models can also be made using fuzzy regression and fuzzy operators. Hence, fuzzy operations include both logical operations and numerical operations. Another useful feature of fuzzy logic is its ability to make inferences. Propositions are readily represented by fuzzy values. Since implication is also a fuzzy operator, approximate reasoning can be carried out naturally as fuzzy computations.

The concepts of fuzzy logic clearly complement those of neural networks. While fuzzy logic provides simple data representation, neural networks provide none. Where fuzzy logic can be used to model a system, neural networks are well suited to provide sophisticated models for diverse type of systems. However, if there is prior knowledge about the underlying system, fuzzy logic can readily encapsulate the knowledge in terms of rules and relations, while it is not particularly easy to preprogram a neural network with prior knowledge. Given a set of training samples, it is not simple to train a fuzzy model, but many algorithms have been developed in the past for training neural networks.

Another aspect of computational intelligence is evolutionary algorithm. This type of algorithm is biologically inspired. The principal idea is that a solution can be produced through genetic reproductions among a population of viable individuals, each individual representing a possible solution. There are two main classes of evolutionary algorithms: genetic algorithms and evolutionary programming. Genetic algorithms use genes, collectively called chromosomes, as the basis to represent possible solutions. Solutions are paired using crossover operations to produce new solutions. Mutations are used to enrich the genetic pool of the population and explore unchartered territories of the search space. Evolutionary programming places less emphasis on the genetic structure and uses mutation as the primary operation to reproduce offspring.

Evolutionary programming is a search methodology and is suited for solving open-ended optimization problems. While neural networks have been shown to solve open-ended problems such as the traveling salesman problem, detailed analysis shows that the neural network spends significant amount of time converging to a local minimum. Simulated annealing has been proposed as a method to cause the neural network to settle on a global minimum, but the technique is computation intensive because the annealing temperature must be lowered very slowly. Evolutionary programming provides a significantly more efficient way to search since each step of the algorithm produces a whole new generation of solutions. In neural networks, the objective function and all subsequent constraints must be explicitly programmed into the weights. In evolutionary algorithms, the algorithm is independent of the objective functions and associated constraints. The algorithm requires only that a cost function be associated with each solution.

Evolutionary programming with fuzzy logic are complementary. In fuzzy logic, open-ended search can be obtained through forward or backward chaining performed in an orderly fashion. Quite often the search is exhaustive, hence the technique is good for problems with a small solution set. In evolutionary algorithm, the solution is obtained by randomly generating individual solutions; hence the technique is ideally suited to problems with a large solution set.

For complex systems, no single technology can easily satisfy all the requirements of the problem. In the quest for a solution to the problem at hand, it is natural to combine more than one technology to create hybrid systems. Hybrid systems are designed to take advantage of the strengths of each system and avoid the limitations of each system. For example, it is natural for neural networks to learn but it is cumbersome for a fuzzy system to learn. Hence a combination of the two would result in a rule-based system that can learn and adapt. On the other hand, learning in neural network is slow. Hence there are many proposed hybrid systems where a fuzzy system is used to tune the learning rate and momentum terms in an effort to speed up the convergence rate. In systems where prior knowledge is available, what is known can be easily coded in rules and facts, but it is not a simple matter to encode prior knowledge in a neural network. These are only a small sample of applications where hybrid systems would be ideal. In this chapter we examine the synergism between neural networks and fuzzy logic.

8.2 NEURONS PERFORMING FUZZY OPERATIONS

One of the simplest types of hybrid systems involves training a neural network to perform fuzzy logic operations. The main advantage of this is the reduction of time complexity. Since there are many neural network chips available through many vendors, these chips are capable of executing billions of neural connections a second. If a neural network can be trained to perform fuzzy operations, then the fuzzy operations can also be performed at the same speed. This is a definite advantage to emulating the fuzzy operations using microcontrollers or simulating the operations using computer instructions.

The three most basic operations in classical set theory are AND, OR, and NOT operations. The corresponding operations in fuzzy logic are min, max,

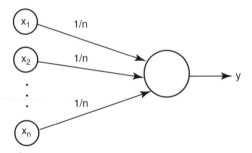

Figure 8.1. A neuron for performing the fuzzy *t*-norm operation.

and complement. When a fuzzy variable can only take on the two extreme values (0 and 1), then the fuzzy operations degenerate into the respective classical set operations. In a more general setting, the terms *conjunctive, disjunctive,* and *complement* are used to represent intersection, union, and complement operations.

8.2.1   Neurons Emulating Fuzzy Operations

A simple neuron can be made to perform logic functions with some special arrangement. This section presents the neural network arrangement for conjunctive, disjunctive, and complement networks.

A conjunctive network performs the intersection operation for fuzzy variables. Using the definition of standard *t*-norm, the intersection is the minimum operation on all fuzzy inputs. A standard feedforward neural network with special input arrangement can be used to perform this operation, as is shown in Figure 8.1 [45].

The network is designed to find the minimum of the input fuzzy values. It is assumed that the crisp inputs have already fuzzified. Assume the fuzzified values are p_i, $i = 1 \ldots N$. In order for the network to work, the fuzzy inputs are first ordered giving p'_i, $i = 1 \ldots N$. Then the difference from consecutive inputs are obtained: q_i, $i = 1 \ldots N$.

$$q_i = p'_i - p'_{i-1}$$

where $p'_0 = 0$ by definition. For the conjunctive network, the weighting function is predefined to be $1/n$. Define the connection weights v_i where

$$v_i = \text{hardlimiter } (\text{SUM}_{j=1}^{n} \ w_i - 1)$$

The hardlimiter output is a one whenever the argument is greater than or equal to one, otherwise is a zero. The activation function is simply taken to

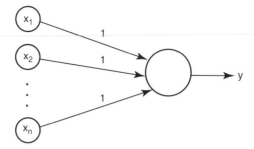

Figure 8.2. A neuron for performing the fuzzy t-conorm operation.

be the linear function. Hence the output of the neuron is simply the weighted sum of the input with the connection weights.

Using the same basic architecture, a disjunctive network can also be obtained. A disjunctive network performs the union operation for fuzzy variables. Using the definition of standard t-conorm, the union is the maximum operation on all fuzzy inputs. A standard feedforward neural network with special input arrangement can also be used to perform this operation, as shown in Figure 8.2 [45].

The network is designed to find the maximum of the input fuzzy values. It is assumed that the crisp inputs have already fuzzified. Assume the fuzzified values are p_i, $i = 1 \ldots N$. In order for the network to work, the fuzzy inputs are first ordered giving p'_i, $i = 1 \ldots N$. Then the difference from consecutive inputs are obtained: q_i, $i = 1 \ldots N$.

$$q_i = p'_i - p'_{i-1}$$

where $p'_0 = 0$ by definition. For the disjunctive network, the weighting function is predefined to be all 1. Define the connection weights v_i where

$$v_i = \text{hard-limiter} \left(\text{SUM}_{j=i}^{n} w_i - 1 \right)$$

The hardlimiter output is a one whenever the argument is greater or equal to 1, otherwise it is a zero. The activation function is simply taken to be the linear function. Hence the output of the neuron is simply the weighted sum of the input with the connection weights.

In a like manner, a complement network can also be designed. A complement operation is a unary operation, in that the complement is applied to only one fuzzy variable. Using the definition of the standard complement operation, the output is simply the difference of the fuzzy input from one. Hence there are two inputs in the complement network: the first is the fuzzy variable and the second is a constant one. The corresponding connection weights for the two inputs are -1 and 1, as shown in Figure 8.3.

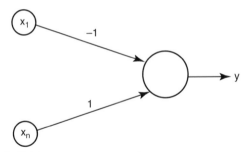

Figure 8.3. A neuron for performing the fuzzy complement operation.

8.2.2   Neurons Performing Fuzzy Operations

A hybrid neuron is also a neuron with crisp inputs and crisp outputs. However, instead of performing a weighted sum followed by a nonlinear transformation, a fuzzy neuron performs one of the fuzzy operations such as the t-norm or the t-conorm operation. While this adaptation of a neuron may not be biologically based, the topology and architecture are certainly biologically inspired.

Corresponding to the crisp inputs, a hybrid neuron also has crisp weights. In general, arithmetic operations such as multiplication and addition are not used in combining inputs and weights because these functions tend to produce resultant values that do not necessarily lie in the interval between 0 and 1. Instead, fuzzy operations are preferred so that the resultant values do lie in the interval between 0 and 1. Each input and its corresponding weight can be combined using a continuous operation such as t-norm or t-conorm. The aggregation of all weighted inputs can also be performed with any of the fuzzy continuous operations. If a nonlinear transformation is required, a continuous function mapping the aggregation value to the output is used.

A hybrid AND neuron takes on two crisp inputs and produces a single crisp output. Corresponding to each input is a crisp connection weight. Each input and its associated weight are combined using a disjunctive (union) operation ($C(x,y)$). The weighted inputs are then aggregated together by a conjunctive (intersection) operation ($T(x,y)$). Using C to denote the t-conorm and T the t-norm operations, the output of the hybrid AND neuron can be denoted.

$$y = T(C(x_1, w_1), C(x_2, w_2))$$

Likewise, a hybrid OR neuron takes on two crisp inputs and produces a single crisp output. Corresponding to each input is also a crisp connection weight. Each input and its weight is combined using a conjunctive (intersection) operation ($T(x,y)$). The weighted inputs are then aggregated together by a disjunctive (union) operation ($C(x,y)$). The output of the hybrid OR neuron can be denoted

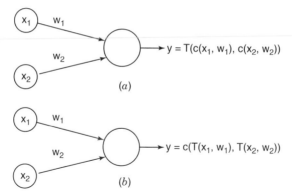

Figure 8.4. A hybrid AND neuron and a hybrid OR neuron.

$$y = C(T(x_1, w_1), T(x_2, w_2))$$

A hybrid AND neuron and a hybrid OR neuron is shown in Figure 8.4.

8.3   NEURAL NETWORK PERFORMING FUZZY INFERENCE

One of the strengths of a fuzzy logic system is its ability to make inferences. Model characteristics are usually written in facts and rules. An example of a rule is:

If x is X_i and y is Y_i, **then** z is Z_i

The rule states that if the input variable x belongs to the membership X_i and the input variable y belongs to the membership Y_i, then the output variable z will belong to Z_i. There are a number of approaches in realizing a rule and a rule set. These approaches are explored in this section.

8.3.1   Regular Neural Network with Crisp Input and Output

The if–then rule points to a system having two crisp inputs and a single crisp output. Though the rule deals with fuzzy variables, x, y, and x are crisp by themselves. The fuzzy value describes the degree that the crisp value belongs in the X_i, Y_i, and Z_i membership functions respectively. Note that the output is also a crisp value. It is now easy to see that the if–then rule can be viewed as a black box with two crisp inputs and one crisp output. As such, the rule can be modeled by a regular neural network such as a multilayer perceptron.

If the membership functions of the input and output variables are know *a priori,* then values of the membership functions can be sampled and used as a training set for the neural network, i.e., $\langle(x,y),z\rangle$ where the first set of values in the double is input parameters and the second parameter of the doublet is the output. If training samples are used to train the if–then rule, then the same training samples can likewise be used to train the neural network. The mapping from the if–then rule to the neural network is direct and straightforward. If there are more inputs and/or outputs, then the corresponding neural network will also have the same number of inputs and outputs.

8.3.2   Regular Neural Network with Fuzzy Input and Output

For some problems, the input may not be a crisp value, but rather a fuzzy value defined by the associated membership functions. A regular neural network can still be used in this case. One approach is to sample the membership function with a discrete number of domain values. Instead of working with a continuous interval, the membership function is sampled at discrete values. In this case, the input to the neural network is a set of membership values at discrete locations of the input parameter. The shape of the membership curve is represented by the function values at the selected locations. Likewise, the output membership curve is represented by a series of function values at discrete points.

Representation in this format is very powerful because a rule can now be formed for the entire membership function.

If X and Y, then Z

Here, X, Y, and Z are membership functions. Using a series of crisp values, each of the membership functions can be sampled. The entire series for X and that for Y serve as inputs to the neural network. Likewise, the entire series serves as the output from the neural network. The training sequence is then a double $\langle(x_1, x_2, \ldots, x_n; y_1, y_2, \ldots, y_n), (z_1, z_2, \ldots, z_n)\rangle$ where the first parameter contains the two sequences for X and Y, and the second parameter contains the sequence for the output Z. The neural network can now be repeated trained using the standard backpropagation method or other standard techniques until the network output yields the desired result.

Uehara and Fujise have proposed a variation on this scheme. Instead of discretizing the domain and sampling the membership functions at those discrete points, they propose that the membership function be represented by a series of α-cuts. Each α-cut represents an interval. In this case, the input to the neural network would be a series of interval values for different α-cut values. Likewise, the output from the neural network would also be a series of interval values for the same corresponding α-cut values. Regardless of the discretization approaches used, the membership function can easily be reconstructed.

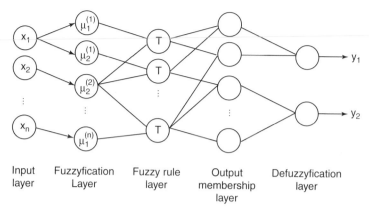

Figure 8.5. A neural network for approximate reasoning.

8.3.3   Fuzzy Inference Network

With some careful rearranging of the inputs, a single neuron has been shown to function as a fuzzy AND, a fuzzy OR, and a fuzzy complement operator. But the real power lies in the ability of a neural network to emulate the fuzzy inference process.

In approximate reasoning, the system is represented by a set of rules and facts. Facts are inputs obtained from the system environment. Rules describe the model characteristics. Using a set of predefined membership functions, crisp inputs are converted to fuzzy variables. Rules relate the fuzzy input variables to fuzzy output variables. The antecedent of each rule is constructed with conjunction and disjunction of the fuzzy input variables. The inference is made using the implication operator based on the generalized *modus ponens, modus tollens,* and hypothetical syllogism. After the inference has been carried out, the fuzzy output variables are defuzzified to yield a crisp number for output.

The process described above can be emulated by a neural network with a topology similar to a multilayer perceptron as shown in Figure 8.5.

Ideally, the input to the network is crisp numbers and the output of the network is also crisp numbers. The first layer of the neural network is to fuzzify the input values. The fuzzification process can be performed by a layer of radial basis function (RBF) neurons or by special subnetworks designed to emulate the membership functions. Each RBF neuron emulates a single membership function, hence a set of RBF neurons is required to produce an array of fuzzy values for each crisp input.

The second layer of the neural network implements the conjunctive and/or disjunctive operation of the fuzzy inputs for the antecedents of each fuzzy rule. Neurons that can emulate conjunction and disjunction have been presented in the previous section. These specialized neurons are used to combine

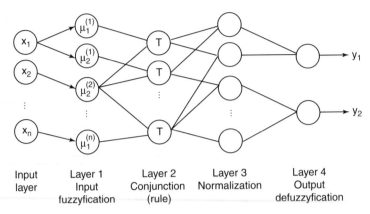

Figure 8.6. An ANFIS network.

the fuzzy input variables produced by the first layer. If the rule antecedents are overly complex, the operations can be emulated by more than one layer here. One suggestion is a conjunctive layer followed by a disjunctive layer.

The third layer of the neural network implements the implication operation. The fuzzy value of the antecedent is used to limit the degree of truthfulness of the output membership functions. This also is a conjunctive operation. To realize the output membership functions, a set of neurons is used to represent the possible crisp output possibilities. The output of the neurons in this layer is limited by the truthfulness of the antecedents obtained from the previous layer.

The fourth layer is the consequent layer. This is a disjunctive layer as the consequent is usually taken to be the t-conorm from all the inferences. The final conclusion is the cumulated truthfulness, i.e., the union from all the inferences.

The last layer is the defuzzification process. A single neuron is used for each crisp output. The weights are arranged in such a way as to emulate one of the defuzzification methods. The most common one is the centroid method, where the crisp output is the centroid of the fuzzy output values.

8.3.4 ANFIS

A more simplified network has been proposed by Shing and Jang [95] and Baglio et al. [6]. The bulk of the network is used for fuzzification using two layers of perceptrons. The inference is based on sigma-pi neurons, and the output membership function is not used. The output of the network directly yields a crisp value. The proposed neural network is shown in Figure 8.6.

The first layer consists of two-input perceptrons with the usual sigmoidal transformation. This layer produces a series of sigmoidal curves. The first input comes from the crisp input value. The second input is always one representing the bias. A bias is needed to offset the crisp input values. This has the same effect as shifting the sigmoidal function to be centered at the desired value. The neurons at this layer are similar to other neural networks using a single layer of perceptrons.

A second layer is next used to collate the sigmoidal outputs together to form membership functions. This layer is composed of two-input neurons with linear activation function. The connection weights are simply 1 and -1. Typically, two sigmoidal functions are needed to make one membership function. A membership function is realized by taking the difference between two sigmoidal function outputs.

The next layer is composed of a set of sigma-pi neurons. The output of these neurons is the product of the weighted inputs instead of the sum of the weighted inputs. The fuzzy inputs are weighted and multiplied to realize the conjunctive relation of the antecedent. In this case, the intersection of the various fuzzy inputs is realized using the product rule instead of the standard (min) rule.

The last layer is simply a set of regular neurons with linear activation functions. The output of each neuron in this layer is the weighted sum of the previous layer. The output of the previous layers represents the strength of activation of a particular rule. This layer collates the strengths of different rule activations together to produce a set of crisp output values.

Another variation on the same network is to eliminate the second layer entirely. If a Gaussian transformation is used as the activation function instead of the sigmoidal function, then the shape of the Gaussian function can be used to represent the membership function. If there are a lot of linguistic variables, this can greatly simplify the network topology.

The key point to observe here is that by emulating the fuzzy rules in neural network architecture, the network can now be trained with standard back-propagation methods in response to training patterns. This means that the shape of the membership functions and the strength of the connection for the rules can be adjusted and learned. When the training is completed, the neural network can simply be converted back to fuzzy rules if desired. This is the primary advantage of using a neural network to emulate fuzzy inference.

8.3.5 Applications

A direct application of emulating fuzzy logic using a neural network is to use the output of the network as a way to tune parameters of another neural network. It has often been observed that the learning rate and momentum greatly affect the ability of a neural network to converge. However, there is no simple way to select the proper values of the learning rate and the momentum factor. It has also been suggested that an adaptive scheme could possibly be more effective during the training phase of the process. This approach has been proposed by Hertz and Hu [1992], who use a second neural network to adjust the learning rate adaptively according to a set of heuristic rules [40]. The second neural network emulates the heuristic rules and produces the recommended values for the learning rate to be used in the first network during the its training process. To accomplish this, a neural network is used with one input and one output parameter. The crisp input parameter is the error for the present iteration. The crisp input value is first fuzzified into seven membership functions (NL, NM, NS, ZE, PS, PM, PL) corresponding to whether the error is positive or negative and whether the magnitude of the error is great or small. Hertz and Hu developed a number of heuristic rules that are preprogrammed into the neural network. The collation of all rules yields the fuzzy values for four membership functions (ZE, PS, PM, PL) for the learning rate. The output of the network is a single variable, the learning rate. The four fuzzy output values are defuzzified into a single crisp value.

Another application was proposed by Baglio et al. in modeling urban traffic noise [6]. The goal is to predict the degree of urban noise from passage of motor vehicles. However, the noise is often mollified due to the shadowing effects of buildings and building elevation. Baglio et al. compared the use of a traditional neural network against the use of a fuzzy inference network. It was found that the performance of the fuzzy inference network is comparable to the traditional neural network. However, the fuzzy inference network has a significantly lower computational complexity than a traditional network.

8.4   CLUSTERING AND CLASSIFICATION

In clustering, while the training patterns are given, the exact grouping of these patterns is unknown. When the training patterns are seen repeatedly, a neural net or fuzzy system is used to categorize the patterns into distinct groups or clusters. In pattern classification, not only are the training samples given, but the cluster that each training sample belongs to is known. The task of the neural network or the fuzzy system is to learn the association so that the system can successfully recognize the input patterns according to the proper class.

If a neural network is used for the recognition process, then the input to the neural net is a doublet $\langle (x_1, x_2, \ldots, x_n), \text{Class} \rangle$ where the first parameter represents the input pattern and the second parameter represents the class that the pattern belongs in. Since a neural network can accommodate large input dimension, it is not unusual for the input set to consist of the original raw data set.

If a fuzzy logic system is used, then the doublet can immediately be written in the form of a rule.

If x_1 is X_1 and x_2 is X_2 and . . . and x_n is X_n, **then** Class.

When rules are used to describe an input pattern, they are more efficient when a small number of antecedents is used. Hence the raw data pattern is often preprocessed to reduce the dimension of the original data set. A number of transforms can be used, including Fourier transform for a one-dimensional signal and two-dimensional images. Other transforms used are principal component analysis and singular value decompositions. If more reduction in data dimension is required, then a feature extraction process is usually performed first. The input to the rules would then be extracted features. In many cases, these features are meaningful to human recognition. Hence the reasoning from a fuzzy logic system can be explained in more recognizable terms to the user.

8.4.1 Classification

Consider a simple two-class system with two inputs. Each dimension of the input space is divided by a set of membership functions. The boundaries of the membership functions separate the input space into distinct areas. Each area can now be labeled with the class number as shown in Figure 8.7.

Further subdividing the input parameters into additional membership functions makes it clear that any clusters can be formed on the input space.

Assume that the input parameters have been set up each with two input parameters, i.e., $x_1 \in \{$Small, Large$\}$ and $x_2 \in \{$Small, Large$\}$. Then there are four areas in the input space. This corresponds to four rules:

If x_1 is Small and x_2 is Small, **then** Class One

If x_1 is Small and x_2 is Large, **then** Class One

If x_1 is Large and x_2 is Small, **then** Class Two

If x_1 is Large and x_2 is Large, **then** Class Two

While the number of membership functions is known and set *a priori,* the exact shape and location of the membership functions can be varied for accurate results. This is when training samples are used to adapt the shape and locations of the membership functions.

The same problem can be cast into a neural network paradigm proposed by Sun and Jang. The neural network would have two input parameters and a single output parameter as shown in Figure 8.8. The inputs to the neural network would be the two input parameters, both crisp. The first layer of the neural network is to compute the degree of likeness between the crisp input parameter and the membership function. These neurons can be radial basis function neurons or regular neurons with Gaussian activation functions. For the Gaussian activation function, the adjustable parameters are the width and centroid of the Gaussian curve. Other membership functions, including triangular and trapezoidal shapes, can also be used. For triangular membership function, the adjustable parameters are the left lower limit, the center upper limit, and the right lower limit. For trapezoidal membership function, the adjustable parameters are the left lower limit, upper limit, right upper limit,

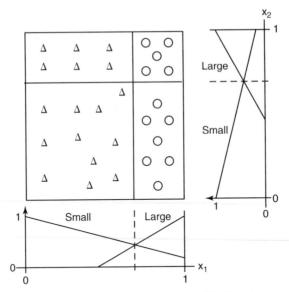

Figure 8.7. Clustering with membership functions.

and right lower limit. Regardless of the activation function used, each parameter of the activation function can be adapted by the standard backpropagation approach.

The second layer of the neural network emulates the conjunctive operation. This is used to connect the various parts of the antecedent together. The output of this layer is the strength of the present rule indicating how closely the input parameters match the stated membership functions. If the match is good, then the strength of the rule is strong; however, if the match is poor, then the strength of the rule is greatly diminished.

The third layer of the neural network is a single-layer perceptron. The output of each neuron is the weighted sum of the firing strengths of the rules

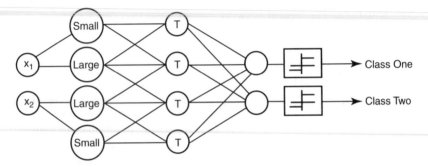

Figure 8.8. A neural network performing fuzzy classification.

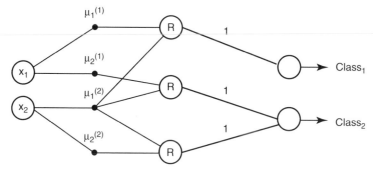

Figure 8.9. A fuzzy perceptron.

in previous layer. The weighted sum is subjected to a nonlinear activation function that is normally taken to be the sigmoidal transformation. In the present case, since there are only two classes, a hardlimiter can be used to indicate whether the output is Class One or Class Two.

During training, the training data consist of the input data and their associated class identification. Since the third layer is a single-layer perceptron, the weights can be adapted by the standard backpropagation approach. The second layer implements the conjunctive operation. Most of the time there are no adjustable parameters in this layer. For the first layer of the neural network, the parameters there can also be adjusted by the backpropagation approach.

8.4.2   Multilayer Fuzzy Perceptron

Nauck and Kruse developed a special three-layer perceptron called fuzzy perceptron [71]. The system is called NEFCLASS, which stands for a neuro-fuzzy system for the classification of data developed. The fuzzy perceptron is designed to learn from training samples the separation for the different classes. The knowledge of the pattern classification is contained in a set of fuzzy rules.

The fuzzy perceptron is composed of three layers, the input layer, the hidden or rule layer, and the output layer, as shown in Figure 8.9. Layer 1 performs the fuzzification of the crisp input parameters. Layer 2 implements the antecedents of the rule set. Layer 3 performs the defuzzification.

Layer 1 performs the fuzzification process. Each neuron in this layer inputs one crisp parameter and outputs a series of fuzzy values according to the set of membership functions defined for that parameter. Each output fuzzy values indicates the degree of match between the input crisp value and the associated linguistic concept. Layer 2 performs the conjunctive operation for selected fuzzy values. Each neuron in this layer implements one fuzzy rule. The output of the neuron is the activation strength of the associated rule and is obtained by a fuzzy AND of the various fuzzy membership values. Layer 3 performs the defuzzification process by combining the activation strengths of all the rules together to form an estimate of the class. It should be noted that the output does not actually yield an estimate of a specific class. Rather, the output shows an estimated possibility of each class. If desired, a fourth layer such as a MAXNET can be used to interpret the results by selecting the class with the largest output.

To start, the user must define the basic structure of the fuzzy perceptron. It is necessary to define the number of neurons in the hidden layer and make an initial estimate of the various membership functions in the input layer. Alternatively, the neurons in the hidden layer can be added iteratively during training. When an input pattern is submitted to the network, a search is performed to see what set of input fuzzy values would yield the best output. The set of selected fuzzy values is then inserted into the hidden layer if there are no other neurons in the hidden layer representing the same set of input fuzzy values. If the system is small enough, then it is possible to start with all possible combinations. After training, a scoring method is used to gauge the effectiveness of each rule and any poorly performing neurons are then trimmed from the system.

9

EVOLUTIONARY COMPUTING

9.1 INTRODUCTION

The area of intelligent computation involves three main aspects: fuzzy systems, which are ideally suited for problem representations and user interactions; neural networks for making models; and evolutionary programming for finding a solution or making an inference. The act of finding a solution is called *optimization*. During the optimization process, a solution is sought that would minimize or maximize an objective function subject to a given set of constraints on the variables. There are a great number of practical problems whose solutions require such an optimization process. In numerical analysis, the solution of even simple problems such as root finding or other problems requiring a search of the local minimum or maximum involves the process of optimization.

Optimization problems can be constrained or unconstrained. In unconstrained optimization, the parameter values are allowed to take on any values as long as the objective function is minimized or maximized. In constrained optimization, one or more of the parameters may be constrained to exist within a specific region or relationship. These constraints are usually written in the form of inequalities. In many circumstances, a constrained optimization problem can be recast into an unconstrained optimization problem by rewriting the inequalities with a penalty function to be included in the objective function. In this manner, the primary objective function is minimized or maximized along with the constraints ensuring that the solution found would satisfy both the desired objective function and the constraints at the same time. This technique is particularly useful and is often used in evolutionary programming.

In most problems dealing with optimization, the solution set can be quite large, and oftentimes the optimal solution is intractable. Depending on the application, there are often good solutions that are close to the optimal solution. In this case, having a good solution is good enough and the additional expense of actually locating the optimal solution for an incrementally small benefit may not be justified. Hence the optimization task becomes finding a suboptimal but good solution that yields a cost close to that given by the optimal solution. Most of the time a solution must be found within a certain allotted time. For example, a metal-cutting machine must find the best way to cut a piece of sheet metal with minimal waste, or an MRP program must arrive at a production schedule within the time available. In these cases, it is particularly crucial to use an optimization algorithm that will give a good solution quickly.

Many search algorithms have been proposed in the literature. The simplest search algorithm is the exhaustive search approach, where the search takes place over the entire search space by checking every possible combination of the search variables. This method yields the optimal solution when the entire space is searched, a luxury that is not often possible. Many proposed pruning techniques allow some of the search space to be trimmed. When the search time is limited, there is no guarantee that a good solution can be found in this case. In an exhaustive search approach, a potential search solution is generated based on what has been generated before.

Another approach is the random search, where possible solutions are randomly generated and checked against the objective function. At any time the best solution is kept. When the search time is exhausted, the best solution found is taken to be the solution. The approach works most of the time because the longer the search time allotted, the better the solution will be. Random search does not work well with combinatorial optimization because there is no relationship between possible solutions. However, there is no guarantee that a good solution or any solution could be found with random search because the potential solutions are generated randomly each time.

An ideal case is an approach where a good solution can be found within an allotted time yet potential solutions are not generated randomly. In other words, the algorithm would learn from past mistakes and propose new solutions that would account for what has been learned from past proposals. Many types of search algorithms have been proposed in the literature based on various principles. In recent years, a set of biologically inspired approaches has been proposed, including simulated annealing and genetic algorithms. In simulated annealing, developed by Metropolis et al. [63] and Kirkpatrick [53], a hypothetical parameter called temperature is used. When the temperature is high, the search is allowed to wander all over the search space. After the search has been carried on for awhile, the temperature is gradually cooled, causing the search to be narrowed gradually to the local minima or maxima. It is commonly accepted that when the temperature is reduced slowly, the solution will more likely converge towards the global solution. The term *simulated annealing* comes from the metal annealing process, where defects in the metal are cured by heating the metal to a high temperature and then cooling it slowly.

Another biologically inspired approach is evolutionary computing. The goal is to learn from previous guesses and propose potential new guesses that would preserve the desirable qualities of previous success. An analogy for this optimization process is searching for a superindividual with the correct genetic makeup. Instead of the entire population being searched for that superindividual, the desired person is obtained through a breeding program with promising parents. Two competing technologies have been proposed in the literature. One approach was originally proposed by Holland [43] and later further developed by Goldberg [31]. This approach is generally referred to as genetic algorithm. Another approach, proposed by Fogel [30], is commonly referred to as evolutionary programming.

9.2   BINARY GENETIC ALGORITHM

In genetic algorithm, the most important aspect of the whole process is to arrive at a representation that will capture the desirable characteristics. The representation is biologically inspired and is based on the genetic system in biology. Search variables are represented by chromosomes. Each gene represents one possible value of a search variable. An individual is a collection of genes and is collectively called the chromosome. A population can now be generated, with each individual having a different chromosome. Each individual thus represents a different solution of the search parameters, hence there is a cost associated with each individual.

A set of random initial population is generated. This population is the initial pool. Each individual is evaluated against the cost objective, resulting in some individuals giving good solutions and others giving bad solutions for the current generation. Most of the individuals giving bad solutions are eliminated from the race and are deleted from the pool. As the algorithm progresses to the next generation, the remaining individuals form the mating pool. Some of the individuals in the mating pool are selected to participate in the mating process. In the mating process, each individual is paired with another. In the simplest case, the match is randomly made. Each successful marriage will produce a number of offspring. Offspring inherit the genetic information from their parents. It is reasoned that those individuals giving good solutions when combined together will yield new individuals or offspring with inherited genes that will give solutions that are just as good if not better than those given by their parents. This idea stems from the argument that if a certain combination of genes yields a good solution, then the descendants ought to also produce a good solution if this combination of genes can somehow be preserved.

The primary operations for combination of genes are crossover and mutation. Crossover requires two parents. The resulting chromosome of the offspring is a combination of the chromosomes of the two parents. Crossover is the primary operation in genetic algorithm since it serves to preserve the

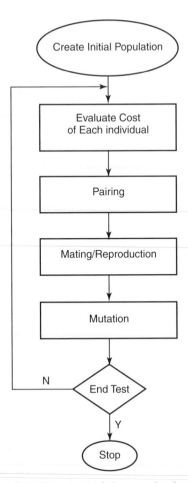

Figure 9.1. Flowchart of the genetic algorithm.

genetic characteristics of individuals with good solutions. Mutation involves the resulting chromosome of the offspring alone. Part of the chromosome is allowed to mutate. This stimulates an excursion to new areas of the search space to keep diversity in the gene pool.

The mating process produces new offspring to replenish the population so as to maintain a constant number of individuals in the population. The new population includes new offspring and other individuals that may or may not have participated in the mating process, depending on the variations in implementations. During the computation for each generation, the chromosome for the best solution is always saved. The algorithm continues until the goodness measure for the desired solution is obtained. Occasionally, the population loses diversity and must be restarted again. The process can be illustrated in Figure 9.1.

9.2.1   Genetic Representation

A key factor in the genetic algorithm is the use of genes to represent the values of the search parameters. In this section, the chromosome for each individual is represented by a string of binary bits. Other representations are possible; these are covered in later chapters. The chromosome contains information related to the values of the parameters. It contains a number of genes, each gene representing the value of one parameter. For example, given two input variables (x, y) and the function $f(x, y)$, the problem on hand is to find the two parameters (x, y) that will give the minimum function value when the input parameters are bounded within the real interval [0, 1].

There are really no unique ways to design the bit string for representing the parameter values. Since the four parameters are all real-valued between 0 and 1, one of the easiest representations is to use the fractional bits. The number of bits required depends on the desired resolution as specified by the application on hand. Assume that a resolution of two decimal digits would be sufficient for the present purpose; therefore in binary, eight bits are required for each parameter. The chromosome for each individual can now be represented by a string of 16 binary bits:

$$[x_0, x_1, x_2, x_3, x_4, x_5, x_6, x_7, y_0, y_1, y_2, y_3, y_4, y_5, y_6, y_7]$$

The binary bits actually represent the quantized and truncated values for x and y.

The order of these 16 bits is not crucial; they can be placed in any order desired. In fact, if x_7 and y_7 represent the most significant bits, it may be of value to put the two most significant bits together and likewise for the rest of the bits between x and y.

$$[x_0, y_0, x_1, y_1, x_2, y_2, x_3, y_3, x_4, y_4, x_5, y_5, x_6, y_6, x_7, y_7]$$

For the purpose of the present example, we will continue to use the first definition. For example, the following binary string

$$[0000111111110000]$$

represents the values $16/256 = 0.0625$ and $240/256 = 0.9375$ for x and y, respectively. Likewise, the binary string

$$[1111000000001111]$$

represents the values $240/256 = 0.9375$ and $16/256 = 0.0625$ for x and y, respectively.

9.2.2   Population

Once the chromosome has been designed, an initial population of individuals can be generated. The size of the population remains constant in the optimization process even though some individuals are being eliminated and new offspring produced. In other words, the number of offspring produced always balances out the number of individuals eliminated from the population. Regarding the initial population, there are two major concerns: the size of the population and the coverage of the population.

Regarding the size of the initial population, the population must be rich enough to preserve the diversity of the gene pool. It is highly desirable that the search space be adequately represented both in the initial population and in subsequent generations. An individual in the population serves to sample the fitness of the search space around that individual. Hence the more individuals there are, the more completely the search space can be covered. However, if the size of the population is large, then the computational complexity will increase at least linearly and consequently slow the generation process. If the population is too large, then the process degenerates into a random search, and the benefits of the genetic algorithm and its ability to learn will be lost. Usually a population of 100 to 1,000 is used. Generally, an initial population of 100 will do. However, if there are a lot of constraints placed on the parameter values, then a larger population size will ensure that there are enough offspring in each generation to keep the population afloat.

The second concern is the coverage of the population. The more completely the search space is covered, the more likely it is that the global solution will be found. If a part of the search space has never been explored, then the algorithm will never be aware of any solution in the unexplored space. If the global solution happens to lie in that unexplored region, then the algorithm will not have been successful in arriving at the optimal solution. Once the algorithm has started, the mutation operation is an attempt to enrich the gene pool by spawning individuals in unexplored regions.

There are two ways to generate the initial population: stochastic and deterministic. The simplest way is to generate bits randomly for all the chromosome of the individuals. Usually a uniform random number generator is used and the random numbers are properly scaled to represent the entire search space. The problem with generating samples randomly is that there is no guarantee that the search space will be covered adequately. This is particularly true when the population size is small. On the other hand, if coverage of the search space is important, then individuals in the initial population can be deterministically generated simply by defining a grid that will canvass the entire search space.

9.2.3   Fitness Check and Cost Evaluation

Once the initial population is generated, the legitimacy of each individual must be checked to ensure that it can be a possible solution. For unconstrained optimization, this step is not necessary. For constrained optimization, the constraints on each parameter can be explicitly checked. If an individual does not satisfy the constraints, then the invalid individual will not be counted and included as part of the population.

After checking for legitimacy, the next step is to evaluate the objective function of each individual. During this step, the parameter values are computed from the binary representation. The parameter values are then passed to a function and used to evaluate the cost. The computed cost is then associated with this individual. Note that the algorithm really does not need to know the exact relationship of the cost and the parameters, only what the cost is for this set of parameters. It is precisely for this property that the genetic algorithm has found widespread usage. In many applications it is not desirable or even possible to find the input–output relationship.

Once the cost has been evaluated for all individuals, the best solution is found by finding the individual that matches most closely to the desired objective. In this case, since we are looking for the maximum of the function, the function itself is the objective value. The individual with the highest objective value is the one desired. The algorithm saves the parameter values for this individual. This set of parameters represents the best solution at this generation.

At this point, the algorithm is similar to a random search except that the parameter values are first generated in terms of binary strings and then converted to real parameter values. For a random search, one merely continues to generate more potential solutions, always recording the best solution found. However, for the genetic algorithm, the power of the algorithm and the learning process comes from the next three steps.

For the present example, the problem is to find the minimum value for the given function. The objective function can be defined as the function value. When the cost is minimized, the function is also minimized at the same time. Note that if the problem is to maximize the function, then the objective function can be constructed to be the negative of the function value. In this case, when the objective function is being minimized, the function is being maximized at the same time.

9.2.4 Mating Pool

Since the objective function for each individual is known, there is a rough idea of something about the search space. With this population of individuals on hand, the next step is to generate more individuals without losing what is already known about the search space and the associated objective function. In this step, suitable individuals are chosen to be part of the mating pool. The goal of the selection process is to choose a number of individuals to be part of the mating pool. A number of strategies are commonly used at this point.

The simplest and most obvious strategy is to use the entire population as the mating pool. In this case, all the individuals will be used as parents and all will be replaced by offspring. The danger of this strategy is that there is no guarantee that the offspring will be better than the parents.

Since the goal is to breed those individuals with good solutions, the tendency is to use only the individuals with good solutions. This can be easily done by first sorting all individuals according to their respective cost functions, then using only a percentage of the individuals at the top of the list with the highest objective function values. The intention is to put two good individuals together, resulting in an offspring that will inherit all the good parts of the chromosome from both parents. At each generation, a fixed percentage of the best individuals can be used for the mating pool. Since the algorithm maintains the best solution and its associated objective value, this value can be used as a measure of the goodness of individuals in the population. This is called the threshold scheme. For an individual to be selected for the mating pool, the individual's objective value must be above a certain percentage of the best objective value.

One difficulty is that it may be possible for the entire population or most of the individuals to have gone bad. This can be detected by checking the objective values of the individuals in the population. If the bulk of the population has degenerated to a poor condition, then a restart is needed. In other words, the entire population will be scraped and a new initial population again generated.

While the natural tendency is to use only the best individuals for the mating pool, it has been shown that it is also beneficial to include individuals with bad objective values. Just because that individual is bad does not imply that the entire region where that individual resides is bad. It is quite possible that some part of that gene may be exactly what is needed to make a better individual. For example, the most significant bits of a bad individual may be incorrect and the least significant bits correct, hence the objective value will be poor. At the same time, the most significant bits of a good individual may be correct and the least significant bits incorrect, hence the objective value will be higher. By combining the genes from both the good individual and the bad, it is possible to have a perfect chromosome, at least in theory.

Another reason why bad individuals are sometimes included in the mating pool is to keep the diversity of the gene pool. Quite often, the whole population can converge very quickly to small variations of the same super-individual. Hence, marriage between two individuals with very similar chromosome can only result in offspring that also have very similar chromosomes to their parents. In this case, diversity of the gene pool is important and must be maintained.

9.2.5   Pairing

Once the mating pool has been established, mating begins with a pair of parents in the pool. To do this, two individuals must be selected to be the

TABLE 9.1. Computation of Cumulative Distribution Function

Chromosome Number	Objective Value	Probability	CDF	Interval
1	8	0.5	0.5	[0, 0.5)
2	4	0.25	0.75	[0.5, 0.75)
3	2	0.125	0.875	[0.75, 0.875)
4	2	0.125	1.0	[0.875, 1.0)

parents. Given a number of eligible individuals in the mating pool, a number of ways are available to select pairs of individuals.

The simplest way to pair individuals together is to select individuals sequentially. To start, the individuals in the mating pool are sorted according to their objective values. Then pairing starts sequentially from the top. The first individual is paired with the second one, the third paired with the fourth, and so on. Another way is to pair the first individual with the last one in the pool and the second individual with the second-to-last one in the pool. This approach is simple to implement and ensures that everyone in the mating pool is used and is used once.

Another way to pair individuals together is to select two individuals randomly from the mating pool and repeat the process until the desired number of pairs has been reached. One problem with this implementation is that there is no guarantee that everyone in the mating pool will be used. In fact, there is no guarantee that the best individuals in the mating pool will be used for pairing, in forming other ways survive to the next generation. Nor is it possible to ensure that an individual will not be selected more than once for mating. To remedy the situation, once a pair has been selected, it is removed from the mating pool. All pair selections are taken from the remaining pool to ensure that every individual from the mating pool is used.

A third approach to mating is to favor probabilistically those individuals that are better than the others. This is called weighted pairing, or the roulette wheel selection strategy. This approach begins with a sorted list of the individuals according to the objective values in the mating pool. Then a probability value for each individual can be assigned by normalizing the associated objective value of that individual by the sum of all objective values. Using the cumulative distribution function (CDF), each individual is now assigned an interval in the CDF. The length of the interval is different according to the objective values. If the objective value is high for a particular individual, then the probability of that individual being selected is high. Correspondingly, the interval for that individual is large. For example, assume that there are four individuals in the mating pool with their corresponding objective values. The probability and the CDF can be computed as shown in Table 9.1.

Given a random number drawn from a uniform distribution, the interval in the table shows which chromosome would be selected. In the event that the objective values are very similar to one another, the probability will be similar and the interval will be almost the same. Another way to spread out the CDF is to use the rank of the objective values instead of the objective values directly.

When the mating pool is large, the above approaches are less effective. First, sorting and ranking a large array is time-consuming. Secondly, the differences in probability values would be minuscule. Another approach to pairing is by means of tournament. When a parent is needed, a small subset from the mating pool is randomly selected. The individual with the highest objective function wins the competition and becomes a parent. The process continues until all needed parents have been chosen.

9.2.6   Mating

In mating, the chromosomes of two individuals must be combined to produce one or more offspring. After two individuals have been selected from the mating pool and marked for paring, the chromosomes for these two individuals can be combined to produce offspring. The two original individuals are the parents. Newly produced individuals are called offspring. The simplest way is for each offspring to use parts of one chromosome combined with parts of the other chromosome to make a whole chromosome. This is called crossover.

In a one-way crossover operation, a single split is used to mark the location of the exchange. Before the crossover operation, a random number is drawn from a uniform distribution and scaled to the number of bits in the chromosome. This random number marks the location of the split. The first offspring takes the first part of the chromosome before the split from the first parent and the second part of the chromosome after the split from the second parent. Likewise, the second offspring takes the second part of the chromosome after the split from the first parent and the first part of the chromosome before the split from the second parent. For example, suppose we have two parents with the following chromosomes:

Parent A: [0000111111110000]

Parent B: [1111000000001111]

A random number is selected to mark the location of the split. Assume that the split location is between the fifth and sixth digit as marked by the separator. The offspring thus produced would be as given below:

Parent A: [00001|11111110000]

Parent B: [11110|00000001111]

Offspring A: [00001|00000001111]

Offspring B: [11110|11111110000]

There is really no reason why only two parents are used to produce two offspring. The same technique can be used for more than two parents to produce more than two offspring. For example, if three parents are used, then, keeping the first part of the first chromosome, the second part can be exchanged with two other parents. Likewise, keeping the first part of the second chromosome, the second part can also be exchanged with two other parents. Also keeping the first part of the third chromosome, the second part can also be exchanged with two other parents. Carrying out these crossover operation with three parents yields a total of six offspring:

Parent A: [00001|1111110000]

Parent B: [11110|00000001111]

Parent C: [10101|01010101010]

Offspring A: [00001|00000001111]

Offspring B: [00001|01010101010]

Offspring C: [11110|1111110000]

Offspring D: [11110|01010101010]

Offspring E: [10101|1111110000]

Offspring F: [10101|00000001111]

In a two-way crossover operation, two splits are used to make the exchange. The two splits mark the pieces of chromosome to be exchanged. Before the crossover operation, two distinct random numbers are drawn from a uniform distribution and scaled appropriately. The first offspring takes the chromosome from the first parent but exchanges the chromosome piece marked by the two splits from parent B. Likewise, the second offspring takes the chromosome from the second parent but exchanges the chromosome piece marked by the two splits from parent A. This operation is illustrated below. Using the same two parents as the previous example, assume that the split now occurs at the fourth and tenth bit.

Parent A: [0000|111111|110000]

Parent B: [1111|000000|001111]

Offspring A: [0000|000000|110000]

Offspring B: [1111|111111|001111]

It is possible to use additional splits to exchange more pieces of the chromosome. It is not clear whether more splits and exchanges in the chromosome would increase the efficiency of the process other than merely increasing the computational complexity.

9.2.7   Mutation

While mating is analogous to bisexual reproduction requiring two parents, mutation is analogous to asexual reproduction involving a single parent. Offspring produced by mating inherit chromosomes from its parents. When the parents have many common genes, then the offspring will also contain many common genes. This condition occurs quite often. As the population evolves, quite often the entire population gradually becomes stale, with all individual having close to the same genetic makeup. Since all the individuals are so similar to one another, very little additional learning can be gained. In order to keep up the diversity of gene pool, the mutation operation is employed. Mutation is a way to produce offspring that will contain genetic material not contained in the chromosome of their parents. Mutation causes an offspring to explore areas not covered by the search space of the current population.

One of the simplest mutation operations is a single-bit complement operation. In this operation, a single bit of the chromosome in the selected offspring is complemented. Take a random number and scale it properly. This random number marks the location of the bit in the chromosome, and one simply complements the selected bit. For example, if an offspring produced by the crossover operation has the following chromosome:

Original offspring: [0000000000110000]

Assume that the random number obtained points to the eighth bit. Since the eighth bit was originally a 0, the complement of that bit is 1. The chromosome of the mutated offspring is as follows:

Mutated offspring: [0000000100110000]

A bit change in the least significant bit of a gene would not cause much change in the parameter value. A bit change in the most significant bit of the same gene would cause significant change in the parameter value.

Using the same approach, one can also have multiple bit mutation also. One simply selects multiple random numbers and complements the corresponding bits. For more random effects, one can also use random number to select the number of random bits to mutate. Depending on the length of the chromosome, a single bit may not be sufficient to cause offspring to mutate enough to begin explorations in new areas of the search space. In this case, multiple-bit mutation would be needed.

Not all offspring are submitted to mutation. Only a small percentage of the offspring is submitted to the mutation operation. This percentage is called the mutation rate. In normal conditions, the mutation rate is kept small. Excess mutation rate defeats the purpose of crossover and inheritance. Excessive mutation rate causes the algorithm to degenerate into random search with little learning from generation to generation.

9.2.8 The Next Generation

After mating and mutation, a new set of individuals or offspring has been added to the population. Some of the offspring could represent a better solution than what is known up to the present time. Most of the time, the offspring represent variations of their parents. These new offspring are now checked for legitimacy and fitness. Any offspring that do not satisfy the constrained requirement are immediately eliminated from the pool. In some implementations, any new offspring produced are immediately checked for legitimacy and eliminated when they do not satisfy the constraints. In this way, only legitimate offspring are added to the population.

At this point the population now contains three types of individuals: parents, unused parents, and offspring. The population size is twice or more than the original. Some individuals must be retired from the population in order to keep the population constant. A number of strategies have been proposed for culling the pool.

One method is to retire all parents and use the offspring instead. This method is simple to implement. Any time when two parents are used to generate two offspring, the parents are immediately eliminated from the pool, to be replaced by the offspring. The question remains as to whether the offspring are better than parents. If two seemingly good parents produce two bad offspring, then the genetic material of the two good parents will be lost.

A second method is to let the parents and offspring compete according to the objective values. In other words, the new population with all parents, unused individuals, and new offspring is sorted and the top half of the population is kept. Any individuals with objective values below a threshold are discarded. This method ensures that there is always a good set of individuals to be used for breeding.

After the population has been culled back to the original size, the best solution is compared with the saved solution. If the new best solution is better than the saved solution, then the new best solution is saved along with the chromosome information as the saved solution. This saved solution represents the best solution up to this generation. The intelligence of everything learned up to this point is contained in the individual chromosomes of the current population.

If the best solution at this point is satisfactory, then the algorithm terminates. If additional time is allowed, the algorithm repeats itself for another generation. As generations progress, it is expected that the best solution up to that point will get better and better. Since at any generation the best solution is kept, one always has the best solution up to that point, regardless of whether that best solution comes from the first generation or the latest generation. In other words, the best solution is the best and will not be worse than any solutions found up to that point. However, as is typical of other iterative schemes, the convergence rate may slow considerably as time progresses. Initially, it does not take too many generations for the best solution to become a good solution. However, as the algorithm continues, it is often observed that more and more generations are required before a new best solution is found. Furthermore, the new best solution found may not be significantly better.

A number of stopping strategies have been proposed. The simplest way to stop the algorithm is when the best solution is good enough. This is somewhat subjective and highly dependent on the application. In the case where one is trying to locate the root of a polynomial, with the best solution providing a polynomial function value that is within ϵ of 0, this error condition can be used to stop the algorithm. However, if we are trying to find the maximum or minimum value for a particular function, there is no hint *a priori* what the maximum or minimum value would be. In this case, it is extremely difficult to set the stopping criterion according to the function value.

Another way to set the stopping criterion is to allocate a fixed number of generations. This is often used when there resources are limited and the best solution is sought within the allocated time frame. This strategy is easy to implement.

A third way to arrive at a stopping criterion is to observe intrinsically within the algorithm in terms of improvements in the best solution. As expected, the best solution improves quickly initially and the improvement becomes less dramatic as the algorithm progresses. This is measured by the convergence rate. Traditionally, the convergence rate is defined as the average change in mean squared error as a function of generation number. It is usually defined as the slope of the mean squared error curve as a function of the generation number. For genetic algorithm, convergence rate can be estimated by the ratio of the percentage of improvements in the objective value over the number of generations since the last update. As the improvement slows down, the convergence rate decreases. When the convergence rate falls below a threshold value, the stopping criterion is said to have arrived.

9.2.9 Performance

How well the algorithm performs depends on a wide variety of factors. One of the most important factors is the representation of parameter values. If the representation adequately reflects the problem on hand, the problem of convergence to the best solution is made simpler. If the search space is linear, then the parameter values should be represented in a linear fashion. If the parameters have a nonlinear effect on the objective values, then a nonlinear representation of the parameter values may work better.

Once an appropriate representation has been decided upon, the efficiency of the algorithm depends on the population size. The larger the population size, the more the search space is covered and searched. This often leads to better solutions quickly. However, if the size of the population is excessively large, the computational complexity can also be excessive. On the other hand, the population size should not be too small, or the lack of genetic diversity will cause the population to converge to a superindividual very quickly. In this case the algorithm has not been given the opportunity to explore the search space to discover where potential solutions lie.

Another crucial factor in performance is the number of generations. Even though the algorithm tends to retain the traits that give good solutions, the chromosome pieces must first be discovered before they can be retained. The discovery process comes from the crossover and mutation operations. This means that sufficient generations must be given to the algorithm so that it has time to explore the search space to look for a good solution. On the other hand, excessive numbers of generations tend to be unproductive. After the algorithm has sufficient generations to converge, the nature of the algorithm is to retain the top individuals. Soon the entire population becomes descendants of a single superindividual with very similar genetic material. Further generations would only encourage inbreeding but in reality produce no new information. At this point, a restart is needed with a new initial population. To avoid further occurrences of this situation, the mutation should be increased to provide more genetic diversity.

Another factor in the performance is the inclusion of individuals with bad solutions in the mating pool. The tendency of the algorithm through the crossover operation is to eliminate individuals with bad solutions and keep only individuals with good solutions. After a small number of generations, the population tends to converge to same superindividual. Increased mutation rate helps to maintain the diversity of the genetic pool. Another method is to allow a certain percentage in the mating pool for individuals with bad solutions. Even though an individual may have bad objective values, this does not imply that all bits in the chromosome are unacceptable. Hence keeping a small percentage of individuals with bad objective values provides the diversity for the algorithm to continue searching.

9.2.10 Enhancements

Many enhancements have been proposed in the literature in an effort to increase the performance of the algorithm and speed up the convergence rate. Many of these improvements appear as different strategies to be implemented in different parts of the algorithm and have been covered in previous sections. In this section a number of general strategies are covered.

Individuals in a population represent a certain portion of the search space. After a number of generations, the elimination of the nonperforming individuals tends to restrict the search space to a local region represented by a superindividual. At that point, subsequent generations would only further constrain the search region more and more narrowly within the local region. The algorithm is unproductive at that point. If the convergence rate parameter is used as a stopping criterion, then the algorithm will stop. If the local region is a local minimum, then the problem is far from being solved. A new restart is needed to move the algorithm to another part of the search space in the hope of locating a better solution.

Another strategy is to start with multiple initial populations. There is no reason why the algorithm should only have a single population. If each population represents a search in a local region, then multiple populations mean multiple local regions are being searched at the same time. In the spirit of competition among multiple individuals in the same population, there is no reason why multiple populations should not also compete among themselves for the best solution. When the algorithm begins, multiple populations are generated. Each population is allowed to evolve for awhile. Then the best solution for each population is compared and those populations with good solutions are allowed to evolve further. Those populations with poor solutions are eliminated in favor of new populations. The advantage of this strategy is that more of the search space can be explored simultaneously.

In order to maintain genetic diversity, a rate schedule can be used to give different rates at different stages of the algorithm. Initially, the goal of the algorithm is to explore the search space. At this point, a high mutation rate is used to encourage the population to spread out in the search space. Towards the end of the algorithm, the mutation rate is reduced so that the algorithm can converge to a solution.

Another strategy is to use the concept of simulated annealing. Initially, the temperature is set high. Correspondingly, the mutation rate is set high and the crossover rate low, so that the algorithm has a chance to explore the search space. Towards the end of the optimization process, the temperature is gradually reduced so that the mutation rate is low and the crossover rate is high. This allows the optimization process to settle on the selected solution.

9.3   CONTINUOUS GENETIC ALGORITHM

In the previous section, a string of binary bits was used as the basic building block for the genes. In this section, the technique for binary genetic algorithm is extended to the case when the genetic representation is based on continuous parameters. In principle both strategies are similar and consequently the algorithm works in similar fashion. However, the change in representation from binary to continuous variables necessitates some subtle changes in the operations. These changes are covered in detail in this section.

In principle, the genetic algorithm for the continuous case is the same as that for the binary case. The algorithm starts with an initial population. Then, the fitness of the population for each individual is computed according to the objective function. Based on the objective values, the population is trimmed. Then, according to the associated objective values for each individual, the mating pool is created. From the mating pool, pairs are selected for mating.

At this point, the strategies mentioned for the binary genetic algorithm in the previous sections are also applicable. Once the pairs are selected, the mating process begins. The mating operations for the continuous case are different and will be discussed in later sections. The mating operations for the continuous parameter case are also different. Once offspring are produced, the fitness of the offspring is calculated and the population is trimmed back to the original size. This part of the algorithm is the same as the binary case.

9.3.1 Genetic Representation

In most optimization problems, the parameter variables can be categorical or numerical. If the variable is categorical, then the representation can be represented in binary or by integers. Suppose the variable can take on one of five different categories. It can then be represented as follows:

$$\text{Binary:} \quad 00001, 00010, 00100, 01000, \text{ or } 10000$$

$$\text{Integer:} \quad 1, 2, 3, 4, 5$$

Note that in the binary case there are actually $2^5 = 32$ possible combinations of those five bits and only 5 of them are valid. This means that many of the offspring would be invalid because the coding of those five bits does not result in one of the 5 legitimate codes above. However, using the integer format, it is simple enough just to constrain the parameter value to be integer and that the integer value is between 1 and 5.

If the parameter value is real, then the binary representation can only be quantized and represented within the resolution depicted by the number of bits allotted in the gene. If more precision is needed, then the number of bits must be increased. Alternatively, a two-stage strategy can be used. Start with an initial representation with a certain number of bits for the parameter values. When the algorithm converges, start another genetic problem with a different representation using the results from the first. For example, given the two-variable function f as a function of x and y. The problem is to find the maximum of the function and the corresponding values of x and y with 32-bit precision. As specified by the application, one can design the genetic representation for x and y with 32 bits. Alternatively, one can use a two-step process. In the first step, design the genetic representation for x and y with 16 bits. Even though the genetic representation does not have sufficient resolution, the algorithm would converge much quicker than if 32 bits were used for representation. As a second step, the problem can now be recast to finding the maximum of the function given that the most significant bits of x and y are specified by what is found in the first step. This is really the same problem except that the interval for x and y has been significantly narrowed.

The multiple-step procedure is needed because the genetic code is represented as strings of binary bits. However, if the genetic code is represented by real numbers, it is not necessary to have multiple steps, because the real number can be represented by the maximum precision allowed in the computer. For the problem of locating the minimum of the function, the genetic code would merely be two real numbers:

$$[x, y]$$

Clearly, this representation is concise and simpler than the representation based on strings of binary bits.

Suppose the problem on hand is to find the maximum value of a four-variable function g. The input parameters are w, x, y, and z. The variables are bound between the 0 and 99. In other words, each variable requires two decimal digits. Using the continuous parameter representation, the chromosome for this example can be represented as a four-variable quartet:

$$[w, x, y, z]$$

9.3.2   Mating

In the binary case, the primary mating operation is the one-way and the two-way crossover operation. The crossover operation produces offspring that inherits the genetic code from both parents. In the continuous case, there are no binary strings that can be split into two or more parts for exchange. If the chromosome is composed of many variables, then the crossover operation can still be applied. However, there are other techniques that are more suited to operations with continuous variables. Many of these techniques are reviewed by Adewuya [1] and Michalewicz [66].

A simple crossover operation for continuous case is the same as the binary case. In a one-way split, a random number is generated and properly scaled to the number of variables in the genetic code. This random number is used to mark the split location. The offspring are generated by swapping parts of the chromosome as before. Assume that the chromosomes for the two parents are given below and assume that the split location is after the first parameter. The offspring thus generated would be given below:

Parent A: [1, |2, 3, 4]

Parent B: [90, |91, 92, 93]

Offspring A: [1, |91, 92, 93]

Offspring B: [90, |2, 3, 4]

While this technique works for the binary case, it only works in a limited capacity for the continuous case. It is obvious from the example that two offspring are produced each inheriting the genetic code from its parents. The algorithm could proceed from this point on. However, after a few generations it is obvious that every individual in the population contains permutations of the same few parameter values (1, 2, 3, 4, 90, 91, 92, 93). In other words, while the crossover operation produces permutations of the parameter values, it is not able to generate new parameter values that are not part of the original set. This places a severe limitation on the efficacy of the algorithm. The same crossover operation can be extended to multiple splits. The swapping operation is the same as the binary case. The difficulties remain the same, however.

Note that if the parameter values are swapped in this manner and as long as the parents contain legitimate values for each parameter in its proper place, the offspring will also be guaranteed to contain legitimate values for each parameter. This is true because the swap leaves each parameter in place. This is a very desirable property for the crossover operation.

In order for the algorithm to be efficacious, it is necessary to generate values that are not in the original population. This strategy is called the linear interpolation scheme. It can be done by combining the values of the parents using a functional relationship so that new values can be generated. One such function is the linear interpretation method:

$$P_{new} = \beta P_A + (1 - \beta)P_B$$

where the values of β ranges from 0 to 1. The value of β controls how much P_A contributes to the new parameter value and the value of $(1 - \beta)$ controls how much P_B also contributes to the new parameter value. The value of β is randomly generated for each parameter at each step. Using the same values for the parents, assume that the four β values have been randomly generated and are 0.1, 0.2, 0.3, 0.4, respectively. The resulting offspring would be as follows:

Parent A: [1, 2, 3, 4]

Parent B: [90, 91, 92, 93]

Offspring: [81.1, 73.2, 65.3, 57.4]

The above operation produces one offspring. To get another offspring, another set of β values must be generated again. There is no particular reason to link one offspring with another.

While the linear interpolation scheme is adept in generating new values for the offspring based on the values of the parents, it is clear that this is an interpolation and therefore the generated values could never be outside the values given by the parents. This is clearly a problem because the operation cannot extrapolate to values outside the interval bounded by the values of the parents. Many suggestions have been proposed to remedy the situation. An obvious solution is an extrapolation scheme, in which the value of β is allowed to be outside the interval of [0, 1]. As long as β is constrained to be within the interval [0, 1], the resultant value is guaranteed to be valid. However if β is allowed to take on values outside the interval, then the resultant parameter value may or may not be valid anymore. As an example, if the values of the two parents take on the minimum and maximum allowable values respectively, then no value of β outside the interval [0, 1] will yield a valid value. On the other hand, if the two values of the two parents take on the same value, then no value of β within the interval [0, 1] will yield any value that is different than that for the parents. This is clearly a problem for the linear interpolation scheme.

Wright proposed a slightly different form of the linear extrapolation formula to allow for values outside the interval governed by the parents [105].

$$P_{new} = \beta(P_A - P_B) + P_A$$

The value of β is still chosen to be in the interval between 0 and 1. However, if $\beta = 0$, then $P_{new} = P_A$, but if $\beta = 1$, then $P_{new} = 2*P_A - P_B$. In the latter case, the value generated is outside the interval $[P_A, P_B]$. Eshelman and Schaffer proposed the blend crossover (BLX-α) [27]. The parameter α determines how far the extrapolated value can stray. Before the interpolation crossover operation is carried out, the values of the parents are extrapolated by a factor of α. Then the interpolation operation produces offspring using the extended range of the parents.

9.3.3 Mutation

In the binary case, mutation is obtained by randomly complementing a bit in the binary string. This scheme clearly does not apply for the continuous case. The object of the mutation operation is to introduce new genetic material to force the algorithm to explore new search space. Hence, any scheme that would generate a new value would work.

The random exchange scheme is the easiest one to implement. Given the chromosome for a particular individual, the random exchange scheme simply replaces randomly one of the parameters with another random value. Select a random number and properly scale the magnitude to the number of parameters in the chromosome. Select another random number and scale the second random number to be within the interval for that parameter. Replace the parameter in the chromosome with the new random value.

If there are many parameters in the chromosome, then a single mutation may not be sufficient to send the individual to an unexplored search space. If so, multiple mutations can be applied to the chromosome so that more than one single parameter is changed and mutated.

9.3.4 Performance

In principle, factors affecting the performance of the continuous genetic algorithm are similar to those for the binary genetic algorithm. De Jong did a comprehensive study of the effects of various parameters on algorithm performance [20]. From the simulation results, De Jong concluded that small population size improves the initial performance while large population size improves the long-term performance. This is not surprising. When the population size is small, convergence is rapid, hence giving good performance quickly. However, because the population size is small, there is insufficient material to explore the entire search space, hence it is easy to get trapped in a local minimum instead of a better local region given a better opportunity to explore a wider search space.

De Jong also concluded that high mutation rate leads to good off-line performance while low mutation rate leads to good on-line performance. Off-line performance is measured by the best objective function value up to the present generation. On-line performance is measured by the average objective function value for all objective function evaluations. De Jong's result is not surprising. When the mutation rate is high, the algorithm is exploring all over the search space looking for the best local minimum region. Consequently, the off-line performance is poor, but the payoff comes from the ability to locate a better local region to converge to. That comes from the sacrifice of a lot of function evaluations. On the other hand, when the mutation rate is low, a solution is reached quickly with not much exploration of the search space, hence the on-line performance is good but the off-line exploration is poor because of the lack of opportunity to explore.

A surprising result from De Jong's experiment is that the type of crossover operations does not affect much of the results. Furthermore, the crossover rate should not be too high or too low. If the crossover rate is too high, the algorithm will bounce around without converging. If the crossover rate is too low, then, convergence is quick but the performance is subpar.

While not many formal studies have compared the use of binary genetic algorithms to the use of continuous genetic algorithms, the experience of many researchers has confirmed that using continuous representations generally gives better performance than the binary case [37]. Furthermore, algorithms using the continuous representation tend to converge much faster than algorithms using the binary representation.

9.3.5 Enhancements

Since the proposal of genetic algorithms back in the 1970s many enhancements have been proposed in the literature in an effort to fine tune the algorithm. In this section, a number of these enhancements are covered.

While the basic algorithm is rather simple to implement and the logic for the generations is rather easy to program, for many applications the main bottleneck lies in the computation of the objective function. For example, consider an application of applying a genetic algorithm to scheduling. The genetic algorithm is capable of generating many potential schedules very easily. What is not so easy is to evaluate the goodness of each schedule generated. To arrive at a goodness measure, an external program is needed to generate the actual schedule, check to be sure that all constraints are satisfied, and then evaluate the schedule according to established guidelines. For this reason, it is not uncommon, while using genetic algorithm to search for a solution, for most of the computation time to be spent in evaluating the objective function of different individuals in the population. Any savings in reducing the number of objective function evaluations translates directly to reduction in the search time or complexity.

One proposal is to eliminate duplicate evaluation of the objective functions. This approach has been proposed by Michalewicz [66] and Davis [19] During the crossover operation, it is unusual for offspring to be identical. This is particularly true when the population begins to converge to a superindividual. Significant time can be saved if identical offspring are spotted and identified. In order to identify twins, it is necessary to check the entire population to see if the same pattern exists. If so, then the objective function is known and the objective function evaluation can be eliminated. Note that identical twins may occur not only among new offspring generated in the present generation but also with parents in the population. In an extreme case, it is possible that the same chromosome has been evaluated before but the chromosome pattern has been eliminated in earlier generations. This means that the algorithm must keep a list of all objective function evaluations. As the generations progress, the list will continue to grow. A point will come when it will be necessary to determine the amount of time in searching a long list versus the amount of time required to perform a single function evaluation.

For some applications, even a single evaluation of the objective function can be extremely time-consuming and complex. If the landscape of the objective function is relatively smooth, then a local interpretation of the objective function could save a significant amount of time. This technique was proposed by Haupt [36]. Before the algorithm starts, a uniform grid is defined on the search space and the objective function values are evaluated for the grid points. These evaluations provide a coarse estimate of the landscape. When a new offspring is generated, the objective function is not actually evaluated precisely. Rather, the objective function is estimated by interpolation from the landscape, from the neighboring points closest to the desired chromosome. While this approach may not produce a solution, due to the imprecise estimate of the objective function, the approach can be used to narrow down the search space rather quickly.

When the algorithm begins to converge, it is often observed that the individuals in the entire population gradually become very similar to one another. When this happens, the algorithm loses its power to explore the search space, due to the lack of genetic diversity. To remedy the situation, Michalewicz [66] proposed attaching a lifetime to each individual. Each individual is allowed to live for a minimum amount of time and is not allowed to live beyond a maximum amount of time. The implementation of a lifetime ensures that no superindividual is allowed to persist and permeate throughout the population for an indefinite amount of time.

9.4 EVOLUTIONARY PROGRAMMING

Evolutionary programming is an approach based on simulated evolution and is similar in operation to genetic algorithms [30]. Rechenberg [86] and Schwefel [91] have also developed a similar technology, called evolution strategies. The basic principle of evolutionary programming arises from the observation that evolution involves reproduction, mutation, competition, and selection. Fogel argued that natural selection occurs not according to the genetic materials (genotype), but according to the expressed and exhibited behavior (phenotype). In genetic algorithms, coding structures are called chromosomes. These coding structures are manipulated directly by crossover and mutation operations. In evolutionary programming, coding structures are rather abstract structures, which are primarily modified by the mutation operation to produce new behaviors.

9.4.1 Evolutionary Strategies

The evolutionary strategies (ES) approach was developed by Rechenberg [86] and Schwefel [91]. It was initially designed to solve optimization problems involving real-valued problems. The process can be summarized as follows:

1. Define an objective function for the problem.
2. Define a coding strategy for representing the solution. Typically the representation is a series of real numbers.
3. Randomly initialize a population of individuals.
4. Compute the objective function values for all individuals.
5. Generate offspring by mutation.
6. Compute the objective function value for each offspring.
7. Select a set of individuals with good solutions.
8. Repeat step 5 unless stopping criteria are met.

From the above flowchart, it can be seen that the process is similar to genetic programming, with the distinct difference that there is no mating. The primary operation for producing offspring comes from mutation. This is denoted as a $(1 + 1) - ES$, where $1 + 1$ indicates one parent giving one offspring. The operation was later extended to multiple parents and multiple offspring. The extended approach is denoted by $(\mu + \lambda) - ES$, i.e., μ parents are used to product λ offspring. The process is called recombination. In the competition, all $(\mu + \lambda)$ individuals are involved in the competition for natural selection.

In the evolutionary strategies approach, mutation is performed by Gaussian perturbation to the parameter values. Note that the perturbation is applied to all parameters. It is argued that behavioral traits are affected by more than one gene. Hence the perturbations are applied to all the parameters. Recom-

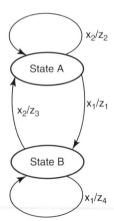

Figure 9.2. A finite state machine.

bination is performed by exchange (crossover) and linear interpolation. Note that the primary search operation is through mutation. Recombination is added only to accelerate the search.

In the natural selection process, the best solution is always kept. In the $(1 + 1) - ES$ case, only the best solution is kept, regardless whether it is the parent or the offspring. In the $(\mu + \lambda) - ES$ case, the best μ solutions are kept out of the λ offspring. All parents will be replaced by the best offspring.

9.4.2   Evolutionary Programming

The evolutionary programming (EP) approach was developed by Fogel as early as 1962 [28]. The goal of EP is to simulate evolution as a learning process. The basic concept is to learn to predict the environment and to translate what has been learned to formulate a suitable response towards the specified goal. The basic mechanism for this prediction is a set of finite state machines (FSMs). A population of FSMs is evolved that can provide better predictions of an environmental sequence towards a given goal. An FSM is shown in Figure 9.2.

In the broadest sense, evolutionary programming defines an environment as a sequence of symbols taken from a finite alphabet. From this given information, the problem is to predict future symbols based on what is already known. It is reasoned that not all correct predictions contribute equally to the same learning. Likewise, not all errors carry the same penalty. In other words, the cost function can be modeled by a cost matrix, which defines the goal.

A finite state machine is defined by a set of states and transitions to and from the set of states. An FSM is defined by a state transition diagram. The current status of the environment is represented by the current state of the machine. Upon an input, the machine will transition to another state as governed by the state transition diagram. The following figure shows an FSM in terms of its state transition diagram.

In the state transition diagram, a state is marked by a circle and a transition is marked by an arc. All transition is identified by a doublet (input/output). The base of the arc is the current state. The head of the arc is the next state or the new state. The doublet notation indicates that when the specified input is received, the FSM will transition from its current state to its next state with the specified output. In much of the digital logic literature this is called a Mealy machine.

The basic process for EP is as follows:

1. Choose the symbolization, i.e., the symbols that appropriately describe the environment.
2. Determine the maximum number of states for the FSM.
3. Select the population size.
4. Create random machines with random initial states. Each input symbol has corresponding randomly selected state transitions and output states.

A flowchart of this process is shown in Figure 9.3. The above formulation requires no *a priori* information, although if such information is available what is known can be programmed directly into the FSMs.

Initialization. Initially, the observed environment must be coded as a sequence of symbols. Based on the application on hand, the alphabet is defined and the symbol sequence is defined according to the problem. In EP, the actual representation of the symbols is not important as long as the representation is unique and can adequately represent the problem space, the observed environment.

After the symbols for the environment have been defined, as part of the initialization an initial population must also be generated. Each individual in the population is an FSM. Each initial FSM is generated with a random number of states, with random transitions, and with random outputs for each transition. In addition, each FSM is also given a random starting state.

Fitness Evaluation. This sequence of symbols is next fed to each FSM. Each FSM has been initialized already with a certain starting state. From the given symbol, the next symbol is predicted and compared with the sequence. After the entire sequence is fed, the fitness of each FSM is evaluated in its ability to predict by counting the number of correct predictions. The actual objective function value is determined by the cost matrix based on the number of correct predictions.

Competition and Selection. After the fitness evaluation, the next step is to trim the population. This is synonymous with selecting the parents for the next generation. The selection can be accomplished either deterministically or stochastically. In the deterministic approach, the best individuals are kept. Both the parents and the offspring participate in the competition.

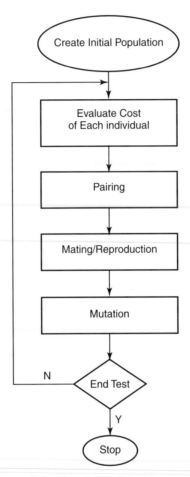

Figure 9.3. Flowchart of the EP process.

In the stochastic approach, those solutions with greater fitness are given more chance to survive than those with lesser fitness. Some of the solutions with lesser fitness should also be allowed to propagate to keep the diversity of the pool. This is done by performing a pairwise competition conducted in a round-robin format. In a pairwise competition, the competition is limited only to neighboring individuals. Hence, some less fit individuals will still survive. At the same time, learning is present due to the competition.

Next Generation. After the competition, the population is brought back into the proper size. The best solution is saved. If the best solution is within the accepted tolerance, then the algorithm stops. If the number of generations exceeds the maximum number allowed, then the algorithm also stops. If not, the algorithm is allowed to proceed.

Population Generation. To generate offspring for the next generation, the main operation used is mutation. The goal of mutation is to improve the performance of the FSMs. Changes to FSM can be applied on any parts of the machine. There are five obvious places for mutation:

1. Change the output symbol.
2. Change the state transition, the arc.
3. Add a state.
4. Delete a state.
5. Change the start state.

Each one of the above changes can cause significant change in the output sequence and hence the prediction accuracy. These changes are probabilistically applied during the mutation process. Variations of the EP approach include the use of multiple mutation operations.

9.5 SUMMARY

In this chapter, two similar and competing technologies, genetic algorithm and evolutionary programming, have been discussed. In operation, both technologies appear to be quite similar. There are a number of similarities between them. But in principle there are significant differences between the two.

In terms of similarities, both GA and EP use a population of individuals to explore the search space. Each individual represents a potential solution as well as some arrangement of the search parameters. An objective function is used to evaluate the fitness of each individual. The objective function is application dependent and problem dependent. Some individuals yield good solutions as measured by the objective function, while others yield poor solutions. In both GA and EP, offspring are generated. The generation of offspring is the primary mechanism used in the search for a better solution. In both technologies, some selection mechanism is also used to cull the population.

In terms of differences, in principle, GA is a simulation of evolution on the genetic level, while EP is a simulation of evolution on the phenotypic or behavioral level. In the early stage of GA development, chromosome representation is primarily by binary strings. This is not true in later stage. GA has been extended to the continuous-variable case. On the other hand, EP has always been developed using real-valued parameters. In GA, reproduction is primarily due to crossover operations and some mutation operations to preserve genetic diversity. In EP, the primary reproduction is due to mutation with crossover operation for speedy convergence.

10

INTELLIGENT STRATEGY GENERATION IN COMPLEX MANUFACTURING ENVIRONMENTS[1]

10.1 INTRODUCTION

Numerous applications exist in which the solution methods and outputs contain a language that is foreign or difficult for the end user. In addition, many real-world environments have time-varying constraints and objectives. Many of the time-varying objectives may run counter to others. Typical of this description is a manufacturing environment in which products are being fabricated to meet a set of orders, commonly referred to as a job shop. In this setting, materials, facilities, and personnel are the primary resources and should be appropriately utilized for achieving maximum profitability. Emphasis is often placed on finding optimum product sequences to achieve one or more (often conflicting) objectives: maximum throughput, maximum revenue, maximum machine utilization, fewest missed ship dates, and so on. Models and methods often consist of linear (integer) programming, stochastic linear programming, dynamic programming, queuing theory, heuristics, and stochastic simulation [41, 70]. For some settings, these methods may not provide an acceptable solution due to several difficulties, namely (1) unavailability of model parameter data, (2) computational time necessary for solution generation, (3) inability to quantify pertinent elements or constraints, (4) solution regeneration in real time if an operational deviation or environment change occurs, or, in the case of stochastic simulation, if the solution represents the long-run average, it may not reflect current shop conditions.

---

[1]This chapter contributed by Monte P. Tull, School of Electrical & Computer Engineering, University of Oklahoma, Norman, Oklahoma.

Model flexibility is an advantage in real applications such as manufacturing processes. Rapidly changing priorities (daily, perhaps even hourly) may be common. External customer pressure, order alteration, personnel and machine availability, part shortages, quality problems, and transportation difficulties are a few of the reasons for production plan deviations. A model that easily accounts for these conditions and provides a timely updated production plan is a valuable tool. Permitting the user to control and dynamically alter objectives is a beneficial model attribute. This capability is necessary for off-line studies and may be essential for real-time applications if current process conditions are to be considered. Difficulties can arise for process managers in attempting to relate business objectives to production schedules and sequences, such as dispatching rules. The three-stage model presented here permits user manipulation of business objectives via a fuzzy logic model and generates a near-optimal production plan using an evolutionary programming algorithm (EA) and an agent-based simulation model for determining fuzzy input parameters. The model can be applied in less complex environments without the simulation step, but typically a process simulation or translator stage is required to map the EA output into the fuzzy evaluator.

Agent-based modeling methods provide a means for representing both internal and external parameters that affect a process and constitute one method for providing an evaluation of the EA output and translate results for input to the fuzzy evaluator [9]. Generally, agents are goal oriented and interact, constructively or destructively, with other agents. Interaction among agents is defined by rules or functions. Emergent behavior of the system is often observable even from very simple agents and interaction rules. The Swarm simulator is an agent-based software package that can be used to develop models of simple or complex processes [98]. Applying this methodology to a manufacturing process allows both internal and external process parameters to be represented as agents. Various types of agents are required. A resource agent represents labor or a machine. Product agents represent the various products that are manufactured. External agents that interact with product and resource agents may represent management or expediting pressure, worker attendance, machine breakdown, and machine maintenance. Each agent is an object possessing attributes that determine its actions and reactions with other agents.

10.2 MODEL DESCRIPTION

Combining simulation with artificial intelligence and genetic algorithms has been proposed as an optimization and scheduling tool [48, 85]. Kewley suggested a decision support model for battlefield settings termed fuzzy-generic decision optimization (FGDO) [51]. A similar approach is used here for a manufacturing environment. A high-level view of the proposed model is shown in Figure 10.1. Initial condition inputs are supplied manually or automatically. Manual input can be used for off-line studies; automatic loading

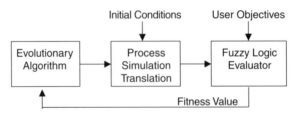

Figure 10.1. High-level model.

is necessary for real-time execution. It is very common for modern factories to have automated product tracking and process state parameters. Process managers supply user objective parameters to the fuzzy logic evaluator. To accomplish this, the user can adjust the fuzzy logic membership functions or modify the fuzzy rule base. These actions are discussed in Section 10.5.

A primary advantage of the model is that it permits the process managers to determine the production plan using business objectives rather than requiring them to specify or interpret operations research types of production rules. Further, the business objectives are stated using fuzzy functions that permit visualization of the relative importance of each objective. It is believed that process managers can make better decisions using business objectives rather than production rules. Process-management decisions based on production rules may lead to myopic local optimization within the various process steps and fail to achieve overall acceptable performance. With the genetic algorithm evolving the production rules and the resulting schedule, the process managers need only evaluate the outcomes. Business objectives are cast as fuzzy membership functions that can be altered by the process-mangement team. Example fuzzy functions are the number of late orders, throughput, machine utilization, back-schedule size, and production interval. For a given rule set generated by the genetic algorithm, the simulation will compute these parameters and pass them through for evaluation by the fuzzy model. The fuzzy model assesses how well the rule set meets the objectives by assigning a fitness value, which in turn is passed back to the evolutionary algorithm. The fitness value is used by the evolutionary algorithm to determine if the rule set is good relative to other rule sets and use the fitness value for further evolution. See Section 10.3.

An example application of the proposed model is a multiproduct, capacity-limited assembly line for electronic modules. Up to 100 different circuit types can be assembled and tested on the facilities. A minimum batch size of 20 is desirable. Assembly kits are queued at the head of the line prior to the first process step. In this discussion we will consider only primary operations with no batch splitting or combining. The sequence of manufacturing operations is shown in Figure 10.2.

Q1 and Q2 represent two primary queues for which dispatch rules are applied. O1–O4 are in-line operations, where the O3 operation is bypassed

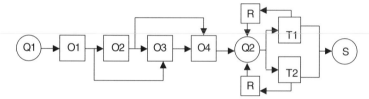

Figure 10.2. Assembly line operation sequence.

by some assemblies. The route through the line and the testing resources are dependent on the product technology utilized and the assembly type. T1 and T2 are testing operations that process unique assemblies. Assemblies that pass test are sent to stock (S). Failing assemblies route through the repair operation (R) and reenter Q2, often after the batch has completed testing. This phenomenon complicates the dispatching rules for Q2.

10.3   EVOLUTIONARY ALGORITHM

Holland proposed genetic algorithms as a method for function optimization [43]. Based on the Darwinian metaphor, potential problem solutions are members of a population P, consisting of N individuals. Each member of the population possesses a genotype or chromosome, v_i, composed of binary strings. The fitness, f_i, of the ith member is determined by a fitness function. Generally, for each generation only the fittest individuals are bred. Both genetic crossover and mutation operators can be employed to produce new individuals. Selection of parents for mating is often performed by the roulette wheel method [6], where the probability of selection of a member is proportional to the fitness of that population member. Let ρ_i be the probability of selecting the ith individual and F be the total fitness of all population members. Then,

$$F = \Sigma_i \, f_i$$

and

$$\rho_i = f_i / F$$

Mating of selected parents is accomplished by crossover of genes from one parent to the other, typically producing two offspring. Crossover points are selected randomly, generally with equal probability for each gene location within the chromosome. Mutation is accomplished by randomly selecting, with a user-prescribed probability, a gene and complementing its value. At each generation, the population size is pruned, using the fitness values, to a maximum population size. Elitist strategies preserve the highest fitness individual(s).

Evolutionary algorithms (EAs) extend the genetic algorithm chromosome to include integer and real gene values [98], as well as qualitative values and functions [48]. Both crossover breeding and mutation are possible with EAs. Crossover points are restricted to gene field boundaries. Mutation operators may vary depending on the mutated gene. Further development of EA chromosome structure permits a parse tree representation. Koza presents a general parse tree structure consisting of nodes that are either functions or variables [57]. These parse trees are equivalent to S-expressions in the LISP programming language. Functions consist of arithmetic operations, mathematical functions, Boolean operations, logical operators (IF-THEN-ELSE), and iterative operators (DO-UNTIL). Variables or terminal elements represent data or information used by the functions and form the leaves of the tree. Mating is performed by randomly generating a cut point in each parent tree, cutting the trees, and attaching the left or right subtree to the other parent. Two offspring are produced for each mating operation.

Let S be the set of functions and T be the set of terminal elements used by the EA. For this application, select the functions, minimum (min), maximum (max), and complement (compl), for S. These functions will combine the dispatching rules that comprise T. We assume that the rule values are normalized between 0 and 1 so that the complement is found by subtracting the value from 1. The following dispatching rule parameters are chosen:

DD Due date
TQ Time in queue
BS Batch size
BT Batch processing time
ST Setup time
TY Test yield rate

Now,

$$S = \{\text{min, max, compl}\}$$

and

$$T = \{\text{DD, TQ, BS, BT, ST, TY}\}$$

Clearly, more complex dispatching rules [84], and hence, terminal elements can be chosen for T; however, for illustration purposes, we will limit our discussion to these sets. Note that, for simplicity, we have not included any

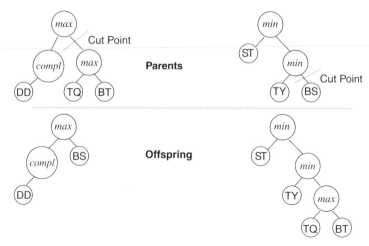

Figure 10.3. Parse tree mating operation.

product characteristic parameters, e.g., type of circuit board assembly. A parse tree representation and mating of parents are shown in Figure 10.3.

10.4 PROCESS SIMULATION

In this decision support system, an agent-based simulator is used to determine the outcome of a particular input queue structure. Simulations using multiple agents allow us to model typical manufacturing situations more easily than can be done with more traditional stochastic simulations. For example, we may wish to include parameters in the worker human character agent that account for decreased productivity near quitting time. In addition, by restricting the stochastic nature of the model, we can significantly reduce the number of runs required to determine outcomes with an acceptable level of confidence.

The basic agents used in our model are classified as shown in Figure 10.4. Using object-oriented programming, each class is a subclass of the class above it in the hierarchy. More agents could be included to incorporate additional factors found in a typical process environment.

Internal agents are used to model the manufacturing facility and the products being produced, while the external agents are used to model external pressures and effects that are not part of the normal manufacturing. For this manufacturing line model, we include both product agents and resource agents. The product agents represent the circuits being manufactured, either analog or digital and may include other parameters such as electronic component types, single or double-sided boards, hand-inserted components, and

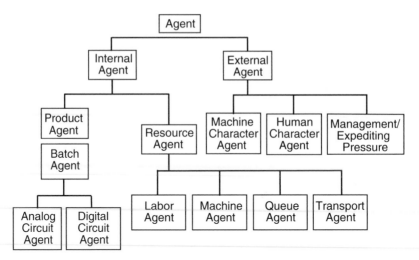

Figure 10.4. Agent hierarchy.

soldering difficulty. The process route is specified for each product agent object. In Swarm simulation terminology, the batch agent represents a swarm of circuit agents. The product agents specify setup times and latency for each station. The resource agents are the human workers and the machine at a particular station. In this approach, these agents are relatively simple and are used primarily to determine machine availability and utilization; however, these resource agents can be acted upon or influenced by the external agents. For the input queue, Q1, and the test queue, Q2, the evolutionary algorithm will present different queue orderings for simulation and evaluation. The queue agents will follow the dispatch rules presented by the evolutionary algorithm.

We define external agents as those modeling all effects that are external to the typical operation of the manufacturing line. These could include machine character, human character, and management/expediting pressure. Machine character includes breakdown and maintenance of the machines for each station. Human character includes absenteeism, as well as time-of-day effects, day-of-week effects, overtime effects, and holiday effects on productivity. We can model either generic workers or individuals. Modeling of individual workers is more appropriate if the productivity varies significantly with the worker, as in the case of highly skilled jobs with workers of various levels of experience. For example, second-shift workers might be less skilled than first-shift workers.

In addition to commercial stochastic simulation tools, a number of agent-based simulators can be used, including Tierra [85], MANTA [33], and Swarm [9]. Tierra is an advanced platform for the study of the evolution of artificial organisms at the level of the genome. The software was developed by Thomas Ray, formerly with the University of Delaware and the ATR Human Information Processing Research Laboratories in Kyoto and currently with the University of Oklahoma. Tierra represents a bottom-up approach to general agent-based simulation and evaluates the environment in which Darwinian evolution can proceed within a computer. MANTA (Modeling an ANTnest Activity), written by Alexis Drogoul in the laboratory of J. Ferber at the University of Paris, is intended to provide a software environment in which questions concerning collective, social computation can be addressed. MANTA addresses many of the difficulties resulting from the cross-disciplinary nature of agent-based simulation. Swarm was developed by the Santa Fe Institute under Chris Langton. The Swarm project is aimed at the development of a fully general-purpose artificial-life simulator. Swarm provides a well-developed platform for the simulation of artificial worlds populated with agents and contains a large library of design and analysis tools and a kernel to drive the simulation [33]. It is written in Objective-C.

The multiagent simulation will result in several measures that are used by the fuzzy evaluator to determine the fitness of the dispatching rule sets. These include machine utilization, late orders, revenue, and throughput. Specific information can be generated for each product batch, as well as production performance over a period of time. If Swarm is used as the simulation vehicle, collection of this information is often performed through the use of simulator probes [9].

10.5 FUZZY LOGIC EVALUATION

The fuzzy logic evaluator receives business and performance parameter inputs from the simulation model. Typical business measures include total processing interval, throughput, late orders, order fill, and revenue. Performance measures are maximum queue size (Q2), queue time, down time, yield rates, and efficiency. The fuzzy model illustrated here is targeted primarily for evaluating business parameters, but it can be easily extended to include factory performance measures. The output of the fuzzy evaluator is the fitness value of the dispatching rule set that is fed back to the evolutionary algorithm (EA).

A fuzzy logic model is a type of expert system that utilizes input parameter membership functions and a linguistic variable rule set to determine the value for one or more crisp outputs [47, 54]. The membership functions for a parameter cover the universe of discourse, U, of that parameter. Membership functions are generally defined by a human expert and are often depicted graphically as shown in Figure 10.5. The late orders (LO) parameter and the throughput (TP) parameter are two outputs, among others, of the simulator. The fuzzy model evaluates these values to determine the extent of membership in membership functions such as GOOD, FAIR, or POOR. Here we consider only convex normal membership functions with fuzzy values in the range from 0 to 1 [54].

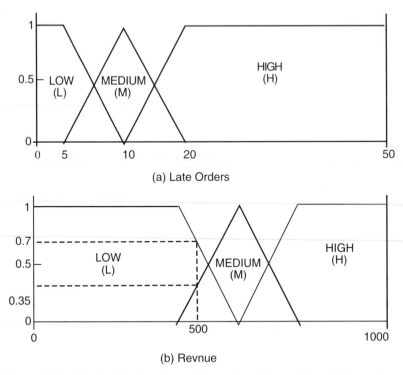

(a) Late Orders

(b) Revnue

Figure 10.5. Membership functions: (a) number of late orders; (b) throughput.

Each input parameter value will have a degree of membership, μ, in one or more of its membership functions. For example, a late-order value of 10 has membership values of $\mu_L = 0$, $\mu_M = 1$, and $\mu_H = 0$ for the three functions in Figure 10.5(a), whereas in Figure 10.5(b) a revenue value of 500 has $\mu_L = 0.7$, $\mu_M = 0.35$, and $\mu_H = 0$. The linguistic variables, LOW, MEDIUM, and HIGH, are used in rules to determine the fitness output, f, of the fuzzy evaluator. The output, f, may be described by fuzzy sets or by a set of singleton values that are nonzero at only one point. Any number of sets or singleton values can be specified [103]. If output fuzzy sets are used, then a defuzzification method, such as center of gravity [54], must be employed to compute a crisp output value. Using singleton output functions is computationally less demanding and is the method used here. Figure 10.6 depicts singleton outputs used to evaluate f. The crisp fitness output value will be in the range 0 to 1 (x-axis).

Let rule j be a conjunctive rule as follows:

If LO is LOW and RV is HIGH, **then** Fitness is EXCELLENT

This rule considers the degree of membership of late orders (LO) in its fuzzy set LOW and the degree of membership of revenue (RV) in its fuzzy set

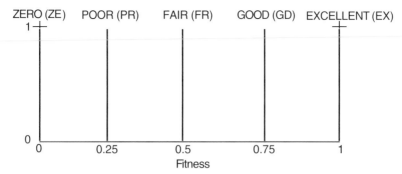

Figure 10.6. Singleton outputs for fitness, f.

HIGH. The conditional part of the rule is the antecedent, and the action part of the rule is termed the consequent. The rule will activate only if the degree of membership for LO in LOW and the degree of membership of RV in HIGH are nonzero. For the conjunctive rule, the min operation is performed. For the jth rule above let $w_j(EX)$ represent the result of the min operation. Then

$$w_j(EX) = \min [\mu_L(LO), \mu_H(RV)]$$

All of the rules that activate will have a nonzero w_i. The crisp fitness output, f, is calculated using the weighted average method,

$$f = \frac{\Sigma_i\, w_i(ZE) \cdot ZE + \Sigma_i\, w_i(PR) \cdot PR + \Sigma_i\, w_i(FR) \cdot FR + \Sigma_i\, w_i(GD) \cdot GD + \Sigma_i\, w_i(EX) \cdot EX}{\Sigma\, w_i}$$

where, as shown Figure 10.6,

$$ZE = 0,\ PR = 0.25,\ FR = 0.5,\ GD = 0.75,\ \text{and}\ EX = 1.0$$

The crisp fitness value computed by the fuzzy model is fed back to the evolutionary algorithm. This computational feedback is required once for each offspring member of the population, P. Based on the fitness values returned, the EA will eliminate low-fitness population members and begin selection of survivors for mating. The algorithm can be stopped after a prescribed number of EA generations or when a prescribed fitness level is achieved.

In this chapter we presented a framework for computational discovery of near-optimal product dispatching is proposed. The overall model incorporates evolutionary algorithms, agent-based simulation, and fuzzy logic. The method is flexible and permits the user to choose optimization parameters based on extrinsic objectives that are different and separate from those used by the evolutionary algorithm. The approach is useful as a stand-alone modeling tool for complex environments and may be utilized as a powerful real-time decision support system.

11

PRODUCT DEMAND FORECASTING USING GENETIC PROGRAMMING[1]

11.1   INTRODUCTION

The ability to forecast long-term future sales of specific products accurately is highly desirable for many companies operating in the increasingly volatile technology sector. Such a capability allows companies to avoid surpluses and shortages in manufacturing resources, including materials, capital equipment, and personnel. By long-term, we mean forecasting of monthly or quarterly sales at a forecasting interval ranging from a few months up to a few years. If forecasts of this type indicate a sharp increase in product demand several months in advance, a company could hire and train additional personnel, increase material safety stocks, and install additional manufacturing capacity. Conversely, if forecasts indicate an impending sharp decline in product demand in coming months, the company could reduce inventories, encourage employees' early retirement, or implement other measures to reduce expenses and improve efficiency for the upcoming slow period.

In recent years, such long-term forecasting for telecommunications and computer network-related products has proven to be an extremely difficult problem due to increasing volatility in the telecommunications industry brought on by numerous factors, including deregulation, the Telecommunications Act of 1996, and ever-expanding global competition. Whereas simple heuristic location-estimation techniques, including exponential smoothing, were in the past at least marginally adequate for developing long-term predictions in this market, we have found them to be wholly inadequate in recent years. Moreover, due to the highly nonstationary, evolutionary, and indeed

[1]This chapter contributed by M. P. Tull, J. J. Sluss, Jr., and J. P. Havlicek, School of Electrical & Computer Engineering, University of Oklahoma, Norman, Oklahoma.

sometimes even chaotic nature of telecommunications product sales, the effort required to reformulate continuously more sophisticated parametric methods including linear regressions, classical Box-Jenkins ARMA models, and Kalman filters, can rapidly constitute an insurmountable burden.

Packard proposed methods for prediction of high-dimensional chaotic time series using genetic algorithms based on conditional intervals for the independent variables [64, 77]. Chromosomes composed of independent variable vectors and their conditional value intervals are used to derive the dependent variable forecast. In the case of a single time series, the vectors are windowed historical values to the time series. Information-theoretic objective measures are used for fitness determination. This method does not guarantee production of conditions for all possible future dependent variable values, regardless of future step size. Moreover, the method fails to relate the dependency of the forecast variable functionally to the independent variables, thus making it difficult to formulate a deterministic model.

Other studies using advanced neuro-fuzzy techniques have been proposed [52, 101], but again these methods fail to produce an interpretive model of market dynamics. We therefore opt for methods that guarantee wide coverage for future prediction values and prediction step sizes, as well as produce a deterministic model that can be studied in-depth for dependencies. One such method is Koza's genetic programming algorithm, which relies on functional combinations of independent variables to yield (empirically discover) a model for predicting the dependent variable [56].

In this study, we present results wherein long-term monthly sales of a particular widely deployed telecommunications product were forecast using genetic programming. These results provide a significant improvement over our previous forecasting study using a commercial software package [97]. In both the current and previous study we used the same independent economic variables. For these extrinsic time series, we elected to use readily available leading economic indicators, reasoning that these should be related to both deployment of new telecommunications infrastructure and growth of existing infrastructure. With this approach, the inherently self-organizing, unsupervised nature of GAs frees the analyst from the need to explicitly model rapidly changing nonstationary structure in the time series.

In the previous study [97], historical values of the actual sales time series themselves were not considered by the GAs; however, in this study the actual product demand figures are permitted into the empirical equation. The previous software was not capable of deriving the time lag or phase shift between the dependent variable and each independent variable. This capability in the new software avoids the need to perform correlation studies to establish the time lags and offers a dynamic time lag selection capability within the algorithm. The new software is written in C++ and operates on a Linux platform.

11.2   ALGORITHM DESCRIPTION

The independent variables are 12 time series of economic indicators selected from among the many such series available on the Economic Time Series website (http://www.economagic.com). The 12 indicators used were originally selected based both on correlation studies with the actual quarterly sales data of the product of interest and on intuitive expectations derived from extensive historical experience with the particular product.

11.2.1   Chromosome Structure

Each individual in the population has a single chromosome representing a LISP S-expression, or parse tree, containing both operands and operations [56]. The admissible operations are basic binary and unary calculator functions, including add, subtract, multiply, divide, roots, logarithms, trigonometric transcendental functions, and simple-order statistics.

Admissible operands include numeric constants, time-lagged independent variable values of one or more of the economic indicators, and one or more time-lagged dependent variable values. The maximum chromosome size for an individual is limited to 40 operations. Note that the number of operands in any given chromosome is determined by the number of operators and the operator types (unary or binary). In the initial populations, both the chromosome lengths and the values of individual genes are generated randomly. Multiple populations are often employed, and a population-to-population migration rate can be specified.

11.2.2   Fitness Evaluation

The fitness of individuals was evaluated based upon their ability to predict monthly sales data correctly for the product. Let x_k represent the actual monthly sales for month k and $\hat{x}_{k,i}$ represent the forecast of individual i for month k, where $k \in [1,N]$ defines the evaluation set. We define f_i, the fitness of individual i, according to

$$f_i = \frac{1}{1 + \alpha} \tag{11.1}$$

where

$$\alpha = \frac{1}{N} \sum_{k=1}^{N} (x_k - \hat{x}_{k,i})^2 + \Lambda \tag{11.2}$$

and where $\Lambda = 10^{-5} \times$ (chromosome length) is a penalty term that favors shorter genetic programs over longer ones. We do not consider the length of the genetic program to be a particularly important factor in our application; hence the small weight given to Λ in (11.2) indicates that this term will be significant only in cases where two or more individuals are equally fit. When this occurs, the individual with the shortest genetic program will be deemed most fit.

11.2.3 Reproduction and Generation Evolution

The GA permits individuals to reproduce both sexually and asexually. In sexual reproduction, two offspring are created with gene sequences derived from those of the parents by single-point crossover reproduction [69]. A crossover point is chosen at random to divide each parent's chromosome into two gene sequences. Each offspring receives one gene sequence from each parent, and the sequences were concatenated to create the offspring's chromosome.

At each new generation, individuals are mated as parents for sexual reproduction using fitness proportionate selection, also known as roulette wheel selection [66, 69]. At each generation, let

$$F = \sum_i f_i$$

be the total fitness of the population. Then $\rho_i = f_i/F$ defines the fraction of the roulette wheel assigned to individual i, namely the probability that individual i will be selected as a parent in a particular sexual reproduction. Sexual reproduction continues until a number of offspring equal to a specified fraction of the current population have been produced.

The GA can implement asexual reproduction using both mutation and inversion [43, 69]. Mutation creates an offspring's chromosome by first copying the parent's chromosome and then randomly choosing a gene to be replaced with a randomly selected value of the same type (operator or operand). Like mutation, inversion first copies the parent's chromosome to the offspring. Two randomly selected genes in the offspring's chromosome are then swapped. As in the case of sexual reproduction, individuals are selected as parents for asexual reproduction by fitness-proportionate selection.

Subsequent to the production of offspring by sexual reproduction, the GA subjects offspring to random mutation as described above. After mutation, all offspring produced from a given population are placed in a new generation pool for the population. When the new generation pool is filled, the fitness of each individual in the new generation pool is evaluated. Hill-climbing algorithms are then applied to the fittest individuals from the pool. In these hill-climbing processes, a mutation, possibly random, is sequentially applied to each gene in the chromosome of the selected individual and is retained only if this mutation results in improved fitness. For a tree-structured chromosome, operator hill-climbing exchanges the operations within the chromosome from the pool of operators, either unary or binary. Operand hill-climbing exchanges one independent variable for another independent variable. Lag-factor hill-climbing varies the phase or time lag of the independent variables. Constant-factor hill-climbing modifies any constant operands in the tree by multiplying and/or dividing the constant value by a randomly chosen value. Although this multiple-point-mutation hill-climbing is computationally expensive, we believe its use results in good genetic program models being produced in the early generations. To reduce some of the computational load, the hill-climbing methods can be applied every nth generation instead of every generation. Not all of the hill-climbing methods need be applied at the same generation nor at the same generation interval. For example, operator hill-climbing can be specified every 10th generation, independent variable hill-climbing every 15th generation, and time-lag hill-climbing every 25th generation, and so on.

11.3   EXPERIMENTS AND RESULTS

Figure 11.1 shows the actual product demand time series, plotted by month, where the data have been scaled to protect the proprietary nature of the absolute values. The forecast interval is defined to be 12 months. The product demand time series is divided into two segments. The first and largest segment is used for the model evolution, i.e., the GA evolves the population of individuals using this segment. The second segment is the evaluation segment and was chosen to be the last 12 months of the demand time series. This segment is used only for fitness calculations and is not available for evolution of the model.

The algorithm described in Section 11.2 represents a reasonably sophisticated GA, for which a number of constants such as percent sexual reproductions, percent asexual reproductions, and mutations rates must be specified.

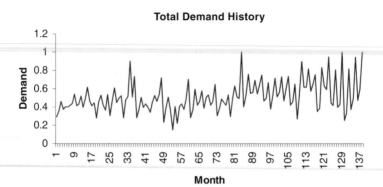

Figure 11.1. Monthly product demand time series.

After empirically adjusting these constants over a period of several GA executions, the following values delivered the best forecasting results observed to date. Initial and sustained population sizes used were 100 to 400 individuals. Up to 10 populations were permitted, with the population-to-population migration rate dependent on the population sizes. For population sizes of 100 individuals the rate was 0.4%, with the migration restricted to the fittest individuals replacing the least-fit individuals. The maximum fraction of the reproductions that were sexual was 50%, while the fraction that were asexual was 71%. Of the asexual reproductions, 70% were small mutations in which only one operator or independent variable was permitted to change, and 1% were large mutations wherein two to five mutations were permitted. Independent variable mutations rely on precomputed correlation coefficients of the independent variable with the dependent demand variable, whereby an independent variable with a high correlation has a proportionately higher chance of being chosen for the mutation.

The mutation rate used here is quite high when compared to other studies. Our observation is that the sexual reproduction using subtree crossover tends to select two high-fitness parents and results in two low-fitness offspring being produced. Mutation, coupled with hill-climbing, tends to rapidly improve high-fitness individuals in each population. Note that sexual reproduction is still necessary to produce new individuals that span the broad solution landscape and cannot be eliminated in favor of pure asexual reproduction.

Hill-climbing was performed every 40 generations. Applying hill-climbing more often than this tended to nullify the diversity of the population. Only individuals that were within 1% of the fittest individual were selected for hill-climbing. Operator hill-climbing and operator-operand replacement hill-climbing were employed. Independent variable hill-climbing, while available, was not used. Operator hill-climbing simply cycles each operator node through the set of operators looking for fitness improvement. Operator replacement hill-climbing uses simple constant values, such as 0, 1, 2, pi, 10, to replace operators and operands in a special type of hill-climbing meant to reduce the complexity of the individuals. Subsequently, these constants were subjected to hill-climbing that would multiply or divide each by a random value in the range of 1.25 to 1.75.

The GA was stopped when, after at least several hundred generations, only negligible improvements in fitness were observed. In all cases, this occurred after fewer than 500 generations had evolved. This number of generations is considerably lower than in other published studies and is subject to further research and evaluation as to the reasons why good models evolve in such a low number of generations as compared to other studies.

Forecasting performance of the best individuals produced by the GA is illustrated in Figures 11.2 and 11.3. The comparison shows the actual demand versus the model's predicted demand over the 12-month evaluation period. In both models the error is quite low. Notice that both models capture the cyclic

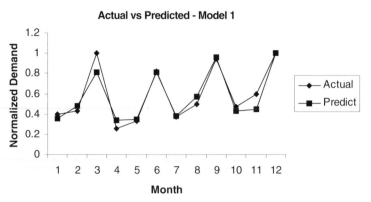

Figure 11.2. Model #1: Actual versus predicted demand over the 12-month evaluation interval.

nature of the demand. Overall, both of these models had average percent errors between 1 and 2%. For any given month, the largest demand error did not exceed the single-day factory production capability.

Subsequent runs of the GA continued to produce models that were comparable to the two shown above. Out of thousands more generated, no superior model emerged for several months. Thus, these models continued to be used for the monthly demand prediction. Each month new demand data became available, and the models were used to extend the prediction for 12 more months.

The management opportunities afforded by the accuracy of these forecasts are many and varied. The cyclic nature of the demand for these products is a challenge to the production facility. The factory would normally prefer a level production schedule that followed a level demand pattern. Since this is

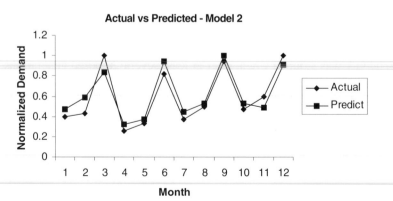

Figure 11.3. Model #2: actual versus predicted demand over the 12-month evaluation interval.

not the case, the factory encourages workforce vacation and liberal leave during the low-demand periods, while a no-vacation policy and overtime are utilized for the peak periods. One of the largest impacts of this accurate demand prediction is in the raw materials inventory. Material planners are provided with a breakdown of these long-term forecasts. Both long-term and short-term material plans are impacted. Material planners provide vendors with material due dates that correspond to the quarterly demand cycle. In addition, vendors are provided with a more accurate one-year forecast for their raw material.

Of course, revenue and sales are primary concerns, and an accurate forecast can provide time to plan for periods of reduced demand. The forecast may offer opportunities to offer sales discounts or other sales incentives to prevent the realization of the reduced demand. Peak demand periods may offer opportunities to maximize profits. In either case, the forecast provides managers the data necessary to plan months in advance. Proper planning and synchronization of the corporate strategy can win new or retain existing customers while maximizing asset utilization and profits.

11.4   CONCLUSION

This chapter is a case study for using evolutionary programming techniques to develop long-term forecasting models for product demand. The method uses 12 extrinsic independent economic variables to develop an empirical formula-based model. The product demand time series studied here is difficult and time-consuming to model and predict using traditional statists-based methods.

The accuracy of the GA-generated models is extremely good and represents a significant improvement over previous studies. The models not only provide valuable data for resource planning, but also offer insight as to what economic factors drive the business being modeled. Several strategic business units can use the product demand prediction data to formulate proactive plans and initiatives.

REFERENCES

[1] Adewuya, A. A., *New Methods in Genetic Search with Real-Valued Chromosomes,* M.S. thesis, Massachusetts Institute of Technology, 1996.

[2] Amari, S., Mathematical foundations of neurocomputing, *Proceedings of the IEEE,* vol. 78, no. 9, September, 1990, pp. 1443–1463.

[3] Atkins, M., Sorting by Hopfield net, in *Proceedings of the International Conference on Neural Networks,* 1986, pp. II-65–II-68.

[4] Badiru, A. B., "A New Computational Search Technique for AI Based on Cantor Set," *Applied Mathematics and Computation,* vol. 55, pp. 255–274, 1993.

[5] Badiru, A. B., Set theory and knowledge base organization, presented at the ORSA/TIMS Fall Conference, St. Louis, MO, October, 1987.

[6] Baglio, S., L. Fortuna, M. G. Xibilia, and P. Zuccarini, Neuro-fuzzy to predict urban traffic, in *Proceedings of EUFIT94, Aachen, Germany, 1994.*

[7] Barto, A. G., R. Sutton, and C. Anderson, Neuronlike adaptive elements that can solve difficult learning control problems, *IEEE Transactions on Systems, Man, and Cybernetics,* vol. SMC-13, no. 5, September/October, 1983, pp. 834–846.

[8] Buchanan, B. G. and E. H. Shortliffe, editors, *Rule Based Expert Systems: The MYCIN Experiments of the Stanford Heuristics Programming Project,* Addison-Wesley, Reading, MA, 1984.

[9] Burkehart, R., The Swarm multi-agent simulation system, OOPSLA '94 Workshop on the Object Engine.

[10] Caporaletti, L. E., R. E. Dorsey, J. D. Johnson, and W. A. Powell, A decisions support system for in-sample simultaneous equation systems forecasting using artificial neural systems, in *Proceedings of the MIND Conference,* 1992.

[11] Caudill, M., Neural networks primer, part I, *AI Expert,* pp. 46–52, December, 1987.

[12] Caudill, M., Neural networks primer, part II, *AI Expert,* pp. 55–61, February, 1988.

[13] Caudill, M., Neural networks primer, part III, *AI Expert,* pp. 53–59, June, 1988.

[14] Caudill, M., Neural networks primer, part IV, *AI Expert,* pp. 61–67, August, 1988.

[15] Caudill, M., Neural networks primer, part V, *AI Expert,* pp. 57–65, November, 1988.

[16] Caudill, M., Neural networks primer, part VI, *AI Expert,* pp. 61–67, February, 1989.

[17] Caudill, M., Neural networks primer, part VII, *AI Expert,* pp. 51–58, May, 1989.

[18] Caudill, M., Neural networks primer, part VIII, *AI Expert,* pp. 61–67, August, 1989.

[19] Davis, L., editor, *Handbook of Genetic Algorithms,* Van Nostrand Reinhold, New York, 1991.

[20] De Jon, K. A., *Analysis of the Behavior of a Class of Genetic Adaptive Systems,* Ph.D. dissertation, University of Michigan, 1975.

[21] De Silva, C., *Intelligent Control,* CRC Press, Boca Raton, FL, 1995.

[22] Dempster, A. P., A generalization of bayesian inference, *Journal of the Royal Statistical Society,* Series B, vol. 30, no. 2, 1968.

[23] Di Piazza, J. S. and F. A. Helsabeck, Laps: cases to models to complete expert systems, *AI Magazine,* vol. 11, no. 3, Fall 1990, pp. 80–107.

[24] Dreyfus, A., *What Computers Still Can't Do: A Critique of Artificial Reason,* MIT Press, Cambridge, MA, 1992.

[25] Engelmore, R. and T. Morgan, editors, *Blackboard Systems,* Addison-Wesley, Reading, MA, 1988.

[26] Ercal, F., A. Chawla and W. V. Stoecker, Neural network diagnosis of malignant melanoma from color images, University of Missouri–Rolla, CSC-93-04, 1993.

[27] Eshelman, L. J. and J. D. Schaffer, Real-coded genetic algorithms and interval schemata, in L. D. Whitley, editor, *Foundations of Genetic Algorithms Z,* Morgan Kaufmann, San Mateo, CA, 1993, pp. 187–202.

[28] Fogel, L. J., Autonomous automata, *Industrial Research,* vol. 4, no. 2, 1962, pp. 14–19.

[29] Fogel, D., Evolutionary programming tutorial, IEEE International Conference on Neural Networks, 1993.

[30] Fogel, L. J., A. J. Owens, and M. J. Walsh, *Artificial Intelligence Through Simulated Evolution,* Wiley, New York, 1966.

[31] Goldberg, D. E., *Genetic Algorithms in Search, Optimization, and Machine Learning,* Addison-Wesley, Reading, MA, 1989.

[32] Golden, B. L., E. A. Wasil, and P. T. Harker, editors, *The Analytic Hierarchy Process: Applications and Studies,* Springer-Verlag, New York, 1989.

[33] Gutowitz, H. A., Santa Fe Institute, at http://alife.santafe.edu/alife/topics/simulator.

[34] Hallam, J., Blackboard architectures and systems, in Mirzai, A. R., editor, *Artificial Intelligence: Concepts and Applications in Engineering,* MIT Press, Cambridge, MA, 1990, pp. 35–64.

[35] Harmon, P. and D. King, *Expert Systems: Artificial Intelligence in Business,* Wiley, New York, 1985.

[36]   Haupt, R. L., Optimization of periodic conducting grids, in *Proceedings of the 11th Annual Review of Progress in Applied Computational Electromagnetics Conference,* March, 1995.

[37]   Haupt, R. L. and S. E. Haupt, *Practical Genetic Algorithms,* Wiley, New York, 1998.

[38]   Hayes, P., The logic of frames, in Metzing, D., editor, *Frame Conceptions and Text Understanding,* de Gruyter, Berlin, 1979, pp. 46–61.

[39]   Haykin, S. *Neural Network: A Comprehensive Approach,* Prentice-Hall, Englewood Cliffs, NJ, 1998.

[40]   Hertz, D. and Q. Hu, Fuzzy-neuro controller for backpropagation networks, in *Proceedings of the Simulation Technology and Workshop on Neural Networks Conference,* Houston, 1992, pp. 540–574.

[41]   Hillier, F. S., and G. J. Lieberman, *Introduction to Operations Research,* 4th ed., McGraw-Hill, New York, 1986.

[42]   Hoffman, R. R., The problem of extracting the knowledge of experts from the perspective of experimental psychology, *AI Magazine,* vol. 8, no. 2, Summer 1987, pp. 53–67.

[43]   Holland, J. H., *Adaptation in Natural and Artificial Systems,* University of Michigan Press, Ann Arbor, 1975.

[44]   Hopfield, J. J. and D. W. Tank, "Neural" computation of decisions in optimization problems, *Biological Cybernetics,* vol. 52, 1985, pp. 141–152.

[45]   Hsu, L. S., H. H. The, P. Z. Wang, S. C. Chan, and K. F. Loe, Fuzzy neural-logic system, in *Proceedings of the International Joint Conference on Neural Networks,* Baltimore, 1992, pp. I-245–250.

[46]   Hush, D. R. and B. G. Horne, Progress in Supervised Neural Networks, *IEEE Signal Processing Magazine,* vol. 10, no. 1, January, 1993, pp. 8–39.

[47]   Jang, J.-S. R., C.-T. Sun and E. Mizutani, *Neurol-Fuzzy and Soft Computing,* Prentice Hall, Upper Saddle River, NJ, 1997.

[48]   Jones, A. and L. Rabelo, Integrating neural nets, simulation, and genetic algorithms for real-time scheduling, in G. Fandel, T. Gulledge, and A. Jones, editors, *Operations Research in Production Planning and Control,* Springer-Verlag, Berlin, 1993, pp. 551–566.

[49]   Josin, G., Integrating neural networks with robots, *AI Expert,* pp. 50–58, August 1988.

[50]   Kandel, A. and G. Langholz, *Fuzzy Control Systems,* CRC Press, Boca Raton, FL, 1994.

[51]   Kewley, R. H., "Computational intelligence for support of military tactical decision making, Ph.D. dissertation, Rensselaer Polytechnic Institute, 2001.

[52]   Kim, D. and C. Kim, Forecasting time series with genetic fuzzy predictor ensemble, *IEEE Transactions on Fuzzy Systems,* vol. 5, no. 4, November, 1997, pp. 523–535.

[53]   Kirkpatrick, S., C. D. Gelatt, Jr., and M. P. Vecchi, Optimization by simulated annealing, *Science,* vol. 220, 1983, pp. 671–680.

[54]   Klir, G. J. and B. Yuan, *Fuzzy Sets and Fuzzy Logic: Theory and Applications,* Prentice Hall, PTR, Upper Saddle River, NJ, 1995.

[55] Kohonen, T., The self-organizing map, *Proceedings of the IEEE,* vol. 78, September, 1990, pp. 1464–1480.

[56] Koza, J. R., *Genetic Programming of Computers by Means of Natural Selection,* MIT Press, Cambridge, MA, 1992.

[57] Koza, J. R., The Genetic Programming Paradigm: Genetically Breeding Populations of Computer Programs to Solve Problems, in *Dynamic, Genetic, and Chaotic Programming,* B. Soucek, editor, Wiley, New York, 1992, pp. 203–321.

[58] Kuipers, B. J., A frame for frames, in Bobrow, G. and A. Collins, editors, *Representation and Understanding,* Academic Press, New York, 1975.

[59] Lewis, H., *The Foundations of Fuzzy Control,* Plenum, New York, 1997.

[60] Liebowitz, J., *Introduction to Expert Systems,* Mitchell, Santa Cruz, CA, 1988.

[61] Lippman, R. P., An introduction to computing with neural nets, *IEEE ASSP Magazine,* pp. 4–22, April 1987.

[62] Maxwell, T., C. L. Giles, Y. C. Lee, and H. H. Chen, Transformation invariance using high order correlations in neural net architectures, in *Proceedings of the Systems, Man, and Cybernetics Conference,* 1986, pp. 627–632.

[63] Metropolis, N., A. Rosenbluth, M. Rosenbluth, A. Teller, and E. Teller, Equation of state calculations by fast computing machines, *Journal of Chemical Physics,* vol. 21, 1953, pp. 1087–1092.

[64] Meyer, T. P. and N. H. Packard, Local forecasting of high-dimensional chaotic dynamics, in *Nonlinear Modeling and Forecasting,* M. Casdagli and S. Eurbank, editors, Addison-Wesley, Redwood City, CA, 1992, pp. 249–263.

[65] Michalewicz, Z., Genetic Algorithms + Data Structures = Evolution Programs, 1st edition, Springer-Verlag, Berlin, 1992.

[66] Michalewicz, Z., *Genetic Algorithms + Data Structures = Evolution Programs,* 2nd edition, Springer-Verlag, New York, 1994.

[67] Minsky, M., A framework for representing knowledge, in Winston, P., editor, *The Psychology of Computer Vision,* McGraw-Hill, New York, 1975, pp. 211–277.

[68] Minsky, M. and S. Pappert, *Preceptions: An Introduction to Computational Geometry,* MIT Press, Cambridge, MA, 1969.

[69] Mitchell, M., *An Introduction to Genetic Algorithms,* MIT Press, Cambridge, MA, 1998.

[70] Murty, K. G., *Operations Research: Deterministic Optimization Models,* Prentice-Hall, Englewood Cliffs, NJ, 1995.

[71] Nauck, D. and R. Kruse, NEFCLASS—a neuro-fuzzy approach for the classification of data, in *Proceedings of the 1995 ACM Symposium on Applied Computing,* Nashville, 1995, pp. 461–465.

[72] Newell, A. and H. A. Simon, *Computer Simulation of Human Thinking,* The RAND Corporation, April 20, 1961, p. 2276.

[73] Newell, A. and H. A. Simon, *Human Problem-Solving,* Prentice-Hall, Englewood Cliffs, NJ, 1972.

[74] Newquist, H. P., The new crime stopper's notebook: the expert system, *AI Expert,* March 1988, pp. 19–21.

[75] Nguyen, D. and B. Widrow, The truck backer-upper: an example of self-learning in neural networks, in W. T. Miller, R. S. Sulton, and P. J. Werbos, editors, *Neural Networks for Control,* MIT Press, Cambridge, MA, 1990, pp. 287–299.

[76] Nii, H. P., Blackboard systems: the blackboard model of problem solving and the evolution of blackboard architectures, *AI Magazine,* vol. 7, 1986, pp. 38–53.

[77] Packard, N. H., A genetic learning algorithm for the analysis of complex data, *Complex Systems,* vol. 4, 1990, pp. 543–572.

[78] Patyra, M. and D. Mlynek, *Fuzzy Logic,* Wiley, New York, 1996.

[79] Pedrycz, W. and F. Gomide, *An Introduction to Fuzzy Sets,* MIT Press, Cambridge, MA, 1998.

[80] Pierreval, H. and L. Tautou, Using evolutionary algorithms and simulation for the optimization of manufacturing systems, *IIE Transactions,* vol. 29, no. 3, 1997, pp. 181–189.

[81] Poli, R., S. Cagnoni, R. Livi, G. Coppini, and G. Valli, A neural network expert system for diagnosing and treating hypertension, *IEEE Computer,* March 1991, pp. 64–71.

[82] Poliac, M. O., E. B. Lee, J. R. Slagle, and M. R. Wick, A crew scheduling problem, in *Proceedings of the International Conference on Neural Networks,* 1987, pp. IV-779–IV-786.

[83] Prerau, D. S., Knowledge acquisition in the development of a large expert system, *AI Magazine,* vol. 8, no. 2, Summer 1987, pp. 43–51.

[84] Raman, N., R. V. Rachamadugu, and F. B. Talbot, Real-time scheduling of an automated manufacturing center, *European Journal of Operational Research,* vol. 40, no. 2, pp. 222–242, 1989.

[85] Ray, T. S., Neural networks, genetic algorithms and artificial life: adaptive computation, in *Alife, Genetic Algorithm and Neural Networks Seminar Proceedings,* 1994, pp. 1–14.

[86] Rechenberg, I., *Evolutionstrategie: Optimierung technischer Systeme nach Prinzipien der biologischen Evolution,* Frommann-Holzboog Verlage, Stuttgart, 1973.

[87] Saaty, T. L., *The Analytic Hierarchy Process,* McGraw-Hill, 1980.

[88] Sagan, H., *Advanced Calculus,* Houghton Mifflin, Boston, MA, 1974.

[89] Schank, R. C. and R. P. Abelson, *Script, Plans, Goals, and Understanding,* Lawrence Erlbaum Associates, Hillsdale, NJ, 1977.

[90] Schank, R. C. and P. G. Childers, *The Cognitive Computer,* Addison-Wesley, Reading, MA, 1984.

[91] Schwefel, H. P., *Numerical Optimization of Computer Models,* Wiley, Chichester, 1981.

[92] Shaffer, G. A., *Mathematical Theory of Evidence,* Princeton University Press, Princeton, NJ, 1979.

[93] Shannon, C. *A Symbolic Analysis of Relay and Switching Circuits,* [n.p.], 1938.

[94] Shepanski, J. F. and S. A. Macy, Teaching artificial neural systems to drive: manual training techniques for autonomous systems, in *Proceedings of the Neural Information Processing Systems,* 1988, pp. 693–700.

[95]   Shing, J. and R. Jang, ANFIS: adaptive network based fuzzy inference system, *IEEE Transactions on Systems, Man, and Cybernetics,* vol. 23, no. 3, 1993, pp. 665–685.

[96]   Silverman, B. G., Critiquing human judgment using knowledge-acquisition systems, *AI Magazine,* vol. 11, no. 3, Fall 1990, pp. 60–79.

[97]   Sloan, S., J. Sluss, M. Tull, and J. Havlick, Long term business forecasting: a genetic algorithm approach, ANNIE '99, Rolla, MO, October, 1999.

[98]   Swarm, 1.0.5, ftp://ftp.santafe.edu/pub/swarm, Santa Fe Institute, Santa Fe, NM.

[99]   Tesauro, G. and T. J. Sejnowski, A "neural" network that learns to play back-gammon, in *Proceedings of the Neural Information Processing Systems Conference,* 1988, pp. 794–803.

[100] Vandamme, F., Knowledge extraction from experts in view of the construction of expert systems, *Proceedings of the NATO Advanced Research Workshop on Expert Judgment,* Porto, Portugal, 1986.

[101] Wan, E. A., Time series prediction by using a connectionist network with internal delay lines, in *Times Series Prediction,* A. S. Wiegand, and N. A. Gevshenfeld, editors, Addison-Wesley, Redwood City, CA, 1994, pp. 195–217.

[102] Weizenbaum, J., *Computer Power and Human Reason: From Judgment to Calculation,* W. H. Freeman, San Francisco, 1976.

[103] Welstead, S. T., *Neural Network and Fuzzy Logic Applications in C/C++,* Wiley, New York, 1994.

[104] Widrow, B. and M. A. Lehr, 30 years of adaptive neural networks: peceptron, madaline, and backpropagation, *Proceedings of the IEEE,* vol. 78, no. 9, September, 1990, pp. 1415–1442.

[105] Wright, A., Genetic algorithms for real parameter optimization, in. G. J. E. Rawlins, editor, *Foundations of Genetic Algorithms,* Morgan Kaufmann, San Mateo, CA, 1991, pp. 205–220.

[106] Zadeh, L. A., Fuzzy logic, principles, applications, and perspectives, public lecture, University of Oklahoma, Norman, OK, April 18, 1991.

[107] Zadeh, L. A., Fuzzy sets, *Information and Control,* vol. 8, 1965, pp. 338–353.

[108] Zurada, J. M., *Artificial Neural Systems,* West, St. Paul, MN, 1992.

INDEX